William of Auvergne and Robert Grosseteste

NEW IDEAS OF TRUTH
IN THE EARLY THIRTEENTH
CENTURY

WILLIAM
OF AUVERGNE
AND ROBERT
GROSSETESTE

New Ideas of Truth
in the Early Thirteenth
Century

Steven P. Marrone

PRINCETON UNIVERSITY PRESS

PRINCETON, NEW JERSEY

Copyright © 1983 by Princeton University Press

Published by Princeton University Press, 41 William Street,
Princeton, New Jersey 08540
In the United Kingdom: Princeton University
Press, Guilford, Surrey
All Rights Reserved

Library of Congress Cataloging in Publication Data will
be found on the last printed page of this book

This book has been composed in Metroset Garamond No. 3

Clothbound editions of Princeton University Press books
are printed on acid-free paper, and binding materials
are chosen for strength and durability
Paperbacks, while satisfactory for personal collections,
are not usually suitable for library rebinding

Printed in the United States of America by Princeton
University Press, Princeton, New Jersey

To Olga

Table of Contents

Preface

WHEN, NINE years ago, I began the research that would ultimately lead to this book, I had it in mind to look at scholastic
figures of the late thirteenth century, in particular at the way
they used the image of divine illumination to talk about
knowledge. Only after some time spent on this project did I
come to realize that if I were ever to succeed in sorting things
out for the period after Thomas Aquinas, I would first have to
turn back and explore more closely the works of thinkers who
preceded him. Here, there were assumptions historians had
long made about the nature of early thirteenth-century scholasticism that needed to be cleared away as well as a number of
new issues to be investigated before the stage could be set for
the high-scholastic days of Thomas and beyond.

Among the new issues that needed examining, the most important appeared to be those having to do with theoretical
questions of method and epistemological criteria, matters fer-
vently discussed by scholars in the thirteenth century. A little
work on such subjects soon brought me to recognize the central role played by the problem of defining truth. It was in
working out the definition of truth and explaining how it applied to human knowledge that thinkers actually developed the
set of assumptions, the common working principles, that were
to guide scholastic discussion and dispute for several hundred
years to come.

The present book is the result of my efforts to understand
the concern for these issues in the decades when they first became critical for intellectual debate in the medieval West. I

hope it is only a beginning, and that it will lay the groundwork for further research into the way these early ideas were expanded and reworked in the years that followed. Perhaps more important, I would like it to be seen as a contribution to the current re-examination of high-medieval scholastic thought—a re-examination occasioned, in large part, by the works of historians of logic, who have taught us to look at scholasticism with new sensitivity to its analytical precision and its methodological awareness.

As is the case in all works of scholarship, there are many people besides the author whose efforts have contributed to the final result. I must thank most of all Giles Constable and John Murdoch, who have guided me from the early days of my graduate study and whose support and advice I still rely upon. The debt of gratitude I owe them goes far beyond my appreciation for their help with this single work. In my numerous attempts to bring a large manuscript down to size I have also benefited from a number of perceptive and generous readers, including Michael Contrada, Reverend William A. Wallace, and two whose names I do not know but whose comments have added greatly to my understanding of the history and the philosophy I have tried to describe. Elisabeth Bouché provided invaluable assistance in getting my rough drafts into shape and helping me to meet deadlines along the way. Paul Meyvaert I must thank for his counsel and encouragement, and for being such an amiable colleague at a time when the academic world sometimes seems to be under siege. Finally I thank Tufts University, not only for giving me a home as a scholar but also for defraying the cost of some of the typing, and Princeton University Press for making it such a pleasure to turn a book into print.

Arlington, Mass.
February, 1982

Abbreviations

===

Beiträge	Beiträge zur Geschichte der Philosophie des Mittelalters (Now: Beiträge zur Geschichte der Philosophie and Theologie des Mittelalters)
CC	Corpus Christianorum, Series Latina
CSEL	Corpus Scriptorum Ecclesiasticorum Latinorum
PL	Migne, J. P. Patrologiae Cursus Completus, Series Latina (Paris, 1841-91)

William of Auvergne
and Robert Grosseteste

NEW IDEAS OF TRUTH
IN THE EARLY THIRTEENTH
CENTURY

Introduction

===

Philosophers have always puzzled over the nature of truth; indeed, the matter has generally fascinated intellectuals of any sort. Yet there have been times when the need to define truth carefully has loomed more important, or perhaps seemed more problematic, than usual. One such time came among intellectuals in Europe during the later Middle Ages. The search to determine the nature of truth in human knowledge assumed an exceptional urgency for scholastics of the thirteenth and fourteenth centuries and animated the best minds the new universities could produce. Despite what is often held to be the overwhelming religious bias of that age, the issue that interested scholastics most was not the problem of characterizing the truth men held on faith, whether that faith was induced by authority or by the testimony of Scripture. Instead, they focused on the problem of defining the truth that could actually be grasped and known by means of human understanding. Scholastics of the thirteenth and fourteenth centuries wanted to know how to identify that true knowledge which any intelligent person could have merely by exercising his or her natural intellectual capabilities.[1]

Out of this concern arose a prolonged philosophical discussion over the nature of truth and over certain issues of episte-

[1] Scholastics of the later Middle Ages divided the functions of the mind into two categories, speculative and practical. In a strict sense only speculative thought pertained directly to truth; practical reason was oriented toward the good. The present study will concern itself exclusively with the mind as related to truth—that is, with man's speculative reason.

3

mology related to it, and modern historians have for some time recognized the importance of this later-medieval discussion for the history of Western thought.[2] The view of what happened that has come to be most generally accepted is that over the thirteenth century there occurred a shift in doctrine.[3] According to this interpretation, medieval thinkers had traditionally

[2] This is not to say that there has been general agreement about the weight this episode ought to be given. The most famous debate over the matter arose out of Maurice De Wulf's criticisms of Etienne Gilson, who thought epistemological matters of the sort involved here were among the most fundamental elements of medieval intellectual history. See Gilson, "Pourquoi saint Thomas a critiqué saint Augustin," *Archives d'Histoire Doctrinale et Littéraire du Moyen Âge* 1 (1926–27), 5–127; "Les sources gréco-arabes de l'augustinisme avicennisant," *Archives d'Histoire Doctrinale et Littéraire du Moyen Âge* 4 (1929), 5–149; and "Réflexions sur la controverse S. Thomas-s. Augustin," in *Mélanges Mandonnet* (Paris, 1930), I, 371–83; and De Wulf, "L'augustinisme 'avicennisant,' " *Revue Néo-Scolastique* 33 (1931), 11–39; and "Courants doctrinaux dans la philosophie européenne du XIIIᵉ siècle," *Revue Néo-Scolastique* 34 (1932), 5–20.

[3] The classic statement of this view was given by Etienne Gilson in "Pourquoi saint Thomas a critiqué saint Augustin," p. 5. Gilson's position—and here one must include views sympathetic to it published even a bit earlier—has had enormous influence on how historians have evaluated and, indeed, investigated the course of medieval intellectual history, especially in the thirteenth century, and it has left its mark on the way many have organized scholastics into schools of thought and regarded vicissitudes in their teaching. See, for instance, before Gilson, Otto Keicher, "Zur Lehre der ältesten Franziskanertheologen vom 'intellectus agens,' " in *Festgabe zum 70. Geburtstag Georg Freiherrn von Hertling* (Freiburg im Br., 1913), pp. 173–82, and Berard Vogt, "Der Ursprung und die Entwicklung der Franziskanerschule," *Franziskanische Studien* 9 (1922), 137–57 [trans. in *Franciscan Studies* 3 (1925), 5–23]; and after Gilson, Bernhard Jansen, "Quomodo Divi Augustini theoria illuminationis saeculo decimo tertio concepta sit," *Gregorianum* 11 (1930), 146–58; Efrem Bettoni, "La dottrina bonaventuriana dell'illuminazione intellettuale," *Rivista di Filosofia Neoscolastica* 36 (1944), 139–58; Léon Veuthey, "Les divers courants de la philosophie augustino-franciscaine au moyen âge," in *Scholastica ratione historico-critica instauranda,* Acta Congressus Scholastici Internationalis, Rome, 1950 (Rome, 1951), pp. 627–52; Giulio Bonafede, *Il pensiero francescano nel secolo XIII* (Palermo, 1952); Alonzo M. Hamelin, *L'école franciscaine de ses débuts jusqu'à l'occamisme* (Louvain, 1961); Pasquale Mazzarella, *La dottrina dell'anima e della conoscenza in Matteo d'Acquasparta* (Padua, 1969); and Leonard J. Bowman, "The Development of the Doctrine of the Agent Intellect in the Franciscan School of the Thirteenth Century," *The Modern Schoolman* 50

explained truth by means of a theory of epistemology scholars call divine illumination, generally considered to be only one part of a broader intellectual current known as Augustinianism.[4] This theory claimed that whatever one held to be true even in knowledge attained naturally—that is to say, without the special intervention of God as in prophecy or in glorification—one knew as such because God's light, the light of Truth, shone upon the mind. It was in the thirteenth century, so the account goes, that this doctrine was first challenged, most emphatically by Thomas Aquinas and his followers in the Dominican Order. For a while, traditional teachings and their new competitor jockeyed for position in the schools, and in

---

(1972-73), 251-79. The same view has also frequently been incorporated into general surveys of intellectual history during the Middle Ages. See Bernhard Geyer, ed., *Friedrich Ueberwegs Grundriss der Geschichte der Philosophie,* II: Die patristische und scholastische Philosophie, 12th ed. (Basel, 1951), esp. pp. 342, 381, 400-1; Etienne Gilson, *History of Christian Philosophy in the Middle Ages* (New York, 1955), p. 362; Gordon Leff, *Medieval Thought. St. Augustine to Ockham* (Baltimore, 1958), pp. 182-94, 211-12; Paul Vignaux, *Philosophy in the Middle Ages. An Introduction,* trans. E. C. Hall (Westport, Conn., 1959), pp. 117-19; Frederick C. Copleston, *A History of Philosophy,* II: Medieval Philosophy (New York, 1962), pt. 1, pp. 246, 255-57; and Julius Weinberg, *A Short History of Medieval Philosophy* (Princeton, 1964), p. 159. For a view that raises questions about Gilson's basic schema, see below, n. 8.

[4] Divine illumination, in the sense in which it is used in this study, refers to any of the various medieval theories that sought to explain man's acquisition of speculative knowledge in terms of an enlightenment by God as a higher truth. It differs from illuminism, another notion common in the Middle Ages, which has to do with the special state of grace enjoyed by contemplatives and mystics when God revealed Himself or His secrets to them. Medieval writers sometimes called this latter process illumination, but it can be distinguished from the sort of illumination under consideration here since it was directed toward the practical reason, not the speculative, and it was limited to the few. For a discussion of these two different ways the mind could be held to relate to God, see Brian Stock, "Experience, Praxis, Work, and Planning in Bernard of Clairvaux: Observations on the *Sermones in Cantica,*" in *The Cultural Context of Medieval Learning,* ed. John E. Murdoch and Edith D. Sylla (Dordrecht, Netherlands, 1975), pp. 236-37. Stock associates the first kind of illumination with the thought of Augustine, and he says that an example of the second kind, what is here called illuminism, can be found in Bernard's use of the notion of illumination.

fact illuminationism found its classical formulation at this time in the writings of Bonaventure or, perhaps more accurately, in those of his disciples, John Pecham and Matthew of Aquasparta at Paris and Roger Marston at Oxford.[5] Soon, however, the older epistemological explanations lost their appeal, so that they either died out completely or maintained only a feeble existence into the fourteenth century.[6] As for new doctrines of truth, several varieties quickly arose in addition to the Thomistic solution, and they led eventually to the rigid, more narrowly dogmatic schools of the late Middle Ages.

Although this standard view has served to point out that the thirteenth century witnessed a change in the way thinkers defined truth and human knowledge of it, it can no longer stand without considerable modification, for it seriously misconstrues the nature of the change it describes. First of all, there never was a traditional doctrine of divine illumination, if what is meant by a doctrine is a coherent theory with a constant philosophical purpose. Admittedly, the image of divine light had a continuous history in Western thought, stemming from a few basic sources, but that does not mean it was always used with the same sense in mind. It was primarily a metaphor and, like any such figure of speech, could find diverse applications. Over the centuries, theologians had used it to describe phenomena as dissimilar as the gift of grace or prophetic revelation, both extraordinary events, and the common agreement of everyone about certain formulas of everyday speech, most notably value-laden words like good, beautiful, or even big and

---

[5] See Gilson, *History of Christian Philosophy*, pp. 340–43, and Jean Rohmer, "La théorie de l'abstraction dans l'école franciscaine de Alexandre de Halès à Jean Peckam," *Archives d'Histoire Doctrinale et Littéraire du Moyen Age* 3 (1928), 105–84, for two prominent accounts of this classic theory of illumination.

[6] Martin Grabmann, in *Der göttliche Grund menschlicher Wahrheitserkenntnis nach Augustinus und Thomas von Aquin* (Münster, 1924), p. 41, was the first to recognize that illuminationist theories, and in particular the notion of intellectual vision in the divine ideas, declined in the late thirteenth century, but subsequent scholars have been divided as to whether or not they disappeared altogether in the form they had taken before.

small. Rather than try to force all these into a philosophical straitjacket, it seems preferable to regard them separately. The historian must examine each case where the language of illumination appears and identify its function before he can assign it any particular philosophical meaning.

Yet the difficulty with the conventional account goes beyond the fact that it presupposes a more coherent tradition than there actually was. On a more basic level it tends to misinterpret the nature of intellectual development. Implicit in this account lies the assumption that except for a dark period, when very little philosophy was discussed at all, the Middle Ages witnessed a single and continuous philosophical debate over the issue of truth. A doctrine advanced in the fifth century could be countered by another one in the thirteenth because throughout the whole period those who were concerned with the problem agreed about the nature of the question to be asked; they differed only over how the question was to be resolved. The fact is, however, that at different times in the Middle Ages thinkers were interested in different kinds of speculation, and therefore they often faced radically different sorts of questions, even over what may appear at first sight to be the same philosophical issue. In this instance the discussion of truth in the fifth century, or even in the early twelfth, was not commensurate with the discussion of truth by the mid-thirteenth, precisely because the nature of the philosophical interest in and approach to that problem had changed. What had originally been loosely a question of epistemology with strong theological implications had become much more a matter of critical philosophy, tied to the syllogistic logic developing in the schools.[7] Naturally, doctrines designed to accommodate

[7] It must be admitted that for all Gilson's talk about an Augustinian tradition, he did at times give evidence he realized that the philosophical nature of the theory of divine illumination may have changed over the centuries. In "Sur quelques difficultés de l'illumination augustinienne," *Revue Néoscolastique de Philosophie* 36 (1934), 321–31, he noted that the theory as Augustine used it was less noetic than epistemological—that is, it was concerned with the problem of judgment more than that of the formation of concepts. Efrem Bettoni, apparently picking up on this,

the problem of truth as it was conceived in the early period would have no precise counterpart or competitor in the later period, when the nature of the philosophical problem had changed. By the same token, language associated with a specific doctrine early on might easily be used in the later period, but for a different purpose and thus to express a totally different philosophical idea. The conventional account, by focusing exclusively on doctrines and giving more attention to the externals of philosophical diction than to the context in which it is found, condemns itself to seeing continuity where there was none and to interpreting every novelty as a change in the content, but not the form, of philosophy. In this way it not only errs; it also overlooks a most significant development in medieval thought.[8]

---

suggested that it was Bonaventure who applied the theory to ideogenic as well as criteriological problems. See Bettoni, "La dottrina bonaventuriana dell'illuminazaione intellettuale," and *S. Bonaventura* (Brescia, 1945), pp. 121–25.

[8] Fernand Van Steenberghen has been the one medieval historian to argue most consistently and coherently for the view that the nature of intellectual discourse changed radically over time, even within the high Middle Ages. He has maintained that philosophy in the strict sense of the word came to be practiced quite late in the medieval West and that genuine philosophical systems emerged only in the later thirteenth century. Consequently, he has claimed that the attempt to define philosophical schools for the early thirteenth century, along Augustinian, Arab, or Aristotelian lines, is misguided. This position is defended throughout Van Steenberghen's works, but it is argued most forcefully in English in his *Aristotle in the West,* 2nd ed. (Louvain, 1970). The present study, while moving in much the same direction as Van Steenberghen's work, differs in that it attempts to show a much greater degree of sophistication on the critical issues of the nature of truth and the theory behind scientific argument than Van Steenberghen would admit for the early thirteenth century.

Among general introductions to the history of medieval thought in English, David Knowles's *The Evolution of Medieval Thought* (Baltimore, 1962), stands out as making the fullest use of Van Steenberghen's ideas. Frederick Copleston, in his latest general survey of the period, *A History of Medieval Philosophy* (London, 1972), considers Van Steenberghen's views with some sympathy, but he eventually settles on a position very close to the more conventional one he held before—that one can speak of a traditional Platonic-Augustinian philosophy leading up and into the thirteenth century. See his *History,* pp. 156–59, 161, 165.

In fact the thirteenth century witnessed a major transformation in the form of scholarly thought. For a large number of intellectuals the tenor of philosophical discourse changed, and with this change arose the problem of truth as it had not existed before. It was during this period that scholars, working in the universities, committed themselves, at least in theory, to Aristotle's model of science (*scientia*).[9] For Aristotle science provided the paradigm of cognitive certitude, and according to strict Aristotelian terminology, scientific knowledge meant knowledge that had been arrived at by means of demonstration. An assertion could be held with the certitude of science only if it had been proved according to the rules of demonstrative logic.[10] This vision captivated thirteenth- and fourteenth-century thinkers, and they too began to speak about "science" as if it were the only worthy form of human thought. Although at the beginning many understood only imperfectly what Aristotle had meant by this term, they all used it with Aristotle in mind, and with a sense of the prestige that attached to the special category of knowledge he had wanted to define.

The idea of "science" and the desire to be "scientific" shaped the scholasticism of the thirteenth century and signaled it as something new in the medieval West. What is important for this study is that the new interest in science posed a number of philosophical problems, in particular that concerning the nature of truth, in a way that would have been previously inconceivable. By adopting the model of scientific thought, thinkers

---

[9] The desire to apply the canons of science extended to practically all forms of thought. Marie-Dominique Chenu, in *La théologie comme science au XIIIe siècle,* 3rd ed. (Paris, 1957), pp. 17–18, and *La théologie au douzième siècle,* 2nd ed. (Paris, 1966), pp. 376–77, and Jean Leclercq, in *Etudes sur le vocabulaire monastique du moyen âge* (Rome, 1961), p. 72, have noted that it was in the thirteenth century that medieval scholars made the study of theology a scientific discipline. See also Albert Lang, *Die theologische Prinzipienlehre der mittelalterlichen Scholastik* (Freiburg im Br., 1964).

[10] For an introduction to Aristotle's ideas about science, see Jonathan Barnes, Malcolm Schofield, and Richard Sorabji, eds., *Articles on Aristotle,* I: Science (London, 1975), especially the article by Barnes, himself, "Aristotle's Theory of Demonstration," pp. 65–87.

of the thirteenth century committed themselves to construct-
ing a theory of truth that could underlie the methods of argumentation they intended to promote. And this endeavor posed
philosophical issues medieval thinkers had not faced before. It
is one of the achievements of thought in the thirteenth century
that scholars of that time first came to grasp the nature of this
new problem of truth and began to work out their own
theories of how the problem should be solved.

To explain exactly how the general transformation in
thought influenced speculation about truth, it is necessary to
compare the role of epistemology and ideas of truth before and
after the adoption of the scientific model. Historians customar-
ily speak of the traditional thought of the Middle Ages as Augustinian, and although this oversimplifies things[11]—for
among sources alone there were many currents besides that dependent on Augustine[12]—it is true that for centuries Augustine exerted a preponderant influence and that his works had a
solid hold on the educated imagination. They had been the
mainstay of intellectual activity since the ninth century at the
latest and constituted, after the Bible, the literary corpus that
every medieval thinker would have known best. The tone of

[11] Odon Lottin, in *Psychologie et morale aux XIIe et XIIIe siècles*, I
(Louvain, 1942), 502, has even argued that there was no such thing as an
Augustinian current of thought before the time of Thomas Aquinas,
whose teachings triggered the formation of such a current in opposition.
What Lottin meant was that before this time there was no single, coherent current of thought associated with the teachings of Augustine as
there would be later in the thirteenth century. Fernand Van Steenberghen has advanced a similar argument in both *Aristotle in the West*,
pp. 126–30, and *La philosophie au XIIIe siècle* (Louvain, 1966), pp.
156–57, 170, 187–89. Their point is well taken and should be considered
in conjunction with the assertion made above that there was no classic
doctrine of divine illumination before Thomas.

[12] Among these other sources, perhaps the most important for the history of medieval thought from the twelfth century on were Neoplatonic
works by Arabic and Jewish philosophers and theologians. They were
particularly influential on questions of epistemology, where they combined with and indeed reinforced many of the themes and images drawn
from Augustine's works. For the sake of simplicity they have not been
included in this brief sketch of attitudes in epistemology before the thirteenth century, but any full investigation would have to give them the
greatest consideration.

Augustine's thought suited perfectly the devotional and doctrinal orientations of the early Middle Ages, when scholars engaged in high-level speculation, largely theological in content, found in his vocabulary a comfortable vehicle for the expression of their ideas.

One area where Augustine's language had the greatest effect was in epistemology. Since he had addressed himself frequently to problems concerning human knowledge, his works were rich in concepts and images that could be employed to talk about the mind. Many of them involved some sort of illumination or intervention from above, and Augustine's metaphors of light and of the impression of a seal in wax were firmly established, taking on even added vigor with the interest in Neoplatonism in the twelfth century. The use to which he put them, and for which they were designed, harmonized with current intellectual needs.

It hardly needs to be said that Augustine was not interested in demonstrative science, nor was his thought scientific in any strict sense of the word. Not only did he not generally concern himself with careful logical analysis. There are also innumerable places crucial to a systematic rendering of his thought where he spoke ambiguously, and in fact it was rare that he worked a philosophical problem out to a final solution. Insofar as he needed a theoretical foundation, he simply borrowed doctrines from earlier writers, leaving it to his readers to iron out the inconsistencies. Consequently, Augustine's handling of truth was free from the burden of precise definition and formal explanation. And this explains why it is never clear exactly how he thought divine illumination worked. No matter how often one goes over his works, the mechanism by which God's light influences human cognition remains vague; only the fact that it does so is sure.

All this can be traced back to the purpose of Augustine's work. Whenever he was not expounding Church dogma, Augustine was less interested in explaining theories than in making clear the proper ends of human behavior. His philosophical reasonings served the purposes of practical religion; they were intended more for exhortation than elucidation. Indeed, the primary preoccupation of almost all his writings was to lead men back to God.

Given this proclivity, it is not hard to understand why he found the metaphor of divine illumination so congenial or why he used it so often. He nearly always examined the nature of truth within the framework of some larger discussion of man's relation to God or of God's economy of salvation.[13] In such cases the image of divine illumination permitted him to make his point in a way that was concise and would appeal to his Late-Antique readers. Since the notion that human knowledge depended on a divine light made the existence of truth metaphysically, and even conceptually, inseparable from the fact of divine assistance in all higher cognitive endeavors, Augustine could argue—as he often did—from any commonly accepted truth, the validity of which he felt no one could deny, to the existence of God. Thus, in the *Soliloquies,* one of his earliest works, Augustine had reason demonstrate God's existence to the mind: "Reason, speaking to you now, promises that it will demonstrate God to your mind, just as the sun can be demonstrated to your eyes. For ... the most certain principles of learning are just like all things that the sun shines on ... : and it is God, Himself, who shines on them."[14] Beyond this, however, divine illumination also implied that God was within reach of the human mind, for if God was involved in the simple act of knowing the truth, then Augustine could say that everyone could find Him and find Him within himself. In *On Free Will,* after he had demonstrated God's existence, Augustine continued by pointing out that the divinity was naturally available to all:

Therefore, since the Highest Good is known and held in Truth, and since that Truth is wisdom, let us discern in it and hold to the

---

[13] See, for instance, in the former case, the last four books of *De Trinitate,* and in the latter, *De libero arbitrio,* especially bk. II.

[14] *Soliloquia,* I, 6, 12 (PL, 32, 875). Unless otherwise noted, all translations from the Latin sources have been made by the author.

Highest Good and fully enjoy it. . . . For just as those who choose to gaze freely in the light of the sun and find joy in such sight, if they were provided with more vigorous, healthy and strong eyes would gaze on nothing more willingly than the sun itself, which indeed illustrates those other things in which weaker eyes take delight, so the mind, if it is made strong and vigorous, after it has looked on many true and immutable certainties, will direct [its gaze] into the Truth itself by which all other truths are shown, and inhering in that Truth it [will] forget all the others and in it find joy in them all.[15]

A train of thought that began with a doctrine about knowledge ended by showing how close God was to man. Augustine employed worldly speculation in hopes that his audience would quickly leave it in order to search for God Himself.

In both its subservience to questions of moral ends and in its formal imprecision, Augustine's bearing toward the idea of truth set the pattern for early medieval thought. For him as well as for early-medieval thinkers, there was no genuinely critical problem of truth—that is, there was no concern to define truth logically and then see whether this definition could be applied to human knowledge and to any reasonable explanation of how it was acquired—because there was no interest in establishing knowledge along the strictly logical lines that would have made such a critical approach attractive. In fact, Augustine was not really posing a problem of truth at all. He was instead using a definition of truth to make a point about God's relation to man.

Yet circumstances would change when scholars committed themselves to science. Ever since the twelfth century educated men in the West had come to put an extraordinary emphasis on knowledge as one of the key mediators between man and his world, material and spiritual. Indeed, it can be argued that one of the peculiar traits of twelfth- and thirteenth-century Europe was its overwhelming conviction that the accumulation

[15] *De libero artibrio,* II, 13, ed. William M. Green, CSEL, 74 (Vienna, 1956), pp. 72-73.

of speculative wisdom was one of the primary ends of man. What encouraged thinkers in this belief, and perhaps contributed to its sudden urgency, was the rapid proliferation of Latin translations from Arabic and Greek sources, beginning early in the twelfth century, a phenomenon that put at scholars' disposal a body of thought for which their educational traditions provided no precedent. In scope and subtlety as well as sheer quantity the new learning of the twelfth century went far beyond anything the Latin world had seen up until then.

Confronted with burgeoning aspirations and a mass of undigested intellectual material, twelfth-century thinkers began to devote a large part of their energies to organizing the knowledge that lay before them. Most of these early attempts consisted of adopting a world-view, frequently some form of Christianized Neoplatonism, into which one could fit all the accumulated bits of conventional wisdom. There were also significant efforts to identify and arrange the various disciplines of knowledge in order to give shape to an otherwise confusing array of practical and speculative pursuits. In either case, the search was for a predetermined structure that would embrace all accepted truths and bring them together into a coherent whole. By the thirteenth century, however, the interest in these old external structures had begun to wane, and there was evidence of a new urge to look for more purely formal and internal ways to organize what men knew. Perhaps the change came about because the body of knowledge had expanded so far that the old world-views were no longer capable of tying everything together; perhaps it was because more than a century of painstaking work in logic had begun to convince men that a new kind of logical ordering was possible. At any rate, one sees more and more often in the thirteenth century the belief that what was needed was an organization of knowledge following universal formal principles. Scholars wanted to systematize their thoughts not by imposing a structure from outside, as had been the case before, but rather by applying purely formal rules of thought out of which a more natural configuration would arise.[16]

To such minds the works of Aristotle seemed like a divine gift; his model of knowledge promised the key they were looking for. What was involved here were not the results of any of Aristotle's investigations into specific fields of inquiry but rather the philosophical groundwork he had laid in order to make those investigations. To Aristotle this meant setting out the spectrum of all possible modes of thought, from the least reliable to the most secure, but the capstone of his efforts was his attempt to isolate that portion of knowledge which was most certain, science or *scientia* itself, and to establish it according to definite formal principles. Even though his speculations about these principles were to be found scattered throughout his works and some of his most profound contributions to scientific theory were merely implied in the books on natural philosophy and metaphysics, he expressed his fundamental views most concisely in his logical writings, particularly in *On Interpretation* and the *Prior* and *Posterior Analytics*. Already by the twelfth century medieval scholars recognized the importance of these works, and the thirteenth century saw their full assimilation into Latin thought with the first systematic attempts to comment on the one most specifically about scientific reasoning itself, the *Posterior Analytics*.[17]

In their efforts to comprehend Aristotle and at the same time work out the principles of science, academics came face to face

[16] On thirteenth-century attempts to articulate a complete structure of speculative thought, see James A. Weisheipl, "Classification of the Sciences in Medieval Thought," *Mediaeval Studies* 27 (1965), 54–90, and "The Nature, Scope and Classification of the Sciences," in *Science in the Middle Ages,* ed. David C. Lindberg (Chicago, 1978), pp. 461–82.

[17] John of Salisbury, writing in the middle of the twelfth century, had commented on the difficulty of understanding the *Posterior Analytics* and added that few minds were keen enough to make much sense of it (see his *Metalogicon,* IV, 6, ed. Clement C. J. Webb [Oxford, 1929], pp. 170–71). Only in the thirteenth century—beginning with Robert Grosseteste's *Commentary*—did this work receive the painstaking analysis it required.

with the classical problem of the nature of truth. For those thinkers with a concern for theoretical rigor, the success of the hoped-for classification of knowledge and the isolation of a certain, scientific body of truths depended on finding a theory of truth and cognitive evidence to serve as a standard, or at least one that would validate the standard already generated by scholastic logic. This entailed not only increased attention to the problem of truth but also a different way of approaching it. Because such thinkers wanted to establish so strictly formal an ideal as science, they had to be careful that their own foundations lived up to the high criteria they had set. Thirteenth-century notions of truth had to be real theories, both precise and complete. In a way that would have been incomprehensible, or merely irrelevant, to thinkers only a few generations earlier, the new theories had to be critical almost in the modern philosophical sense. That is to say, they had to give greater attention to the logical aspects of the problem—as is important in a modern theory of truth—and leave to epistemological questions the subordinate role of explaining how the logic applied in actual cases given the mechanics of human cognition.[18] In every aspect—precision, completeness, criticism—they had no equivalent in preceding medieval speculation. They marked a new stage in the history of thought.

By opting for science and thereby opening a fresh perspective on the problem of truth, the scholastics of the later Middle Ages cut themselves free from the old patterns of thought sympathetic to Augustine. His reflections on truth, designed, like those of the early Middle Ages, to reveal the workings of a standard in the operations of the mind and to show how that standard resided in God, but not to speculate on its formal

[18] Medieval thinkers were never critical to the extent that they worked out the logical problems of truth first and then looked to see whether there was any chance human thought could meet the established criteria. Such an attitude has been seen only in modern times. In the Middle Ages men considered the logical and epistemological problems together, starting with the firm assumption that a way would, or must, be found whereby truth could be said to characterize at least some form of human cognition.

qualities, offered little to those desiring to produce a measure that could actually be applied. But if the old ways of thinking were inadequate, Aristotle himself did not furnish quick answers. Scholars had to cull the fundamentals of his theories painstakingly from his works and fill in the numerous lacunae on their own. Perhaps more important, they had to figure out just what he meant and what the significance of a scientific model would be for their own patterns of thought. Both circumstances, the divergent philosophical direction of previous thought on truth and the interpretative and theoretical difficulties with new sources, made the problem of truth facing the thirteenth century no simple matter of choosing between doctrines or of shifting from one to another, as the conventional account implies. The novelty of the situation forced thinkers to set out on new philosophical ground.

The history of the problem of truth in the later Middle Ages is, therefore, the story of a process of intellectual inquiry and debate by which thinkers came to understand the nature of the new problem that faced them and worked out solutions that were consistent and fully satisfied the philosophical needs for which they were designed. The universities provided the conditions necessary to sustain such a debate, and it was there that the new issue about truth arose and ran its course. The whole process lasted from the early thirteenth century to the first decades of the fourteenth. As with almost any philosophical inquiry, progress depended on maintaining a running dialogue among intellectuals. Over the years there would be false starts that had to be rejected and conceptual dilemmas that needed working out. Since medieval scholars put such a premium on authority, a considerable effort would be required to interpret the sources in a way compatible with the new interests or to recognize when they did not apply. A comprehensive solution, or even a full understanding of what the problem was about, could come only with time, after scholars had laid out all the relevant questions and begun to suggest the doctrinal options with which they could be answered. That stage was not reached until the late thirteenth century, in the generation of scholars after Thomas Aquinas. It is in this period that one finds the greatest proliferation of writings about the problem of truth and the first significant attempts to take opposing sides on the fundamental issues involved.[19] In the scholarly arguments of these years one can already see the outlines of the ultimate crystallization of both problem and solution in the major philosophical currents of the fourteenth century, most notably nominalist and Scotistic thought.

In order to understand these later developments it is necessary to go back to the origins. This study will examine the first stage in the process, the earliest attempts of thirteenth-century thinkers to find a theory of truth suitable to an organization of knowledge as science. In doing so it will occasionally be necessary to discuss epistemological issues not actually part of a theory of truth but upon which a novel conception of the nature of truth was founded. Emphasis will be placed on both the efforts to devise a new language to speak about truth and the attempts to come to terms with traditional notions of divine illumination so as to determine their place in the new perspective.

This first stage in the process extended from about 1220 to the end of the 1240s. As the time when scholars first recognized the existence of a more critical problem of truth, these years manifested greater ambiguity and inconsistency than would be found in subsequent stages. The attachment to a scientific ideal was still young, and even its most enthusiastic adherents devoted considerable time to speculating in the older modes of thought, sometimes intruding this discussion upon their more scientific investigations. Curiously enough, it was in the schools of theology at both Oxford and Paris where the

[19] From this perspective John Pecham and Matthew of Aquasparta, the late-thirteenth-century thinkers commonly associated with the classic doctrine of illumination, can be seen to have shared little more than some patterns of language with their forebears of the twelfth century. Their desire to establish a scientific theory of truth made them define the role of divine light in precise terms that were foreign to the traditional views about truth. The doctrines they espoused were, therefore, not reformulations of an older theory but rather new theories worked out under the pressures of the philosophical issues of their time.

greatest achievements were made in elucidating the nature of truth, and among theologians of the time there were two whose work stands out: William of Auvergne (ca. 1180-1249), bishop of Paris from 1228 to 1249, and Robert Grosseteste (1168?-1253), bishop of Lincoln from 1235 to 1253. They were the ones who began the task, who laid the foundations for the developments of the later thirteenth century. This study will focus exclusively on their work.[20]

Before turning to examine the thought of these men, however, it is necessary to introduce a few categories that will serve to organize the exposition. When thinkers set out to find a workable theory of truth, they faced two basic questions. First, they had to determine the nature of truth itself: What was truth, and how could it be defined? Second, they had to discover the kinds of evidence for true knowledge: How could one arrive at truth in this life, and when could one be sure of having found it? Admittedly, the difference between the two problems was sometimes a subtle matter. In the simplest case, immediate knowledge of self-evident truth, the evidence was nothing more than the perceived fact that the conditions defining truth had been met. Yet when it came to derivative knowledge, such as that arrived at by logical inference, the mind attained certain knowledge without simultaneously perceiving the fundamental conditions that made it true, and in such cases the rules of evidence had to be considered separately from the terms set in the formal definition of truth.

Furthermore, in order to answer these two questions there had to be some agreement about the number of cases to which they should be applied. Since knowledge can take several forms, a theory accounting for truth and its evidence in one form will not do for another; thinkers needed a taxonomy of cognition to guide their efforts. Just as scholars in the thirteenth century looked to Aristotle for the key to science, so it

---

[20] It may come as a surprise that the eminent theologians William of Auxerre, Alexander of Hales, and for the last years of this period John of la Rochelle do not appear in this study. In fact, their writings contain very little that pertains to the subject.

was natural for them to adopt the formal categories he employed.

Working from an analogy with language, Aristotle divided knowledge into two basic forms. As in speech one could distinguish individual words from the sentences they went together to comprise, so in thought it was necessary to separate single ideas from the more complicated mental configurations that combined them.[21] This simple scheme rested on the assumption that concepts were like images, each referring to a single subject, and that such concepts were the atoms of all human thought. Depending on whether these atoms were regarded individually or as combined into larger units represented by propositions, one could speak of simple or complex cognition. In the words of the Latin Middle Ages, knowledge was either *incomplexum* or *complexum*.

Since people expressed what they knew in the form of statements, it was the second kind of knowledge, complex cognition, that interested Aristotle most, and within complex cognition it was that part which was also most certain—that is, scientific knowledge—to which he gave the greatest attention. Here, he had to make room for inference. The principal way— strictly speaking, the only way—to obtain science was by demonstration.[22] But if this was so, then it would seem that the paradigmatic form of certain knowledge had to be inferred from something else already known to be true, for demonstration was a formal process of logical inference. The question was, therefore, how one could explain this previous knowledge upon which the inference was based without falling into the

---

[21] See *De interpretatione*, I, 1 (16a9–15) (for the Latin version of this text used most commonly in the Middle Ages, the translation by Boethius, see *De interpretatione*, Aristoteles Latinus, II, 1–2, ed. Lorenzo Minio-Paluello and Gérard Verbeke [Bruges, 1965], p. 5). The *locus classicus* on simple and complex cognition was found in Aristotle's *De anima*, III, 6 (430a26–28).

[22] Aristotle, *Posterior Analytics*, I, 2 (71b16–17). See the Latin translation by James of Venice, the version used most commonly in the Middle Ages: *Analytica Posteriora*, Aristoteles Latinus, IV, 1–4, ed. Lorenzo Minio-Paluello and Bernard G. Dod (Bruges, 1968), p. 7.

circularity of saying that all certain truths were demonstrated from others that had in turn been demonstrated from others before.

Aristotle's answer was that there were some basic truths so evident that they did not have to be inferred. Thus, there were in fact two kinds of complex cognition that were certain, and they were not arrived at in the same way. The first kind concerned those complex truths known immediately, what Aristotle called the principles of scientific knowledge. The second was knowledge of truths demonstrated from such principles by the rules of logic; these inferred truths were the conclusions of science.[23] Now, while both kinds of cognition made up the body of scientific knowledge, broadly speaking, Aristotle applied the name *scientia* in the strict sense only to the latter, that concerning demonstrated truths. "Science" referred properly to knowledge of the conclusions. Knowledge of the principles was pure understanding (*intellectus*).[24] The crux of the distinction lay in the discursive process of the act of reason, *ratio* in the strict scholastic sense of the word. To acquire science required the rational processes of syllogistic logic as described in the *Analytics;* the understanding of principles, on the other hand, came through the simple application of the mind's power to comprehend.[25]

Aristotle's scientific plan allowed, therefore, for three basic forms of thought: one form was simple, the apprehension of an uncombined concept; and two were complex, the immediate understanding of a complex principle (*intellectus*) and the demonstrated knowledge of a complex conclusion (*scientia*).[26] It

---

[23] *Posterior Analytics,* I, 3 (72b18–25).

[24] *Scientia* was the standard Latin translation for Aristotle's *epistēmē*—as *intellectus* was for *nous.*

[25] See *Posterior Analytics,* II, 19 (100b7–15) (in the Latin translation by James of Venice [Aristoteles Latinus, IV, 1–4, ed. Minio-Paluello and Dod, pp. 106–7]).

[26] Perhaps the most eloquent description of the three forms of knowledge comes from the thirteenth century itself, from Thomas Aquinas's *Commentary on the Posterior Analytics.* If one keeps in mind that not all of Thomas's contemporaries shared his clarity of thought, his statement can serve as a model for the scheme accepted throughout the late Middle

was to these three types of knowledge that thinkers of the thirteenth century had to address the two questions about the definition of and the evidence for truth.

Yet this did not come to six different questions—two for each of the three types of knowledge—but only five. Since the principles and the conclusions of science were, from a purely formal point of view, epistemologically equivalent, the definition of truth reduced to the same thing for them both. They each consisted of affirmative or negative propositions, and having defined truth for propositions in general, it was not necessary to examine the issue further. Only when it came to the question of the evidence for knowing the truth did the difference between principle and conclusion become significant. The evidence for principles depended immediately on the definition of complex truth. Principles consisted of immediately evident complex truth, and one knew they were true by seeing that the knowledge they provided met the conditions of the definition of truth. Because an examination of this process revealed a good deal about the formal nature of human cognition, it was of considerable importance to those interested in the theory of knowledge. Indeed, explaining how one arrived at the knowledge of principles was a major and controversial issue through-

---

Ages: "Now there are three acts of the reason, of which the first two pertain to reason insofar as it is a kind of understanding (*intellectus*). One act of understanding is the comprehension (*intelligentia*) of indivisible or incomplex concepts, and by this action the intellect conceives what a thing is. And this operation is called by some the information of the intellect or intellectual imagination. And to this operation of the reason is devoted the teaching that Aristotle hands down in the book of *Categories*. The second operation of understanding is the intellectual act of composition or division. . . . And to this act of reason pertains the teaching Aristotle hands down in the book *On Interpretation.* The third act of reason concerns that which is actually proper to reason (*ratio*)—that is, to pass from one thing to another so that through what is known a man comes to knowledge of the unknown. And to this act pertain the other books of logic." *Commentarium in libros Posteriorum analyticorum,* prooemium, §4 in *Opera omnia* (Leonine ed.), I (Rome, 1882), 138b. The translation given here has been arrived at through comparison with that of Fabian R. Larcher in his English edition of Aquinas's *Commentary on the Posterior Analytics of Aristotle* (Albany, N.Y., 1970), pp. 1–2.

out the thirteenth century. Evidence for the knowledge of conclusions, on the other hand, had to do with the rules of logical
inference, so that one had to work out the modes of demonstration in order to explain how it was possible to know when
such propositions were true. This was the task of the theory of
logic, and from the early thirteenth century on medieval thinkers excelled in this field, where they made some of their most
notable contributions to philosophy. Yet such matters had little to do with formal questions of epistemology and the nature
of cognitive certitude. Once one had indicated how a true
knowledge of principles had been arrived at, one could expect
any educated person to concede that true knowledge of the
conclusions would follow by the rules of demonstration.

These were, then, the five basic questions that concerned
thirteenth-century thinkers in their investigations of the problem of truth. For the case of simple cognition they had to ask
what truth was and how it was attained. For the case of complex cognition it was necessary to keep in mind the distinction
between principles and conclusions. A single question with a
single answer sufficed to explain what truth was in both cases.
Yet on the matter of the evidence for such truth—how the
mind could attain it—scholars had to respect the division between the two. The question of the way to knowledge of the
principles was largely a problem for noetics and epistemology;
the question of the way to knowledge of conclusions led back
to the procedures of syllogistic logic. This simple framework
provided the foundation for thirteenth-century theories of
truth, and its categories and questions will guide the analysis
that follows.

PART ONE

William
of Auvergne

WILLIAM OF AUVERGNE was born in Aurillac, France, some-time in the late twelfth century, perhaps around 1180.[1] Although little is known about his early life, it is clear that as a young man he went to study at Paris, first in the school of arts and then, after a period as master of arts, in the school of theology. There he eventually received his licentiate and assumed a chair as regent master. In 1228, Pope Gregory IX appointed him bishop of Paris, and he held that post until his death in 1249.

William's literary activity spanned the time of his professorship and his early years as a bishop. His major work, the *Magisterium divinale ac sapientiale,* was a compendious apology for the Christian view of the world.[2] In it, he proposed to defend all of truth against the errors of impious philosophers, and he said he would do so without making any appeal to Christian faith or the authority of divine revelation, relying only on the way of natural reason and logical proof.[3] The work actually consists of seven different treatises, of which five were probably

[1] For the details of William's biography, see Noël Valois, *Guillaume d'Auvergne, évêque de Paris (1228-1249), sa vie et ses ouvrages* (Paris, 1880); Richard Heinzmann, "Wilhelm von Auvergne," in *Lexikon für Theologie und Kirche,* 2nd ed. (Freiburg i. B., 1965), X, 1127-28; Ernest A. Moody, "William of Auvergne and his Treatise *De anima,*" in *Studies in Medieval Philosophy, Science and Logic* (Berkeley, Calif., 1975), pp. 1-109; Ephrem Longpré, "Guillaume d'Auvergne et L'Ecole Franciscaine de Paris," *La France Franciscaine* 5 (1922), 426-29; and Amato Masnovo, "Guglielmo d'Auvergne e l'Università di Parigi dal 1229 al 1231," in *Mélanges Mandonnet,* II (Paris, 1930), 191-232.

[2] This work is generally referred to simply as the *Magisterium divinale.* William himself, however, called it by many names, and Guglielmo Corti, in "Le sette parte del *Magisterium divinale ac sapientiale* di Guglielmo di Auvergne," in *Studi e richerche di scienze religiose* (Rome, 1968), pp. 293-94), argues convincingly that it is more appropriately designated by the longer title used here.

[3] See William's prologue to his *De Trinitate,* ed. Bruno Switalski (Toronto, 1976), pp. 15-16.

composed before William became bishop, but two, *De universo* and *De anima,* almost certainly date from the early years of his episcopacy, in all likelihood from 1231 to 1236.[4] It is these two late treatises that are most important for this study, for in them William gave the fullest account of his ideas about truth and the nature of true knowledge. Another, minor work that includes some speculation on truth, *De bono et malo,* dates from before 1228.[5]

William wrote at a time when, despite several prohibitions against teaching the natural philosophy of Aristotle and his commentators, Aristotelian science and philosophy were beginning to dominate intellectual discussion. Some modern scholars have interpreted his work as an all-out attack on the

[4] All previous speculation about dating William's work was superseded by Josef Kramp, in "Des Wilhelm von Auvergne 'Magisterium divinale,'" *Gregorianum* 1 (1920), 538–84, and 2 (1921), 42–78, 174–87, who in turn was corrected on a minor point by Ephrem Longpré, in "Guillaume d'Auvergne et Alexandre de Halès," *Archivum Franciscanum Historicum* 16 (1923), 249–50. Ernest Moody, in "William of Auvergne," pp. 9–11, essentially accepts Kramp's conclusions but suggests that the latter part of *De universo* and the *De anima* may not have been completed until around 1240. Amato Masnovo, in "Guglielmo d'Auvergne," *Rivista di Filosofia Neo-Scolastica* 19 (1927), 132, and in *Da Guglielmo d'Auvergne a s. Tommaso d'Aquino,* I, 2nd ed. (Milan, 1945), 38, feels that although the last two treatises of the *Magisterium* were written after 1231 they represent views William developed in his years as a teacher, before 1228, to which he gave a new redaction in the 1230s, but not a new form. There has also been some debate about how William intended his seven treatises to go together to make up the *Magisterium.* Kramp, in the article mentioned above, suggested an order that most scholars have accepted as authentic. Recently, however, Guglielmo Corti, in "Le sette parte del *Magisterium,*" pp. 304–6, has come up with a slightly different order, completely eliminating *De anima* from the original seven. He speculates that when William came to write *De anima* he was not sure how it fit in with the others and perhaps did not care about giving it a definite place.

The edition of *De universo* and *De anima* used in this study is that in the *Opera omnia,* two volumes, the second containing a supplement (Orleans-Paris, 1674, repr. Frankfurt a. M., 1963). Hereafter, this work will be referred to as *Mag. div.*

[5] This work has been edited by J. Reginald O'Donnell in *Mediaeval Studies* 8 (1946), 245–99, which edition will be referred to below as *De bono et malo.* It must not be confused with a second *De bono et malo* written by William and also edited by O'Donnell, in *Mediaeval Studies* 16 (1954), 219–71.

newly discovered body of thought.[6] Others have pointed out, with greater justification, how much he contributed to the early attempts to assimilate Peripatetic and Arabic philosophy by bringing Aristotle's views into line with Christian notions of the universe. They have suggested that he held to a *via media* between rejection and uncritical acceptance, remaining open to the new intellectual currents while retaining full independence with regard to specific doctrines.[7] The latter view is surely closer to the truth, and in fact it may not go far enough to reveal the innovative character of William's thought. For all his wariness about certain peculiarities of doctrine, when it came to language and the principles of scientific procedure he capitulated almost completely to the new ideal.[8] Among his contemporaries he was in the forefront of the move to adopt the terms of Aristotle's analysis.

---

[6] Heinzmann, in *Lexikon für Theologie und Kirche,* X, 1127, identified William as a sharp opponent of the new Aristotelian, Arab, and Jewish influence on medieval thought, and Karl Werner, in *Die Psychologie des Wilhelm von Auvergne* (Vienna, 1873), p. 1, and in *Wilhelms von Auvergne Verhältniss zu den Platonikern des XII. Jahrhunderts* (Vienna, 1873), p. 54, called him a reactionary Platonist sympathetic to the old scholasticism of the twelfth century. Masnovo, in "Guglielmo d'Auvergne," *Rivista di Filosofia Neo-Scolastica* 19 (1927), 145, and Bernard Landry, in "L'originalité de Guillaume d'Auvergne," *Revue d'Histoire de la Philosophie* 3 (1929), 441, have argued that William was more anti-Avicennian than anti-Aristotelian, although Gilson, in "Pourquoi saint Thomas a critiqué saint Augustin," pp. 48–80, claimed William as one of the founders of a scholastic current highly dependent on Avicenna, to which Gilson gave the name *Augustinisme avicennisant.*

[7] The notion that for all his criticism William did much to advance the cause of Aristotle's philosophy in the West can be found in Stephan Schindele, *Beiträge zur Metaphysik des Wilhelm von Auvergne* (Munich, 1900), p. 9, and Aimé Forest, "Guillaume d'Auvergne, critique d'Aristote," *Études médiévales offertes à Augustin Fliche* (Vendôme, France, 1953), p. 79. Amato Masnovo, in *Da Guglielmo d'Auvergne a s. Tommaso d'Aquino,* III, 2nd ed. (Milan, 1946), 211, noted William's respectful independence toward Aristotle, as did Ernest Moody, who, in "William of Auvergne," pp. 13, 105–6, suggested the idea that William followed a *via media.*

[8] Moody, in "William of Auvergne," p. 103, remarked that at the very least Aristotle supplied William with a new terminology, and even Werner, who held him to be a confirmed anti-Aristotelian, recognized that William borrowed considerably from Aristotle's analytical language (see *Die Psychologie des Wilhelm von Auvergne,* p. 1).

It would be hard to exaggerate the difficulty and the complexity such an enterprise entailed. Indeed, it is the very magnitude of the task that makes William such an interesting thinker to read. Yet his position in the history of thought, his coming during a time of profound intellectual change, also makes his work sometimes quite hard to understand.

The scholars of the thirteenth century were heirs to an intellectual tradition that conflicted on many points with Aristotle's method as well as his view of the world, and at each of these points they had to face the sometimes agonizing question of whether to abandon the old or ignore the new. If it had been merely a matter of competing doctrines, the choice would have been clear enough, and for independent thinkers like William, subject to an easy solution. He felt no compunction in rejecting Aristotle out of hand whenever his teachings departed from Christian belief. Yet the problem was often more subtle, as when the analytical foundations of Aristotle's language ran counter to some equally fundamental attitude of traditional thought. In such instances, where a host of assumptions implicit in the new language ran up against a comparable array of assumptions in the old, it was extremely difficult to sort out the issues or even pinpoint the discrepancies. Someone like William, who wanted to employ the categories of Aristotle's thought without thereby commiting himself to all of Aristotle's doctrines, might at times find himself trying to explain his ideas in language largely unsuited to what he had in mind. For instance, how was he to discuss the relation of activity to passivity in the workings of the human mind? For William as for many medieval thinkers steeped in the writings of Augustine, the human capacity to understand something was comprehensible only if one assumed that the mind had the power to relate to what lay outside it by means of an immanent act—that is, by one that was self-generated and self-contained. Yet Aristotle had explained all operational relations solely according to the rules of external action and passive reception, rules he had derived from his view of change in the physical world. It was a constant challenge for William to use the language of agent and receiver that he found in Aristotle's works—which he did wholeheartedly—without having to give up one of the central ideas of his epistemology, and he succeeded only by constantly restating his position and modifying Aristotle's terms until they became his own.[9] To follow him through this procedure the modern reader must be extraordinarily sensitive to shifts in meaning and ambiguities in thought.

But this is not the only obstacle to an easy understanding of William's ideas. Another characteristic, perhaps an outgrowth of his problems in using Aristotelian terms, was his tendency to argue as much by analogy as by categorical analysis. Although the writings of other thirteenth-century thinkers also exhibit this trait, it is particularly marked in William's case.[10] He frequently found it more convenient to suggest what he meant with a series of images rather than to specify qualities or operations with precise definitions and technical terms. As a result, his work often reads like a kind of philosophical pantomime, where similes, analogies, and metaphors are used to conjure up a picture to the mind's eye. Such language requires the reader to pay utmost attention to the context, for it can never be assumed that an image used in the solution of one problem will have quite the same meaning when employed to resolve another. William had a few favorite metaphors and he used them again and again, but not always with the same end in mind.

In short, to read William right one must not be bound by literal interpretation. Nor should one confuse examples with strict categories. Above all one has to remain open to nuances

[9] For a discussion of William's handling of this issue, see below, Chapter II, 2.

[10] Landry, in "L'originalité de Guillaume d'Auvergne," p. 463, asserted that the real originality of William's work derived from an intellectual temperament that was extraordinarily rich in imagination. In a similar vein Corti, in "Le sette parte del *Magisterium*," p. 291, pointed out that William's writings are marked by a special style that in its use of example and description departs from the norm of what is commonly recognized as the scholastic method and often renders his work hard to comprehend.

in meaning that cannot be easily expressed in categorical terms. There is, in William, a flexibility in language that contrasts with the more precise and rigid way some of the same terms were used later in the thirteenth century, after the scholarly lexicon had been more nearly standardized by decades of philosophical debate. Only by recognizing this elasticity for what it is can one hope to penetrate beyond the sometimes enigmatic surface to the real meaning of his thought.

I

The State of Human
Knowledge

===

THE PROBLEM of truth was, in the thirteenth century, only part
of a larger question concerning the value of human knowledge
and the criteria for discerning within it various levels of certitude. What is striking about the thought of William of Auvergne is that he was capable of making substantial progress toward a critical notion of truth while at the same time holding
to a more conservative view that disparaged the powers of the
human mind as exercised by the wayfarer in the world of sin.
This in itself marks him as coming at the very beginning of the
thirteenth-century enthusiasm for science and for a systematic
study of the natural bases for thought, and it makes his ultimate contribution in that area all the more noteworthy.[1]

Whenever he speculated in cosmic terms about the nature of
human cognition, William drew a wide disparity between the
natural capacity of man as he was created and the merger abili-

[1] There are two works that deal at length with William of Auvergne's
theory of mind and knowledge. The earliest, Matthias Baumgartner, *Die
Erkenntnislehre des Wilhelm von Auvergne,* Beiträge, II, 1 (Münster, 1893),
is a careful and exhaustive examination of the sources and the best account of William's doctrines on epistemology. Amato Masnovo, *Da
Guglielmo d'Auvergne a s. Tommaso d'Aquino,* 3 vols., 2nd ed. (Milan,
1945-46), makes a broader study of William's philosophical attitudes
but is not as convincing on the specific question of knowledge. Also of
importance for this subject are Gilson, "Pourqoui saint Thomas a critiqué saint Augustin," and Moody, "William of Auvergne." In addition, see Werner, *Die Psychologie;* Landry, "L'originalité," pp. 441-51; and
Valois, *Guillaume d'Auvergne,* pp. 266-78.

ties left to him after the Fall. He built his epistemology on a well-established position, drawn originally from Augustine but during the twelfth century modified to fit related doctrines from Arab and Jewish authors, that placed the soul on the border of the divine world of pure intelligibles and the sensible world of corporeal substances.[2] In William's own words:

According to Christian doctrine, which is necessarily most true in all things and most free from any falsehood and error, one must hold that the human soul is naturally constituted and ordained as if on the horizon of two worlds. And one of those worlds is the world of sensible things, to which the soul is closely joined by means of the body. The other world is truly the Creator Himself. . . .[3]

[2] See Jean Rohmer, "Sur la doctrine franciscaine des deux faces de l'âme," *Archives d'Histoire Doctrinale et Littéraire du Moyen Age* 2 (1927), 73–77, and Georg Bülow, ed., *Des Dominicus Gundissalinus Schrift von der Unsterblichkeit der Seele,* Beiträge, II, 3 (Münster, 1897), pp. 126–27. These works show that the doctrine took two forms among Arab and Jewish philosophers. One form, found in the works of al-Ghazali, attributed two faces to the soul; the other, found in Avicebron and Avicenna, described the soul as having a single face that it was free to turn to those things either above it or below. In either case the soul had access to the world of intelligibles and the world of sensibles. Avicenna's doctrine was taken up by Dominic Gundisalvi, a Christian philosopher of the late twelfth century (see his *De anima,* ed. J. T. Muckle, *Mediaeval Studies* 2 [1940], 86).

[3] *De anima,* VII, 6 (*Mag. div.,* II supp., 211b). See also the same view expounded in *De universo,* II, 3, 20 and 21 (*Mag. div.,* I, 1056aH and 1057aC). William was likewise familiar with the doctrine of the two faces of the soul (see *De bono et malo,* p. 280). In a separate treatise, *De immortalitate animae* (see the edition in Bülow, *Des Dominicus Gundissalinus Schrift,* p. 56), he made reference to both of the two traditional doctrines. Although Bülow held, along with most scholars, that William's *De immortalitate animae* was essentially a copy of an earlier treatise of the same name written by Gundisalvi (the latter work constitutes the main text in Bülow's edition: *Des Dominicus Gundissalinus Schrift*), Amato Masnovo, in *Da Guglielmo d'Auvergne,* III, 119–23, and Baudoin Allard, in "Note sur le 'De immortalitate animae' de Guillaume d'Auvergne," *Bulletin de Philosophie Médiévale* 18 (1976), 68–72, have made a strong argument that the work Bülow attributed to Gundisalvi was also from William's pen, so that the two versions that have come down to us are variants of a single treatise by William, not the works of two different authors.

Baumgartner proposed the *Liber de causis* as another source for Wil-

As he explained, the soul had it naturally within its power to turn to either of the worlds and to gather knowledge from what was in them.[4]

Traditionally, especially in the works of Jewish and Arab writers, this view had served to explain the basic cognitive activities of the human soul in its earthly life, but for William it stood primarily as a reminder of how far man had fallen from his original state of innocence. Although the soul was created to have equal access to the world above and below, original sin so perverted its nature that man lost the full exercise of his intended powers. Along with freedom of the will the first sinners also forfeited the freedom, which is to say the ability, to direct their intellectual gaze to the intelligibles in God above. William explained that in the present state of misery the soul, weighed and bent down with the body, was no longer able to raise itself to the superior world.[5] He went so far as to say that as long as the human intellect lived in sin it was asleep, even buried so far as the more noble objects of thought were concerned.[6] Only in extraordinary cases, determined by the will and pleasure of God, could men on earth get some glimpse of the luminous region above them; and for this they had to be blessed with a new revelation or an added grace.[7] Otherwise even Christians would have to wait for the Resurrection before they could enjoy the vision in that divine light for which they had been created.

This assessment of the effects of the Fall led William frequently to devalue whatever knowledge the mind could garner on its own while here on earth. Spiritual operations in this life,

---

liam's doctrine. In that work the soul is described as being on a horizon, with eternity above and time below (see Baumgartner, *Die Erkenntnislehre*, p. 19, n. 3). William's notion of a horizon between two worlds would seem to come from this, and on one occasion he even borrowed the idea that the soul was situated between eternity and time (see *De bono et malo*, p. 280).

[4] *De anima*, VI, 33 (*Mag. div.*, II supp., 193a–b).
[5] *De universo*, II, 3, 20 (*Mag. div.*, I, 1056aH).
[6] *De universo*, II, 3, 21 (*Mag. div.*, I, 1057bA).
[7] *De universo*, II, 3, 20 (*Mag. div.*, I, 1053bD–1054aE).

including understanding, were a considerable step down from what they had been created to be, far from the height of their natural brilliance and nobility.[8] Since men had lost the most important aspect of their mental vision, William was prepared to claim that what was left, cognition from the lower world of the sensibles, only deformed their essential humanity.[9] He even discredited science itself, claiming that the system of knowledge men constructed through demonstration did not elevate them and bring them closer to their natural end but instead debased their nature. As William explained it: "The more the mind progresses along the way of demonstration, the more it approaches darkness and distances itself from the light of principles. . . . Therefore, by philosophizing, the mind acquires an ever more imperfect and less luminous knowledge."[10] Philosophy, then, and all rational speculation about the universe could not be admirable disciplines in a scheme of Christian education but were rather obstacles to man's proper development.

It must therefore be clear to you that the way of philosophy is not the way to acquire the perfection of our intellect (*virtus superior apprehensiva*). And if this is true, then it should not be called the way of philosophy, but rather error or, even better, obscurity, since it diverts [the mind] and wrests it far from the light. For whatever is error and blindness is necessarily deformity and imperfection and obscurity.[11]

Given such sentiments, it would seem that the thought of William of Auvergne would be the last place to look for a scientific notion of truth. In fact, however, William's attitude toward knowledge on earth was not without its more positive side, and if the traditions of Christian theology often encouraged him to take an unenthusiastic view of human cognition, he could also be more approving. So long as he was not

[8] *De anima*, V, 19 (*Mag. div.*, II supp., 144a).
[9] *De bono et malo*, p. 281.
[10] *De bono et malo*, p. 282.
[11] Ibid. That William intended the *virtus superior apprehensiva* to stand for the whole intellect is clear from another passage in the same treatise, p. 278.

making an explicit comparison between knowledge in the earthly life and knowledge before the Fall or after resurrected glory, he spoke with a confidence in human intellectual powers that could easily accommodate Aristotle's ideal of science. In the beginning of *De anima* he testified to his esteem for demonstration and his belief that it could lead to certain knowledge: "I realize that the argument from authority alone is merely dialectical and can induce only belief (*fides*). For it is my intention in this treatise, and wherever I am able, to induce demonstrative certitude."[12] He once even admitted that scientific knowledge in itself was good and worthy of praise.[13] Indeed, the whole project for the *Magisterium divinale* was based on the assumption that man could attain scientific truth. Only an authentic enthusiasm for the worldly use of reason could account for a work of such scope.

Clearly, for all his disparagement of the powers of the mind in the world, William held them to be of no mean value in the acquisition of truth. He felt that if knowledge were to command respect among the learned of the world it had to be accompanied by scientific, which was to say demonstrative, argument, and he understood that this required an appreciation of the workings of natural reason and a familiarity with Aristotle's logic.[14] Indeed, since he had denied to man in this life the upper half of his original intellectual vision, he implicitly raised the importance of the cognitive powers that were left. No longer obscured in the shadow of a higher intellectual capacity, man's ability to learn from what he saw in the sensible world had to be taken seriously, for it offered the only way to reliable

[12] *De anima*, I, 1 (*Mag. div.*, II supp., 65b).

[13] *De fide*, I (*Mag. div.*, I, 3aD). See also Gabriel Jüssen, "Wilhelm von Auvergne und die Entwicklung der Philosophie im Übergang zur Hochscholastik," in *Thomas von Aquin im philosophischen Gespräch*, ed. Wolfgang Kluxen (Freiburg/Munich, 1975), p. 199.

[14] This is the reason William gave in the prologue to *De Trinitate* for having chosen to use rational arguments throughout his *Magisterium*. There he set out his intention to meet the learned (*eruditi*) on their own terms with logical proofs. See above, introductory remarks to Part One, n. 3.

knowledge, save Scripture or special revelation, and provided the sole foundation for intellectual discourse. As William was no skeptic and had no intention of forgoing reasoned discussion, he was invariably led to consider the worldly procedures of the mind in terms more favorable than his cosmic epistemological pronouncements would strictly have allowed.

Yet William not only turned to natural reason and relied on the worldly logic by which it was seen to operate; he also took care to examine how it was that these operations were capable of leading to truth. Several times in his *Magisterium divinale* he interrupted his narrative to speculate on the nature of truth and the foundations upon which a knowledge of it could be established, and here again his modification of the old scheme of a two-sided perspective for the human mind, by eliminating man's vision into the eternal world, led him to lay more emphasis on cognition within the concrete and material world of creation. In his analysis of the rational process by which men arrived at certain knowledge he gave less attention to the traditional concern of demonstrating God's active role—now reserved for the resurrected life—and stressed instead the naturalism of Aristotle's epistemology. This meant that his notion of truth was free to develop along critical lines not possible among the currents of Augustine's thought. Thus, despite his proclaimed disdain for knowledge on earth, William gave an account of truth worked out almost entirely in terms of purely rational criteria and leaving almost no place for God's intervention in the processes by which it was attained. In doing this William placed himself in the vanguard of the scholastic thinkers of his time, and he became one of the key figures in the growth of an increasing emphasis on science and the demonstrative method as a model for the highest form of human discourse. This side of his work was to have an enormous influence on subsequent thought.

II

Truth in Simple Knowledge

===

I. THE NATURE OF SIMPLE TRUTH

According to Aristotle, the notion of truth depended on being able to make a judgment, on distinguishing between a sort of cognitive right and wrong. Since simple concepts or simple words merely pointed to an object and gave no further information, even as to whether it actually existed or not, they did not ask for a judgment from the mind, nor could a judgment be made about them. They were, quite simply, intelligible or logical markers standing for an object, either real or mentally contrived, and so they could not be considered to be either true or false.[1] For example, the concepts or words "man" and "mermaid" both indicated some objective content, although in the one case this actually could be some existing thing and in the other it could not. As both concepts or words fulfilled their function in making known the objective content to which they referred, nothing further could be demanded of them. It made no sense to ask if they were true or not, since they acted purely as signs. Stated in more general terms, this meant that simple knowledge possessed significance, but it did not have truth or falsehood. For that, one had to turn to complex cognition and complex speech, where simple things were either combined or disjoined. It was in the soundness or unsoundness of the combining or disjoining that lay the basis for a judgment of truth.

Strictly speaking, William agreed with Aristotle: simple cog-

[1] See Aristotle, *De interpretatione,* I, 1 (16a9–18), and *De anima,* III, 6 (430a26–28).

nition was neither true nor false. Yet whereas for Aristotle this settled the matter, truth being reserved solely for complex knowledge, for William there was still a place for truth, if not for true knowledge, even in his theory of simple understanding. In *De universo* he outlined six different meanings for the word "truth," three of which had to do with the general problem of knowledge.[2] One of these ways, the sixth in William's list, dealt with complex cognition and will be examined later. The other two, the first and the fourth in the text, related to simple knowledge.

As William explained it, truth, when it did not apply to complex cognition, referred to the objective existence of things known. This is clear from both of the relevant definitions given in *De universo*. According to the first, truth stood for the thing in reality (*res*) and was opposed to the sign by which that thing was signified. In this sense the sign could be seen as falsehood, since it was not really the thing to which it referred.[3] The other definition, the fourth on William's list, identified truth as the being of a thing (*ipsum esse rei*).[4] Here, William was drawing on an idea that went back to Boethius, who in a classic passage had spoken about the *esse* of a thing as opposed to *id, quod est*.[5] As Boethius used these terms, *esse* was limited to the formal qualities of a thing or to the form alone, while *id, quod est* referred to the substance as a whole.[6] William followed Boethius to the degree that he, too, associated being or *esse*

---

[2] *De universo*, I, 3, 26 (*Mag. div.*, I, 794bE–95aB). The three ways we shall not be concerned with were the second, truth as the opposite of simulation; the third, truth as purity and opposed to impurity; and the fifth, truth as the Creator.

[3] *De universo*, I, 3, 26 (*Mag. div.*, I, 794bE).

[4] "Quarto modo ipsum esse rei uniuscujusque, hoc est, residuum a tota varietate, et circunvestitione accidentium, et hoc est esse, quod explicat diffinitio, in quam non cadit aliquid de accidentibus, sed ea sola, quae vel sunt rei essentia, sive substantia." *De universo*, I, 3, 26 (*Mag. div.*, I, 794bF).

[5] See Boethius, *Quomodo substantiae* (or *De hebdomadibus*) (PL, 64, 1311).

[6] See above, n. 5, and also Boethius, *De Trinitate*, I (PL, 64, 1250B). For an excellent analysis of Boethius's use of *esse* and *id, quod est,* see Gilson, *History of Christian Philosophy*, pp. 104–5.

with formal qualities—that is, he restricted being to what was essential to the thing, exclusive of all accidental variety—yet he departed from the original usage by insisting that being should somehow involve the substance as well.[7] Indeed, it becomes apparent, if one looks closely at all William's references to simple truth, that his notion of being was actually very far from what Boethius had in mind. For William, being, and therefore simple truth, was much more than the formal nature of a thing; it was in fact the substantial reality of an object in the world, strikingly similar to Boethius's *id, quod est.*[8] Despite the differences in language, therefore, William's two definitions of simple truth were merely variations on a single theme: truth in the simplest sense was nothing other than the true thing itself.

By this definition simple truth was plainly not a measure of human knowledge. Instead, it entered into knowledge as an object of the mind, the plain and simple object to be known, so that in knowing real things one knew the simple truth.[9] Wil-

[7] See n. 4 above, as well as *De universo,* II, 1, 35 (*Mag. div.,* I, 836aE): "Veritas enim uniuscujusque rei non est, nisi vel substantia, vel essentia, sive esse ipsius. Et hoc est, quod ratio, sive diffinitio explicat."

[8] In addition to William's references to substance in the passages cited above in n. 7, see his even more radical language in *De universo,* II, 1, 34 (*Mag. div.,* I, 835bB): "Veritas, et verum semper simul sunt...." Compare *De universo,* II, 1, 35 (*Mag. div.,* I, 836aG), and the passage cited in n. 20 below. In all these cases William identified being or truth with the existing individual object itself. The fact that William could still call this reality "essence" had to do with his identification of essence, substance, and singular reality.

As is shown below, Grosseteste departed even more radically and explicitly than William from a purely Boethian use of the terms *esse* and *id, quod est,* and picking up on a remark of Augustine, he openly defined truth as *id, quod est.*

[9] William once did speak of the true definition (*vera diffinitio*) of a thing, as if in the case of definition it were possible to make a judgment of truth concerning simple cognition (see *De universo,* I, 3, 26 [*Mag. div.,* I, 794bF]). This seems to contradict Aristotle's notion that simple concepts were neither true nor false. In fact, however, William did not have in mind the opposition of truth to falsehood. Instead, he was referring to the difference between a definition that explained the substance of a thing and a definition founded on accidental qualities. Since the substance was the truth of a thing, William found it convenient to call the substantial definition the true one. He did not mean to imply that other sorts of definition besides the substantial one could not serve truly to represent an object.

liam even explained how, with reference to his theory of similitudes or signs. He said that the truth of a thing, its being, could provide the occasion for a similitude or likeness of itself, which likeness referred back to it as image to exemplar.[10] It was by means of such similitudes, in this case the intelligible forms of things, that the mind was applied to the objects of its understanding and thus came to know the things that were in the world outside.[11] In short, the intelligible forms in the mind were similitudes of the external truth and the vehicles by which the mind came to know it.[12] Similarly, written or spoken signs—words—could serve as pointers to simple truth. This was, indeed, what William meant by his first definition of truth, for every sign signified something, and if this something signified were actually a thing (*res significata*), it could properly be considered the truth that the sign was designed to reveal.[13]

It is clear, therefore, that although William had departed from Aristotle by making a place for truth in the business of simple cognition, he had not rejected Aristotle's insistence that no judgment was involved in knowledge on this rudimentary level. For all his use of traditional terminology, William was in fact cutting himself off from the attitudes that had hitherto determined the way medieval scholars thought about what happened in simple cognition, attitudes intimately connected with the epistemological model of Augustine. Like William, Anselm, too, had used Boethius's idea of *esse* to define a kind of simple truth, what he called *veritas essentiae rerum,* but for Anselm this truth in the essence of things implied a comparison

[10] *De universo,* II, 1, 16 (*Mag. div.,* I, 823bA).
[11] *De anima,* VII, 8 (*Mag. div.,* II supp., 213b).
[12] *De universo,* II, 1, 16 (*Mag. div.,* I, 823aB).
[13] See above, n. 3. William held that intelligible forms in the mind and written or spoken words were equally capable of serving as signs for things (see, for example, *De universo,* I, 3, 26 [*Mag. div.,* I, 795aB]). As it appears he maintained that signs signified the *res significata* directly, he would seem to have been one of the earliest medieval thinkers to hold that words or terms referred immediately to objects in the real world and not primarily to ideas. See also below, nn. 23 and 24.

with an ideal in the mind of God, and therefore it was properly denominated a rightness or *rectitudo*.[14] Anselm was, quite simply, still speaking in terms reminiscent of Augustine, where even simple truth and all knowledge of it ultimately reduced to a matter of judgment dependent on some reference to the divine. But William put simple truth solidly in this world, and he made it, so far as the human mind was normally concerned, opaque to illumination from God above. In doing this he opened the way to a new attitude about the nature of human knowledge.

To see how fully this was so, it is necessary to turn to William's speculations about language. Since simple truth was identified with the object of knowledge and not with simple knowledge itself, the question of truth in simple cognition reduced to the question of the reference or, in William's words, the imposition of nouns and words. The way William worked out his theory of imposition shows how far he had come from the earlier views about truth.

When William argued that the truth of a thing was the thing itself, he claimed to be taking a stand in direct opposition to the teaching of Plato. According to William's exposition, Plato had maintained that there was a special world reserved for the truth of things, the archetypal world of exemplars, or of species and forms. In addition, there was the sensible world, and here were located the *exempla* or similitudes of those truths in the higher realm of forms. True earth, true fire, true anything were not located in that lower sphere among men; they existed among the archetypes. Consequently, whatever the eyes perceived did not properly deserve to be called by the name of a true thing but should instead be referred to

---

[14] See Anselm, *De veritate,* 7 (in the edition by Francis S. Schmitt, *Opera omnia,* I [Edinburgh, 1946], pp. 185–86) and 13 (Schmitt, ed., I, 198). Apart from the notion of rectitude and a comparison to the divine ideal, William's description of *veritas rei* was at times remarkably close to Anselm's account of *veritas essentiae rerum.* See, for example, *De universo,* II, 1, 35 (*Mag. div.,* I, 836aE).

obliquely, as, for example, earthlike (*terreum*) or firelike (*igneum*).[15]

William conceded that Plato was right to maintain the existence of a world of archetypes. On this score it was only necessary to add that according to Christian doctrine the archetypal world was Christ Himself, who served as the exemplar for all types of creation.[16] Yet when it came to calling the supersensible archetypes the truth of things in the created world, there Plato had gone too far. William's principle that the truth of a thing was its own essence or substance, its very being and not that of any other, meant that no exemplar could rightly be considered the truth of the thing made like it (*exemplum*).[17] To hold otherwise would have been, as William said, "an intolerable abuse."[18] Even Plato could not deny that any exemplar and its earthly imitator were truly two different beings, essentially diverse and relating to each other something like cause and effect; and if this was so then each had its own truth, just as each had its own essence. Consequently, it was impossible to say that both were of the same truth, or that one was the truth of the other. In William's own words: "It is manifestly impossible that the earth where we are and the exemplary earth, that is, the one that ours copies, be of one truth or of one essence. For, because each one truly exists, they must be two or of two beings, and so of two truths."[19] The truth and the substantial being of a thing could not be separated.[20]

---

[15] *De universo*, II, 1, 16 (*Mag. div.*, I, 823aC). William had in mind Chalcidius's translation of the *Timaeus*, 49D, as well as his commentary on it. See Plato, *Timaeus a Calcidio translatus commentarioque instructus*, Plato Latinus, IV, 2nd ed., ed. Jan H. Waszink (London, 1975), pp. 47 and 320–21.

[16] *De universo*, II, 1, 17 (*Mag. div.*, I, 823bC).

[17] *De universo*, II, 1, 35 (*Mag. div.*, I, 835bD–836aE). See also Gabriel Jüssen, "Idee" (II, B, 3: Wilhelm von Auvergne), in *Historische Wörterbuch der Philosophie*, eds. Joachim Ritter and Karlfried Grunder (Basel/Stuttgart, 1976), IV, coll. 84–86.

[18] *De universo*, II, 1, 35 (*Mag. div.*, I, 836aF).

[19] *De universo*, II, 1, 36 (*Mag. div.*, I, 837aB–C).

[20] "Ubi uniuscujusque veritas, ibi est ipsum, et econtrario." *De universo*, II, 1, 35 (*Mag. div.*, I, 836aG).

The weakness of Plato's notion of truth was equally apparent in his explanation of man's use of language, the audible or visible tokens of knowledge. His views implied that the real referents of simple nouns were to be found in a world beyond the senses. To William, however, it was patently clear that normal language referred directly to the things the senses perceived, that is, to objects in this world. He insisted that "no other man has ever called earth or fire or water anything but those things that are with us and can be seen."[21]

By directing his arguments explicitly against Platonic doctrine William was able to bring his own views into greater relief and at the same time to cast himself as the defender of levelheadedness against the errors of pagan philosophy. In fact, however, William's criticisms also struck another, more immediate target: the earlier medieval attitude about truth. Despite the fact that this implicit attack remained unacknowledged, it is from historian's perspective the more important of the two. William held that the correct Christian interpretation of Plato's archetypal world was to identify it with Christ or the ideas in His mind, but when seen in this way Plato's teaching came to appear closely allied with the way such thinkers as Anselm had explained the nature of simple truth. Anselm's views, interpreted in the light of the Augustinian epistemology from which they derived, implied that God's intervention was necessary every time men came to know the truth. Such was, indeed, the essential characteristic of a theory of divine illumination. The reason for this divine intervention was that the ultimate truth of all things resided in God, and so to know a thing as true one had to measure the ephemeral object in the world against its divine exemplar. Even the knowledge of simple

---

[21] *De universo,* II, 1, 34 (*Mag. div.,* I, 835bD). In *De universo,* II, 1, 35 (*Mag. div.,* I, 836bH), William actually tried to excuse Plato by saying his statements about the nature of species and their location in a higher world were never meant to be applied to the normal language of predication (see below, n. 47). Despite this softening of his position, however, William never really accepted Plato. In *De anima,* II, 2 (*Mag. div.,* II supp., 73b), he warned his readers not to take too much interest in Plato, since he spoke lies, or at best metaphors.

truth therefore rested on a comparison between image and exemplar, and so it could not be just a simple perceiving but had to involve a real judgment. This meant, of course, that knowing the truth required having access to the divine ideas themselves. As a corollary, every concept and every word expressing a knowledge of the simple truth referred to something in God as much as it did to an object in nature.[22]

William's scheme essentially eliminated this divine role. Although he never directly addressed the question, his notion of truth in objective reality and his views on the reference of words left no doubt that he thought divine illumination had no place in most of the normal workings of the mind. By fixing the truth of every created thing in the world and identifying it with the thing's being, its substance alone, he removed the need to appeal to a vision in God. No divine intervention was necessary for the mind to know simple truth because no comparison or judgment had to be made; the intellect merely seized the objective reality facing it and thereby knew what was true. William's theory of reference made the point even more clearly. He explained that the names of simple objects (*essentialia nomina*)—what would later be called nouns of first intention—referred directly to things in the world (*sunt imposita rebus ad nominandum eas*) and in no way to the Creator Himself, except possibly when the prophets used them metaphorically.[23] The same was true of words like the adjectives black and corporeal, used to describe things according to qualities that belonged properly to them (*secundum proprias dispositiones suas*). William expressly denied that any such words (*nominationes*), whether substantive or adjective, implied a comparison with God; they pointed immediately and exclusively to creatures in the world.[24]

---

[22] This is, indeed, the implication of Chapter 13 of Anselm's *De veritate.*

[23] *De universo,* II, 1, 36 (*Mag. div.,* I, 837aC–D). In *De universo,* II, 1, 34 (*Mag. div.,* I, 835bD), William made the point explicitly that they did not refer to ideas in God's mind.

[24] *De universo,* II, 1, 34 (*Mag. div.,* I, 835aB).

There was, however, an important exception to the rule that the exemplary world had no part to play in man's ordinary simple cognition. If the names of created objects and their proper qualities referred directly to things in the world, there were other words that drew their meaning from God or a quality inherent in Him. In such cases, human knowledge made reference, in some way, immediately to the divine.

The basis for this exception to the rest of William's theory of imposition lay in his views about being and simple truth. In this case he wanted to affirm that the truth of some things, and therefore the reference of the words standing for them, lay in God Himself. Yet the way he made this claim seems at first glance to have contradicted everything said so far about the nature of simple truth. According to the fifth of the six definitions of truth in *De universo,* God alone was the truth and all creation nothing but falsehood.[25] Later in the same work William introduced this notion into his discussion of being and the reference of words, and here he cast it in terms borrowed from Avicebron, maintaining that God was the truth of the universe while the universe was by comparison a mere shadow.[26] Put in this way, the position looks exactly like the Platonic exemplarism William was then engaged in refuting. In fact, however, he intended something quite different.

No sooner had William introduced the idea of God as the truth of creation than he began to qualify what he meant. Strictly speaking, God did not represent the truth of all things in the universe but rather of a modest number of objects of the mind. Certain words used to speak about things in the world more properly signified qualities belonging to the Creator Himself, and they found their fullest meaning only when applied to Him. Whenever they were used to describe something in creation, they could not be said to have this full meaning,

---

[25] *De universo,* I, 3, 26 (*Mag. div.,* I, 794bG).
[26] *De universo,* II, 1, 33 (*Mag. div.,* I, 834aF). William himself cited Avicebron. The passage he was referring to can be found in Avicebron's *Fons vitae,* III, 55, ed. Clemens Baeumker, Beiträge, I, 3 (Münster, 1892), p. 201.

since their referents would then be mere shadows of what they were designed to denominate. As William explained it: "When you consider the immensity and the sublimity of the Creator in each and every predicate that implies His magnificence and providence and glory, you will find that the same predicates, when they are referred to the universe or its parts, only signify trifling shadows, hints, traces and mere signs of those things they signify in the Creator, when they are spoken of Him."[27] Most words, on the other hand, directly and properly signified objects in creation. In terms of the language of simple truth this meant that there were two sets of beings or objects of the mind. In one set the truth of the thing, and therefore its real being, lay with God, while only its image or similitude could be found in creation; in the other, larger set truth was in the world, and the image with God.[28]

Reduced to this scope, the notion of God as simple truth did not contradict William's other views about the truth of things, for in those cases where the truth lay in God, He was indeed the objective reality that words signified and to which human knowledge referred. The things or qualities predicated in such instances were truly in God, while their similitudes or images alone could be located in the created world.[29] What had to be kept in mind was that they formed a special category and in no way applied to most of reality or to most of simple cognition. The failure to realize this fact, William claimed, accounted for Plato's mistake. He was right in recognizing that common

[27] *De universo*, II, 1, 33 (*Mag. div.*, I, 834aF-G).
[28] *De universo*, II, 1, 34 (*Mag. div.*, I, 835bB). When William spoke of those things whose truth lay in the world and whose image alone lay with God, he did not mean to deny the Christian doctrine of the temporal and ontological priority of the divine exemplars. In *De universo*, II, 1, 16 (*Mag. div.*, I, 823bB), he had explained how the divine exemplars could be said to be the images (*similitudines*) of the things created from them, not in the strict sense of the word "image," but because, with respect to human knowledge, the divine exemplars were in most cases secondary and known only as similitudes of the existing essences of things, which were known first and most immediately.
[29] *De universo*, II, 1, 33 (*Mag. div.*, I, 834bH). See also above, n. 28.

words could refer to realities in the exemplary world above. The problem was that he took the doctrine too far.[30]

The words William had in mind as properly signifying a truth in God were, as he said, those that implied something of His magnificence, providence, or glory.[31] It seems he meant words used to refer to the supreme attributes of God, perhaps God's proper qualities. As examples, William listed "powerful" and "power," "being" and "existence," "true" and "truth," "good" and "goodness," "beautiful" and "beauty," "wise" and "wisdom," "high" and "height," and "noble" and "nobility"—all qualities or abstract nouns drawn from qualities.[32] In addition, there were some concrete substantives like "king," "lord," and even "creature," the last of these presumably because it entailed prior reference to the Creator Himself.[33] When one considered the fundamental meaning of these words, it was apparent that they, too, implied something belonging more to God than to any substantial form on earth.

In normal speech, of course, all these words were used to describe God's creatures much more often than God Himself, and this despite William's insistence that their only proper signification (*significatio*) was to God alone. Indeed, he held that they could merely be applied (*applicantur*) to things in the world, and even this application had to be made equivocally, in a manner of speaking (*secundum quid*) or by means of a certain similitude.[34] The way this was done was through metaphor or analogy. Toward the end of his critique of Plato, William conceded that it was possible for names signifying truths that ex-

---

[30] *De universo,* II, 1, 34 (*Mag. div.,* I, 835aA).

[31] See above, n. 27.

[32] See *De universo,* II, 1, 33 and 37 (*Mag. div.,* I, 834bF and H, and 837bB). The words William listed included those that would later be known as transcendentals. Note that William's position could be interpreted to mean that such terms could be predicated only equivocally of God and creation.

[33] See *De universo,* II, 1, 34 and 37 (*Mag. div.,* I, 835aB and 837bB).

[34] *De universo,* II, 1, 33 (*Mag. div.,* I, 834bH).

isted in the world to be used to refer to God, although not in the way Plato meant when he said all such words primarily referred to a divine idea. Instead, the names of things on earth could be used "by means of a certain similitude" to describe God, in the way the prophets called Him the Sun of Justice.[35] William used practically the same phrase—"by means of a certain similitude"—when talking about the way words signifying divine realities could be applied to things in creation, and presumably he thought the process was likewise the same, although working in the opposite direction.[36]

Yet William's theory still had not explained exactly what it was in the world men knew when they spoke in a metaphorical way about qualities not properly belonging to creatures or how it was they came to perceive the divine attribute they applied metaphorically. His reference to the prophets was no help here, because the primary object in prophetic language was something in the world, clearly available to the mind, while in this case the real truth lay in God. William never explicitly worked out a solution to this problem. Indeed, he was strangely silent about the epistemological conditions that applied to knowledge of the simple truth where the reference was direct to God and only equivocal to things on earth. Nevertheless, he must have held to some notion of Godly intervention, some version of the traditional doctrine of divine illumination, and this despite the fact that he continued to maintain that man's natural access to the divine world above had been cut off by original sin. Twice he implied that what characterized the normal imposition of words signifying things in the world was that it involved no comparison (*comparatio vel respectus*) to God, as if such a comparison might be a typical aspect of language where words properly signifying something divine were used to refer to creatures.[37] The idea of a comparison between a created ob-

---

[35] See above, n. 23.

[36] See above, n. 34. William used the same language again in the same way just after the passage on the prophets. See *De universo*, II, 1, 37 (*Mag. div.*, I, 837bB).

[37] See above, n. 24, and *De universo*, II, 1, 34 (*Mag. div.*, I, 835aA).

ject and its divine exemplar was a hallmark of the doctrine of divine illumination, and it is nearly certain that behind William's language about equivocal reference in the case of his special qualities lay some such notion of a double object that the knowing mind had to compare before arriving at the truth. As for the mechanism by which the mind came to perceive these objects and the truth, there was not, in the section dealing explicitly with the problem, even this much of an indication of William's views. Again, however, he must have held to one of the traditional notions of divine intervention. There is, in fact, evidence to support this assertion, and it comes where William examined the origin of the principles of science. Further discussion of the question will be possible, therefore, in the section on complex cognition below.[38]

That William held that there were terms primarily signifying something divine but normally used to refer to creatures in the world constituted a considerable concession to the Christianized Platonism against which he otherwise so persistently fought. Yet it is important to remember that it was a limited concession. In terms of the development of medieval thought, what William had done was to reduce the doctrine of divine illumination from its all-embracing significance and limit it to a small section of the cases to which it once applied. The other side of William's theory of human knowledge of the simple truth, which in fact dealt with the majority of the cases men would face in this life, looked forward to future developments in the thirteenth-century appreciation of science and a scientific method of thought. Already, William was fixing human knowledge of things other than the articles of faith solidly in the world and cutting it off from earlier attempts to look for divine criteria to certify its validity. In this way his theory of simple truth laid a new foundation for a worldly notion of truth in complex knowledge and prepared the way for a more critical approach to the whole problem of truth in human cognition.

[38] See below, Chapter III, 3.

2. THE CONDITIONS OF SIMPLE COGNITION AND
THE WAY TO KNOWLEDGE OF SIMPLE TRUTH

By claiming that simple truth was a question of being and not of intellectual judgment, William shifted the focus of the discussion about truth away from simple cognition. For him, as for Aristotle, the problem of true and false cognition applied only on the complex level, and it was there he would have to elaborate a notion of truth adequate to a systematic organization of knowledge. Before going on to consider William's view of complex cognition, however, it is necessary to examine more closely his account of the act by which the mind seized simple concepts. In his explanation of the objective content of knowledge as well as the way the mind attained its object, William established principles on this simple level that would be of considerable significance when it came to considering the truth of propositions.

William insisted that the terms of simple cognition referred immediately to something existing in the world and not to an archetype or Platonic ideal. According to the fourth of his six definitions of truth, this simple object of the mind, the referent for concepts and terms, was the being itself of each thing.[39] More precisely, it consisted of whatever was left to a thing after one had eliminated from consideration all variety and all accidental properties; it was what the definition described and was therefore identical with the essence or substance of the object. Enough has been said to show how, for all the echoes of Boethius as well as Anselm that can be heard in William's language, his views differed substantially from what either of these thinkers had to say about the nature of the simple object or what it was that made this object true. Yet it remains unclear how William could use his notion of the simple object as essence or substance to account for what the mind actually could know about the world, especially how he would make allow-

[39] See above, this chapter, n. 4.

ance for the division of simple concepts into singulars and universals.

William generally used the terms "essence" and "substance" interchangeably.[40] For him, both of them stood for the fundamental reality of each thing. Furthermore, according to the fourth definition of truth, they each stood for the being of the thing, its existential base, excluding accidental properties or whatever else was not necessary in order for it to be.[41] Essence, substance, and being, therefore, were all three identical, and in real terms they all represented the absolute minimum required by each actual object to maintain its purchase on the world of existence.

All this was clearly a considerable departure from Boethius's use of these terms and, in fact, from the way they were frequently used up to William's time. Yet William separated himself even more radically from Boethius's idea of simple reality by going on to maintain not only that these three—essence, substance, and being—were identical but also that they provided the full and exclusive basis for individuality itself. He resolutely denied the Boethian principle that numerical diversity arose from the variety of accidents.[42] Instead, he said that two individuals of the same species did not differ by anything accidental to them or by only part of their substance but rather by their total individual substances or essences.[43] Since in real terms substance was the same as species or specific nature, this led to the initially perplexing conclusion that two things of the same species differed numerically by their species themselves.

---

[40] See nn. 4 and 7 of this chapter. See also, *De universo,* II, 2, 15 (*Mag. div.,* I, 859aA).

[41] See above, n. 4.

[42] See *De universo,* I, 3, 29 (*Mag. div.,* I, 802aE-F), and Boethius, *De Trinitate,* I (PL, 64, 1250B). William realized his words sounded like an attack on Boethius, and so he made the somewhat dubious argument that the passage in *De Trinitate* was, against all appearances, intended to be interpreted somewhat along the lines of the position he was working to defend.

[43] *De universo,* II, 2, 15 (*Mag. div.,* I, 858bG-H).

William was so determined to be consistent that he actually used such language, for all its apparent awkwardness. He spoke of the distinction between two individuals as an essential diversity or difference (*diversitas et differentia essentialis*), in contrast to an accidental one.[44] Once he stated even more baldly that individuals within a single species were numbered or individualized through their very specific essence (*in specie sua*).[45] Here, he recognized how peculiar his language was and felt compelled to clarify his words with a technical distinction. By saying these individuals differed in their species, he did not mean to imply any dissimilarity (*dissimiltudo*) in their specific essence but rather a simple diversity (*diversitas*). Specifically their essences were the same; numerically they were diverse.

These views on singular substance invariably had their effect on William's notion of specific identity. According to what he said in *De universo*, two things belonged to the same species simply because their substances, each one separate and individual, were specifically similar. There was no reason to suppose they shared any part of their substance or participated in some third, external thing. As William explained it, the species, considered as a category or class of things and not as the predicated specific nature, was the substantial similitude of individuals.[46] It was a relation among things and not some super-real substance in itself. Precisely this principle was what accounted for William's rejection of Plato's exemplarism. Since the complete species—this time the predicated nature and not the logical category—was present in each individual, there was no need to involve the divine exemplar in the reference of simple terms. In William's words, the species predicated of individual things in

---

[44] See *De universo*, II, 2, 15 (*Mag. div.*, I, 859aA), and n. 43 above.

[45] *De universo*, I, 3, 29 (*Mag. div.*, I, 802aF-G).

[46] ". . . species est substantialis similitudo individuorum. . . ." *De universo*, I, 3, 29 (*Mag. div.*, I, 802aF). William attributed this definition to a *quidam ex Italicis philosophis*, whom Baumgartner, in *Die Erkenntnislehre*, p. 63, and Roland de Vaux, in *Notes et textes sur l'avicennisme latin aux confins des XIIe–XIIIe siècles* (Paris, 1934), pp. 40-42, have identified as Boethius. See Boethius, *In Isagogen Porphyrii commenta*, ed. Samuel Brandt, CSEL 48 (Vienna, 1906), p. 166 (2nd version, I, 11).

normal speech were necessarily to be found in those individuals themselves.[47] They referred as much to the singular substance as did proper names.

In short, for William the substance of an individual thing was, at the same time and without any real distinction, the foundation for its individualness and the basis for its specific nature. So far as concerned reality and not intentions in the mind, William seemed to be on the verge of obliterating the difference between universality and individuality. To be more precise, he was subsuming universality totally within the world of individual things. His theory of species, and indeed his whole ontology, focused almost exclusively on the individual.[48]

It is easy to imagine how such views would affect William's theory of knowledge. If the specific nature of a thing were identical with its individual being or substance, then it would be possible for the mind to comprehend both the individual and the universal species. Furthermore, it could do this through one and the same intelligible act. All that was necessary was for it to penetrate directly to the substance, and if it knew this, then ipso facto it knew the universal and the singular.

These are, in fact, precisely the conclusions William drew when he came to examine the natural powers of the human mind. Arguing against the Aristotelian view that the mind could seize only universals, he insisted that, in its original or innocent state and in the state of glory, the human intellect possessed direct cognition of singulars as well as universals.[49] Indeed, there was no other tenable position. The intellect

[47] De universo, II, 1, 35 (Mag. div., I, 836bH).

[48] This is what Masnovo had in mind when he said that William's epistemology never really got beyond the individual (see Masnovo, Da Guglielmo d'Auvergne, III, 144).

The conclusions of the present study concerning William's theory of species support the arguments Baumgartner made against Hauréau, who had claimed William was an extreme realist to be compared with a figure like William of Champeaux (see Baumgartner, Die Erkenntnislehre, pp. 76–77). Hauréau's view has more recently been taken up by Etienne Gilson in History of Christian Philosophy, p. 257.

[49] De anima, V, 17 (Mag. div., II supp., 141a), and De universo, II, 2, 15 (Mag. div., I, 859aB). See also n. 45 above.

operated, in contrast to the senses, by penetrating to the substance of created beings, and so it was proper that it should perceive the differences between individuals, which derived from their substantial or essential diversity.[50] The nature of the intellective power, viewed in the abstract, directed it to both particular things and universals; it could perceive each of them with the same inherent facility.[51]

Yet if this was the power of the human mind in its natural state of innocence or glory, conditions were different in the world of sin. Just as the Fall corrupted the intellect's original capacity to see into the realm of the intelligibles above, so it weakened reason's operation in the created world of the sensibles. In fact, this natural intellectual ability was so perverted that William could call it "submerged and as it were buried in the body and darkened by our original corruption."[52] In this life the mind could no longer penetrate immediately to the substances of things; it could not see them "face to face" but only under a covering.[53] Since this covering consisted of sensible properties, the intellect was reduced to begging from the senses whatever it could learn about the world. In a manner of speaking, it had to be illuminated by the senses.[54] It was, William explained, as if the mind had been robbed of its own intellective light and was forced to rely on the feebler glow of the

---

[50] De universo, II, 2, 15 (Mag. div., I, 858bG). In this passage William contrasted sense (sensus), which could not perceive the whole, with reason (ratio) or intellect (intellectus), which saw (perpendit) the something below sensible accident—that is, substance. He cited Boethius as a source for the distinction between sense and reason, and Baumgartner, in Die Erkenntnislehre, pp. 63–64, n. 6, suggested that the reference might have been to Boethius's Philosophiae consolatio, V, pros. 4. See the edition by Ludwig Bieler, CC, 94, 1 (Turnhout, 1957), p. 97.

[51] See De anima, VII, 1 and 3 (Mag. div., II supp., 203a and 205a).

[52] De universo, II, 2, 15 (Mag. div., I, 858bH).

[53] De anima, VII, 7 (Mag. div., II supp., 213a). See also De anima, V, 18 (Mag. div., II supp., 143b).

[54] De anima, V, 18 (Mag. div., II supp., 143b), and De universo, II, 3, 21 (Mag. div., I, 1057aC–D). William had already denied the view that there was some knowledge innate to man (see De bono et malo, p. 282). In De universo, II, 3, 19 (Mag. div., I, 1051bD–1052aE), he explicitly rejected Plato's theory of reminiscence. William agreed with Aristotle that the mind was created devoid of knowledge and had to acquire after birth

sensibles and the senses, in the same way that those who wanted to see at night, when they were deprived of the brilliance of the sun, had to depend on lanterns.[55]

Under such circumstances none of William's generalizations about the natural workings of the mind would hold, although he continued to maintain that even in this life the proper object of the intellect was substance. His account of how this was so constituted one of the most complicated and difficult parts of his philosophy. The problem was to explain how the intellect could learn anything at all from the senses. He insisted that the intellect knew those things external to it by means of their similitudes or images inhering within it, and all he said about the acquired nature of knowledge supported his claim that such images must be received.[56] Here lay the root of the difficulty. In William's own words: "Therefore, either the substances in question here [i.e., the intellective powers] are subject to sensible and particular things and receive from them their signs and similitudes, or no new knowledge at all is generated in them concerning such things. The whole difficulty of the question, therefore, lies in the way such signs are received."[57] It did not seem that the intellect could receive material forms, at least not in the way the senses did. The sense of touch, when exposed to heat, became hot itself, but the intellect certainly did not when it understood what it was to be

---

whatever knowledge it was to have in this life (see *De anima*, VII, 4 [*Mag. div.*, II supp., 208a]). Furthermore, it was not only sensible substances the mind came to know through the senses but also immaterial or spiritual ones, which could be perceived only insofar as they were manifested by definite sensible dispositions. Indeed, this was how one recognized that there were other animate beings in the world and came to attribute to each individual person a particular human soul (see *De universo*, II, 3, 19 [*Mag. div.*, I, 1051bA], and *De anima*, VII, 7 [*Mag. div.*, II supp., 213a]). The only exception to the rule that immaterial things were known here below through the senses came in the case of the intelligible dispositions of the mind itself, for the intellect in which these occurred perceived them directly (see *De anima*, III, 12 [*Mag. div.*, II supp., 102b]).

[55] *De anima*, V, 18 (*Mag. div.*, II supp., 143b).

[56] See above, nn. 11 and 12 of this chapter, and also *De bono et malo*, p. 282, and *De universo*, II, 2, 69 (*Mag div.*, I, 921bD–922aE).

[57] *De universo*, II, 2, 69 (*Mag. div.*, I, 922aE).

hot.[58] How, then, did the mind take something from the senses on its way to knowing the substance of sensible things?

It was an old question, one William was familiar with from the works of Aristotle, but his answer broke completely with the Aristotelian tradition. As William interpreted him, Aristotle tried to account for the origin of human knowledge by positing a separate agent intellect, the tenth of the celestial intelligences, which was responsible for placing the images of things in the mind.[59] William's response was to reject the idea of an agent intellect in any form.[60] Instead, he offered two possible alternatives: "Wherefore, either [the intellect] does not receive [the forms of things] in the way the senses do, as I have said, or it does not receive them at all, as a certain Christian sage has said. And his words were, that the intellect, excited by the senses, forms in itself with wonderful swiftness intelligible forms."[61] The Christian sage was Augustine, who in his *De Genesi ad litteram* explained the formation of mental images in essentially the way reported, although he made no mention of how the senses affected the mind, whether by excitation or not.[62] As could be expected, given his previous account of the dependence of the mind upon sensation, William went on to say that Augustine's extreme solution, altogether

[58] *De universo*, II, 2, 65 (*Mag. div.*, I, 914bF).
[59] *De anima*, VII, 5 (*Mag. div.*, II supp., 210a).
[60] *De anima*, VII, 4 (*Mag. div.*, II supp., 209b). Roger Bacon has often been credited with saying that he heard William maintain in lecture that the agent intellect of the human mind was God Himself. In fact, if one looks closely at the relevant passage in Bacon's *Opus tertium*, one can see that Bacon says literally no more than that twice he heard William attack the view positing an agent intellect as part of the soul. Of course, even if Bacon meant to imply that William also associated the agent intellect with God—which was Bacon's own doctrine concerning the agent intellect—that does not mean we need to take his report as accurate. Above all, it cannot command greater authority than William's own statements on the issue in his own works. See *Opus tertium*, c. 23, in Roger Bacon, *Opera quaedam hactenus inedita*, I, ed. John S. Brewer (London, 1859), pp. 74-75.
[61] *De universo*, II, 2, 65 (*Mag. div.*, I, 914bG).
[62] Augustine, *De Genesi ad litteram*, XII, 16 (33) (PL, 34, 467). William may have borrowed from Boethius the notion that the senses excited the mind. See Boethius, *Philosophiae consolatio*, V, met. IV and pros. 5 (Bieler, ed., pp. 98-99).

to deny reception from the senses, was unnecessary. Augustine had been reluctant to admit that the intellect received anything from the senses because he thought that all act and reception (*agere* and *passio*) had to follow strict rules of similarity: heat could cause only something hot. In fact, William explained, this was not so, for not every received quality had to be similar to the agent that caused it. A case in point was the fact that an unmoved soul could cause a body to move.[63] Here there was no local motion on the part of the mover, and yet the effect was an actual change in the physical location of the body. Thus, a spiritual action in this instance had a physical effect. Similarly, it was possible for the intellect to take up something from the senses without this in any way derogating from the intelligible nature of the intellect or subjecting the soul to any sensible or material properties. The mind could, as William had said, receive the forms of things—receive them even from the senses themselves—but not the way the senses did.

To make sense of such a reception William had to escape the precise language of Aristotelian physics and elaborate new principles of action and passivity. He contended that Aristotle himself had conceded that the intellect, while receptive to knowledge from the senses, was not subject to material forms in the same way the senses were.[64] Yet William's ultimate vision of intellection required a more radical adjustment, for he saw in the act of understanding more than a mere reception. His primary reason for rejecting the notion of an agent intellect, which he felt left the mind in the demeaning position of a passive receiver, was that the intellect, the knowing and receiving power of the mind, had to include an active capability of its own.[65] Otherwise it would be nothing more than a mirror or a

---

[63] *De universo*, II, 2, 65 (*Mag. div.*, I, 914bG).

[64] See *De universo*, II, 2, 74 and 75 (*Mag. div.*, I, 928aE and 928bF).

[65] Steeped in the writings of Arab commentators on Aristotle, especially Avicenna, William never fully considered how "agent intellect" might be taken to refer to one of several powers belonging to the soul. Yet it is unlikely he would have been receptive to such an idea had he explored it further, so insistent was he on the indivisibility of the mind and on the notion that the knowing subject must know through a kind of active, and not purely passive, grasping of the object.

book inscribed with the writing of whatever knowledge it contained; and, he noted, no one would dare attribute to a book or a mirror the power to know.[66] Somehow the mind had to be at once receptive and active, without any division of powers. It could not be just material and receptive of intelligible forms; it had also to be productive of them in itself.[67]

It was not easy for William to find the language or the analytical models to explain how the intellect functioned in this way. Part of the problem arose from his own reluctance to abandon the very Aristotelian principles he had implicitly denied. Indeed, he wanted to keep to Aristotle's terms, even in instances like this where they did not exactly apply. When they proved inadequate, his only recourse was to turn to somewhat less precise analogies. In his attempt to clarify the act of simple understanding, therefore, William alternated straightforward analytical passages with a battery of metaphors and analogical descriptions. The latter are not easy to interpret, and in order to see what William meant by them it is necessary to follow him through them all and then try to discover how they fit together.

The process of simple cognition began with the reception of sensory data by the senses. This initial procedure established the bond between the mind and the substantial world of created things, thereby ensuring the objective reality of primary knowledge. At the very foundation of human knowledge, therefore, was an act of transmission that followed the laws of Aristotelian physics. The sensory organs were material and fully capable of receiving an impression from material objects.

Beyond the first step, however, there could be no more material act and receptivity, and this is what created the difficulty. William said that the senses influenced the intellective power not by impressing some form on it but by exciting it to generate those forms itself.[68] He attributed this view to Augustine,

---

[66] De anima, V, 6 (Mag. div., II supp., 121b).
[67] De anima, V, 7 (Mag. div., II supp., 122b).
[68] De universo, II, 2, 74 (Mag. div., I, 927bD–928aE).

although, as noted above, it seems that the latter spoke only of the activity of the mind and made no mention of how the senses induced it to act.[69] Whatever the origin of the position, it could not stand without elaboration, for it remained to be shown how the senses, which could not act directly on the mind, were capable of affecting it in any way whatsoever. William's answer was that the senses evoked a determinate response in the mind because they were intimately tied (*alligata*) to it.[70] He offered no further explanation of how such intimacy permitted an operation below the level of physical act and reception, but he presumably was relying on the doctrine, also drawn from Augustine, of the identity of the soul and its powers.[71] The proximate linking of two faculties in a single, seamless structure, no matter how disparate they were in nature, made it unlikely that one should be touched without the other in some manner being likewise affected.

Once the senses had excited the mind, they no longer took an active part in the process of simple cognition. All further activity originated solely with the mind itself. William's account of the senses' role meant, therefore, not only that they did not serve as a material agent in simple cognition but that in fact they did not serve as an agent at all in the strict sense of the word. They did not act on the mind but announced things to it and thereby provided what William called the occasion for it to know whatever stood behind these sensible accidents.[72] In

---

[69] See above, n. 62. As for Boethius, although he spoke of the senses exciting the mind, he did not go on to say the mind generated its own intelligible forms.

[70] *De universo*, II, 2, 65 (*Mag. div.*, I, 914aH).

[71] Literally, of course, the senses could not be tied to the soul if they were themselves material or receptive to material images, as William seemed to imply. At this point there was, therefore, a degree of ambiguity in William's work as to the precise nature of the senses. But the main point was clear enough—that the jump from sensation to intelligibility occurred without any passivity on the part of the mind. For William's view on the powers of the soul, see Baumgartner, *Die Erkenntnislehre*, pp. 15–16.

[72] *De universo*, II, 3, 21 (*Mag. div.*, I, 1057bA). See also *De universo*, II, 2, 74 (*Mag. div.*, I, 928aE).

technical terms, they performed the function of an occasional cause. Thus, although William had emphasized the importance of sensory knowledge as a necessary bridge between the intellect and the external world, his epistemology actually left the senses with a modest role. To compensate for this deviation from Aristotle's model he amplified the dynamic capacity of the mind, so that the mind itself, with its active nature, became the sole efficient cause of knowledge. Here, on the side of the intellect, William devoted his greatest efforts to describe human understanding. Because of the difficulty of the task, he turned to metaphorical speech.

Two of the metaphors or analogies William drew to help clarify how the mind worked in simple apprehension involved images that were favorites of his, ones he used again and again to describe various functions of the human soul.[73] The first compared the intellect to a spider and the sensible object to a fly caught in its web. Just as the motion of the struggling victim, passed along a filament of the web, was enough to make the spider realize it had caught a fly, even though it could not see the insect, so sensations sufficed to lead the mind to knowledge of an external substance without any direct perception. The motion in the web, like the sensations, provided the merely occasional cause of knowledge; the efficient cause lay in the innate light (*innatum lumen*) or skill (*ars, artificium*) of the spider—that is, the mind. William likened the process to the way recollections arose from the treasury of the memory or thoughts and passions from speculative or moral habits, given the proper stimulation by a suggestive object in the world. The second example came from Aristotle's *Posterior Analytics* and had to do with a man watching a money-changer speak with another person. In this case the viewer, without overhearing any of the conversation or being told what was going on, would be able to guess that the two men were transacting a

---

[73] *De universo*, II, 2, 75 (*Mag. div.*, I, 928aG–H). See also *De universo*, II, 2, 74 (*Mag. div.*, I, 927bD), and *De anima*, V, 7 (*Mag. div.*, II supp., 122b).

loan.[74] Here, sight gave the occasion to what William, following Aristotle, called the skill or quick wit (*sol[l]ertia*) of the
viewer, and this skill accounted for the knowledge of what was
actually happening. William stressed that under no circumstances could the vision of two men speaking be a cause in itself of the viewer's understanding. Such knowledge could arise
solely from a skill of comprehension subtle enough to take the
sensible image as evidence for something in no way explicitly
contained in that image.[75] On another occasion William called
this skill of Aristotle's a habit or disposition (*habitus*).[76] It was,
as he described it, a spring from which perceptions poured
forth like a stream flowing from its source.[77]

Etienne Gilson has interpreted such passages to mean that
William held God to be the direct cause of human understanding—not only the creator of the innate light, habit, or

---

[74] See Aristotle, *Posterior Analytics,* I, 34 (89b13-14). It is interesting
to note that William used the word *mutuari* for "to lend," while the
translation of the *Posterior Analytics* most commonly used in the Middle
Ages, that by James of Venice, used the word *accommodare*. Perhaps William had looked at the translation by the otherwise unknown "Ioannes,"
which did in fact say that the viewer knew *quod mutuatur*. See *Analytica
Posteriora*, Aristoteles Latinus, IV, 1-4, ed. Minio-Paluello and Dod, pp.
68 and 156.

[75] William's use of the notion of *sol[l]ertia* or quick wit to account for
the primary acquisition of simple concepts violated Aristotle's intention
that it apply to the discovery of middle terms, an element in the theory
of complex knowledge. It was William's need to explain how the mind
used sense data instantaneously, without having recourse to any discursive process or being subject to an actual impression from the senses, that
made such a novel application of the idea so tempting. Even in Aristotle
"quick wit" condensed into a single mental act a process that when analyzed logically expanded into something more complicated. It must be
added, however, that William also used the idea of quick wit properly
when he came to explain the discovery of the middle. Robert Grosseteste
employed the idea, too, but he remained strictly faithful to Aristotle,
giving quick wit a place only among the processes of complex cognition.
When Grosseteste dealt with the problem of how the mind seized simple
concepts—a process that at bottom he viewed very much as William
had—he made the logical complications more explicitly evident in his
noetics and openly described it as a matter of induction.

[76] *De anima*, V, 7 (*Mag. div.*, II supp., 122b).

[77] See above, n. 73.

---

skill but also the real source for the concepts flowing out of it. In other words, God illumined the intellect in the first instance, taking the role of the Avicennian agent intellect to the pure passivity of the soul. It was only after the Divine Illuminator had so to speak filled the soul with the borrowed power to understand, to form the images of knowledge, that the soul itself, in the second instance, overflowed in a multitude of cognitive acts.[78]

Yet Gilson has confused William's metaphysics of creation with his notion of intelligible act, two sides of William's thought it is important to keep apart. To be sure, William used the image of a fountain on occasion to talk about the source of life in the human organism, saying that the soul was a spring pouring out life into the human body.[79] In fact, it was not just life that flowed from the soul into the body but all human activities and operations, sense and motion included.[80] This notion of the soul as the fountain of life probably derived from Avicebron's *Fons vitae,* transmitted through the intermediary of Dominic Gundisalvi. Since William, like Avicebron, held that the ultimate source of life was God Himself, he went on to explain that souls were not the only fountains of life in men, for into them ran also the vivifying stream of the Divine Creator, cause of that abundance by which they overflowed into the body and produced its vital acts.[81] God, as the immediate source of all being, was therefore the foundation for the soul's existence and for its operations as well, and to this extent William could fully adopt Avicebron's language of emanation. In these cases, having to do with the origin of life, the image of a fountain or spring did, consequently, lead directly back to the divine. When, on the other hand, it came to explaining how the mind knew and how it acted in knowing, and not where it derived the vital power to do so, the image of the

---

[78] See Gilson, "Pourquoi saint Thomas," pp. 52, 79–80.

[79] *De anima,* V, 24 (*Mag. div.,* II supp., 152a).

[80] *De anima,* VI, 4 (*Mag. div.,* II supp., 159b).

[81] Baumgartner pointed out the connection with Avicebron in *Die Erkenntnislehre,* pp. 17–18. On God as a fountain, see William's *De anima,* V, 24 (*Mag. div.,* II supp., 152a).

spring served a different purpose. Here, for most normal knowledge, William made no mention of God as illuminator of the mind, and he had no reason to do so, given his views about the sufficient power of the intellect.

Instead of implying a role for God, William's examples of a spider, a money-changer, or a fountain emphasized how sensation performed the role only of stimulating knowledge, not of causing it in the sense of generating it or even accounting for its generation. They indicated that sensations were not gratuitous, for they stimulated the mind to a determinate act; somehow they passed along to the mind enough of an indication of the object to allow the formation of a valid concept. Nevertheless, the productive cause of knowledge, that which really accounted for its presence in the intellect, was the mind itself, or more specifically some skill possessed by the mind. The analogy of the spider suggested that there was a sort of stock or treasury out of which were drawn mental perceptions; that of the money-changer, that there was more simply an ability to make the right perception under the right conditions.

Another example William used to explain what he meant also derived from Aristotle. As William interpreted him, Aristotle held that each naturally moving object—that is, one whose motion was explained by the nature of things—possessed a motive force that tended to a definite place and could be described only as a kind of life to the object, or perhaps a sort of sense.[82] This sense performed an operation—it moved and

---

[82] *De universo,* II, 2, 74 (*Mag. div.,* I, 927bB–D). William referred this example specifically to the intelligences, but as he was trying to explain the active power of intellect, what he said could be applied equally well to the human mind. In fact, in the examples that follow this passage, William expressly drew the comparison with human understanding, where, he said, the problem of explaining knowledge of sensibles was analogous to that in higher substances.

It is interesting to note that the position William attributed to Aristotle is practically the opposite of what Aristotle himself said about natural motion in *Physics,* VIII, 4 (254b33–255a12). The position is, on the other hand, quite close to what Adelard of Bath, in his *Quaestiones naturales,* LXXIV, said was Aristotle's view of eternal motion. See *Die Quaestiones naturales des Adelardus von Bath,* ed. Martin Müller, Beiträge, XXXI, 2 (Münster, 1934), pp. 66–67, as well as Müller's note, p. 88.

acted—without any passive reception on the part of the object to which it belonged. William argued that if such was the case in some material bodies, it should not be surprising that similar operations could be found in nobler beings, whose immateriality would make it all the easier for them to act in some such way. This was in fact precisely what happened in the separate intelligences, and in human intellects as well. Intellection was an act that occurred without any real passivity or material reception in the substance in which the action terminated—that is, in the intellective power.

All these examples in *De universo* suggested aspects of a solution to the problem of explaining how the mind worked in simple cognition, yet it was in *De anima* that William tackled the whole question head-on. There, in a short but complicated series of explanations and images, he gave his fullest statement on the processes of the mind, one that makes it possible to tie together the separate strands of his earlier comments and come up with a final estimate of what he intended.[83] He began by repeating his assertion in *De universo* that not every movement from a potential to an actual state, such as what happened to the intellect in understanding, had to follow the physical laws of action and passivity. Then he explained that the intellectual power was by nature (*nata est*) able to receive the signs of things, the mental images by which it knew them, and that to do so it needed the mere excitation of sensation, not, so the text implied, a true act of the senses on the mind. Given these fundamentals of cognition, William next turned to specify how the powers of the mind operated. He noted that the senses functioned by applying the mind to things in the world, joining it to them by means of a spiritual connection (*conjunctio spiritualis*). As for the operation of the intellect itself, it could be compared to the behavior of two animals: like the chameleon, the mind picked up or took into itself the similitude of any object to which the senses directed it; like the ape, which

[83] See *De anima*, VII, 9 (*Mag. div.*, II supp., 215b). The relevant passage is given below in Appendix B.

imitated what it saw men do, the mind made itself like any object exposed to it.

By this point William's zeal in piling metaphor on top of metaphor might seem to have succeeded only in obscuring what he wanted to say. Yet in fact such language, by drawing back from what William must have felt to be the restrictive precision of the language of Aristotle's physics and psychology, introduced a flexibility that alone permitted him to clarify his vision of the mental process. As always, he insisted in this final passage that the mind first approached the world through intermediaries, one set of which consisted of intelligible signs. William held to the principle, universally accepted since the time of the Greeks, that knowledge meant assimilation, and he interpreted this after the manner of Aristotle to mean that the mind came to know things in the world by receiving mental images representing them.[84] Another set of intermediaries were the senses, and by claiming that they were necessary for intellectual cognition William again affirmed a principle of Aristotle's epistemology. In this case, of course, he gave the principle a non-Aristotelian interpretation, maintaining that the senses were required after the Fall to excite the mind and arouse it to perceive its natural objects.

So far there was nothing in this account William had not said before. What was new was that here, for the first time, he undertook to explain exactly how the mind related to its object through the intermediaries of sign and sense. First came the assertion that the senses joined the mind to the world in a spiritual connection, as if having performed their role of excitation they slipped away and left the intellect face to face with its object. William never explained precisely what this spiritual connection was or how it came about. It seems, though, to have brought the mind into direct contact with created substance and, insofar as was possible after the Fall, to have restored it to some approximation of its natural cognitive state, the difference being that now the initial prodding of the senses was

[84] *De bono et malo,* p. 282.

needed where before the mind acted solely on its own. Perhaps this was what William was thinking of when on another occasion he said that the mind in this life had to be transfixed or illuminated by the senses before it could raise itself to its original power to apprehend the intelligibles or even to care for the body.[85]

Second, and even more important than the notion of a spiritual bond, was the way William accounted for the act of the mind itself. It was here that he broke most completely with the physical principles that seemed to restrict his thought. Through the analogies with the chameleon and the ape, which complemented those he had used earlier in *De universo* but were simpler and more to the point of his thought, he animated the intellect, and this permitted him to solve the Aristotelian problem of action and passivity. Like Augustine before him and like many medieval thinkers who were to follow, William wanted to establish that a power like the mind could reliably relate to what lay outside it solely by means of an immanent act. Thus, the senses and material effects of the external world remained of decisive importance for human knowledge, but they did not act as an efficient cause nor did they subordinate the knowing mind to their materiality. Yet William's final account did more than substitute one kind of psychological mechanism for another. By attributing a kind of personality to the mind itself he altogether escaped the bounds of a mechanical epistemology along the lines of Aristotle's thought. No longer was he forced to describe the intellective power as a simple function of a living soul or as an organ in the human machine, descriptions he felt made it too passive, too lifeless to be the subject of understanding. In his more figurative terms, it was like an independent organism, conscious of the stimuli it received rather than subject to them, so that even the simple act of apprehension became essentially a reflexive process, arising both out of self-awareness and out of an awareness of the external world. This was, however, a process that remained in-

---

[85] *De universo*, II, 3, 19 (*Mag. div.*, I, 1051aD and 1051bB).

divisible and impervious to further philosophical analysis. There was no point in trying to break down the act of understanding into its fundamental psychological constituents, for to do so would destroy its essential subjectivity—hence the tendency to avoid, at least momentarily, the concrete and mechanical terms of Aristotle's analysis and turn to more impressionistic figures of speech. At last, William was able to justify his earlier contention that the intellect must be more than a mirror or receptacle of intelligible forms. Where Aristotle had seen the mind as a blank page on which the signs of things were to be inscribed, William insisted that this was not enough, since before it could be said to understand it had to be given the power to read those images it received.[86] His description of the intellect as an active subject corrected what he saw as Aristotle's error. A conscious mind would be, to be sure, a book of the signs it assimilated, but it would be, in William's own words, a book for itself (*liber in effectu sibi ipsi*).[87] It would not only receive; it would actively respond.

The upshot of all William's examples was, therefore, to subjectify the mind and, in a fashion not unlike that found in the thought of Augustine, to bestow on the cognitive faculty a life of its own. Consequently, for all his Aristotelian insistence on the importance of the external, sensible world as opposed to any exemplary realm, his explanation of simple understanding required a radical rejection of some of the fundamental laws of both Aristotelian and Neoplatonic epistemology. In place of their view of action and passivity he elaborated a theory of spiritual operation founded on the principle of immanent and conscious mental activity.

This was the essence of William's final view of the processes of the mind. Yet a full notion of the way the mind knew simple concepts would also have to account for the difference between particular and universal knowledge. For William this would mean explaining the difference in a way compatible

---

[86] See William's own words in *De universo,* II, 3, 21 (1057aD).
[87] See Appendix B.

with his insistence that the substance of any existing object was in its entirety both singular and determined to a specific nature, that it was at once the individual and the species. Although he was apparently not interested in making the detailed logical analysis a complete solution to the problem would require—in particular, he did not address the question of the logical difference between universal and particular predication—he did make some mention of the way the mind working in the world came to the two basic sorts of simple knowledge. His remarks on this score are sufficient to show how he viewed the nature of reference in each case.

William held that after the Fall the human mind acquired knowledge of singulars by means of the sensible accidents inhering in every real substance.[88] This did not mean that William accepted the theory of individuation through material accident. On the contrary, he was adamantly opposed to such a theory, for he thought that the specific substance lying below accidents was itself already individual.[89] This did not, however, prevent him from holding that the mind came to know singular substance through those very accidental properties in no way essential to it. Indeed, this is exactly what one would expect given the mechanics of his account of simple apprehension. Unfortunately, he did not say precisely what object the intellect confronted in this way. It could not have been the full substance, for then there would have been no need to know particulars by means of material accidents.[90] Yet it would seem that it would have to have been more than an artificial object, constructed by the mind from accidental properties to serve in

---

[88] *De universo,* I, 3, 29 (*Mag. div.,* I, 802aG). See also *De universo,* II, 3, 21 (*Mag. div.,* I, 1057aC).

[89] See above, this chapter, n. 42.

[90] William's remarks were perhaps contradictory on this score. On the one hand, he held that the senses joined the mind to things in the world, presumably substantial things, while on the other he maintained that the fallen mind could never confront substance face to face (see Appendix A). All that is absolutely clear is that the confrontation in the world had to be something less than the direct vision available to the mind in its natural or glorified state.

place of the unattainable substance below. It had to be something in between the two. Whatever the case, the reference of the knowledge attained in this way was clear; it was to the singular reality existing in the world.

The problem was somewhat more difficult when it came to universal cognition. While William maintained the Aristotelian line that it was universals the intellect perceived properly and per se, not the singulars to which those universals were attached,[91] he was just as plain in saying that in the world the intellect could not penetrate directly to the substance of things and thereby see the species as it was.[92] The only place he gave an indication how he would resolve the dilemma came in a passage where he spoke explicitly about the different kinds of simple knowledge available to men on earth. Although the passage actually lists three types of knowledge, it is the first two alone that concern the problem under consideration here.[93] The first type of knowledge followed the lines of William's explanation for human knowledge of singulars after the Fall. He held that the mind had to consider beyond (*perpendere*) the covering of accidents to arrive at some vision of the individual substance that underlay them, although it could not come to see the substance itself face to face.[94] The second type was knowledge of universals or, in William's precise words, knowledge by abstraction, and here he seemed to be trying to approximate Aristotle's explanation of how the mind came to know universal objects. William referred to this abstraction as a spoliation (*spoliatio*) or laying bare (*denudatio*), and he explaned that it consisted in the privation of the apprehension of

[91] *De universo*, II, 1, 14 (*Mag. div.*, I, 821bB).
[92] *De universo*, II, 2, 15 (*Mag. div.*, I, 859aB).
[93] *De anima*, VII, 7 (*Mag. div.*, II supp., 213a–b). The whole passage is given below in Appendix A.
[94] William frequently reiterated his view that the intellect could consider what lay beyond the covering of accidents, and he claimed that the same idea could be found in the works of Boethius, whom he habitually referred to as a certain Latin philosopher. See above, n. 50 of this chapter, and also *De anima*, V, 18 and VII, 1 and 7 (*Mag. div.*, II supp., 143b, 203b and 213a).

individualizing forms. As an example he cited the vision of a statue of Hercules. From up close one could easily see that the statue depicted Hercules, but if it were gradually moved farther away there would come a time when one could no longer recognize who was represented but know only that it was some man. In much the same way the similitudes of things in the imagination sometimes represented to the intellect this or that individual; at other times, when seen abstractly, they called to mind only a specific form.

On its own this explanation of universal knowledge seems perfectly straightforward, but in the context of William's thought it presents enormous problems.[95] First, there is the practical impossibility of accounting for the individualizing forms that William said were to be stripped away. Nothing in his theory of individual substance corresponded to them. He specifically denied that individuals differed by anything other than their substance or essence, and he insisted that this substance contained nothing more than the specific nature itself.[96] Second, there is no clear explanation of what universal knowledge was to be abstracted from. If it was from singular knowledge, that would make the problem doubly hard, for it was shown above that William gave no indication precisely what singular knowledge was, short of some vague and indirect apprehension of the specific substance. Again, as in singular cognition, all that was clear were the general terms of reference— once more to a real object in the world.

In the end, then, there is no way to form an exact idea of what was known in the two cases described, precisely how such knowledge was arrived at, or how the two sorts of cognition related, even which one came first. One can say only that William's thoughts on this subject were incomplete and that, while he turned sporadically to Aristotelian formulas to help

---

[95] It is interesting to speculate that William had in mind something like the process of sensory abstraction Grosseteste was to draw from the works of Aristotle.

[96] See De universo, I, 3, 29 (Mag. div., I, 802aF), and n. 43, above.

him in his exposition, he had not adequately assimilated Aristotle's epistemology and perhaps not even fully understood what it meant. Yet precision on these issues was of only secondary significance for the question of truth. Whatever the specific differences between the conditions of universal and particular cognition, William had established their primary reference beyond the shadow of a doubt. In human cognition after the Fall, concepts and words having to do with the essences and properties of worldly things referred directly to a particular object in the created world. It was this doctrine that would be crucial when it came to developing a theory of complex truth.

III

The Truth of Complex
Knowledge

===

1. THE NATURE OF COMPLEX TRUTH

William accepted Aristotle's view that one should not think of
simple cognition as either true or false because he believed that
simple knowledge did not call for a judgment. The idea of
cognitive truth depended on being able to judge the value of
what was known, but simple concepts and words were cognitively neutral. There was no question of accepting or rejecting
them. They served the function of pointing out an objective
content and made no demands on the mind to assent to anything about that content, even on the important question of
whether or not it actually corresponded with something that
existed or could exist. It was, therefore, only on the level of
complex knowledge that one could pose the question of
whether knowledge was true or false. Complex knowledge
consisted of concepts or words arranged in groups so as to
make propositions, and as Aristotle had pointed out, each of
these propositions not only possessed a field of reference, determined by the sum of the referents of all its simple terms, but it
also made a statement about the way things were, which is to
say, about the way the references of the simple terms fit together.[1] Consequently, every such statement demanded a judgment; it did not merely point but rather asserted something
and had therefore to be either accepted or denied. In making
the judgment one distinguished between true and false knowl-

[1] See above, Chapter II, n. 1.

edge. If one could isolate the criteria by which the judgment was made, they would constitute at least the rudiments of a theory of complex truth.

It was here that the search for a theory of complex truth tied in with the early thirteenth-century interest in a scientific method of thought. Man's knowledge of the world consisted of statements about the natures of things and the way they functioned and related to each other. If it were going to be possible to isolate that part of this knowledge that could be held with certitude—science itself—men would have to find some standard to test the validity of these statements. This standard would, of course, be the measure of complex truth. Applying such a measure demanded, in the first place, a familiarity with the logical rules for making true statements and drawing valid inferences, and second, an understanding of the theory that lay behind these rules. To scholars of the thirteenth century the latter demand came to appear particularly important. The twelfth century had already seen considerable work on the rules of logical argumentation, but the ultimate defense of truth had depended in practice on an appeal to authority and more theoretically on an often vague notion of some sort of divine revelation. The self-styled scientific thinkers of the thirteenth century felt the need for a new theoretical explanation, one that would more clearly justify their increasing reliance on evidence in the world and on the formal principles of demonstration. Here lay the significance of William's speculation about the nature of complex truth. He came at the very beginning of a concerted effort to define such truth critically and to work out the problems involved in showing how the resultant definition could meet the demands of scientific thought. His theory of complex truth, although incomplete and not free of difficulties, was one of the milestones along the way to a more successful resolution of the issue in the later Middle Ages. At the same time, he went a long way toward developing a coherent and precise language to talk about truth in this more critical manner and toward sorting out those ways of speaking about truth that derived from the interests of earlier thinkers and those that suited the more critical aspirations of his own time. On both counts, William's efforts gave evidence of his attachment to the new spirit of science.

The problem of truth in complex cognition occurred to William in *De universo* where he was discussing the idea of fate.[2] He claimed that some thinkers tried to avoid determinism by distinguishing between God's word (*verbum*) and His saying (*dictum*). They pointed out that God predicted many things which, according to Christian doctrine, would not come about by necessity, either the necessity of natural law or the force of inevitable circumstance. Yet God's word, His *verbum*, was His immutable Son, and it was hard to see how anything said by or through this Son would not thereby necessarily come to pass. In order to save chance and the freedom of the will these thinkers maintained that God said some of the things He predicted not by His word or Son but by His saying (*dictum*), which William scornfully interpreted as a lying word (*verbum mentiendi*). According to this theory, whatever God said by His saying, as opposed to His word, remained a contingent event, and if it did not turn out the way God had said it would there would be no loss to His dignity.

A similar difficulty arose, this time without reference to God but only to the idea of truth itself, when one considered propositions referring to future contingent events.[3] William held that it was possible to make a true assertion about a future contingent event without in any way prejudicing its contingency—that is, it was at least theoretically possible for man and quite within the capabilities of God. Yet if this were so, then where should one locate the truth by which such statements were true? It could not be in the real things to which such statements referred, since they did not yet exist when the statements were made. Unfortunately, there seemed to be no other

---

[2] See *De universo*, I, 3, 25 (*Mag. div.*, I, 792aG–792bG).

[3] *De universo*, I, 3, 25 (*Mag. div.*, I, 792bH–793aA). The problem was very likely suggested to William by Anselm's *Monologion*, 18, and *De vertitate*, 1 and 10 (Schmitt, ed., I, 33, 176 and 190). Yet if William took the idea from Anselm, he totally rejected Anselm's solution. See below, n. 4.

place for their truth to reside, for it was their truth and had to have some connection with them. Perhaps, then, they had no truth. In that case how could they be said to be true? William gave as an example the proposition, the sun will rise tomorrow. It did no good to say its truth was in the future, for it had to be true today. To object that the sun actually did exist today and so truth could reside in it in the present was beside the point, for one could always cite as a counterexample the proposition, a certain day has passed, which is no longer; or, a certain day is yet to come. In each of these cases there was no possible present referent. The nearly inevitable implication was that William's original position was mistaken. Such statements could not be true in the present but had to wait until the event occurred.

The solutions given in both these instances were abhorrent to William. Whatever God said must be true, even if it were not necessary, and it must be possible, at least for God, to make a true statement in the present about a future contingent event. Something had to be wrong with the analyses his hypothetical opponents gave. The question was, what was the proper way to talk about truth, specifically in such cases but also, by extension, wherever it applied to complex cognition? What was the truth and where could it be found?

Before giving his own answer, William paused to examine a response that had been traditional up to his time, dependent on the notion of truth drawn from Augustine. According to this view, God, who was Truth itself, provided the standard for human knowledge, and so the truth of complex statements, in particular those where there was no existing referent, was not to be sought in the world but in God. As the First Truth, He was the guarantor of all true propositions, and they were all true through Him. William would have nothing of this solution. What he thought about those who adhered to it is apparent from the way he described them: "Some people, disturbed by these and similar arguments and prevented by their own imbecility from reasoning clearly, have become like wandering blind men, incapable of finding the door to truth. They have said that it is the First Truth by which all other such things are true."[4] They were plainly in error, and William was confident he could dismiss their theory with adequate arguments.[5]

He explained that there were two ways thinkers had held propositions to be true by the First Truth, either formally (*formaliter*) or efficiently (*effective*).[6] By the first, when one called something true, presumably a complex statement, one was actually predicating of it the Creator Himself, and therefore God Himself was essentially in it or in whatever it referred to. By the second, calling a complex statement true meant predicating of it some effect of God, which was consequently in it and in its referents. The traditional way to describe this effect was as an intelligible light (*lux intelligibilis*) radiating from God in much the same way that visible light shone from the sun, and William sometimes spoke of it as an influence or an effusive truth (*veritas effusa*).[7] He noted that both ways of seeing God as the basis for truth involved insoluble difficulties.

When William argued against these views, he generally assumed they held God or His effect to rest in the reality to which statements referred, but occasionally he spoke as if they were seen to reside in the propositions themselves. In either instance his objections were the same. His first argument was that this notion of truth would inevitably mean that sometimes God's essence would have to come to rest in nonbeing.[8] Similarly, if one held all truth to consist in an effect of God, His light, then this light would at times have to fall on something that did not exist. As he had said, the only reality in-

---

[4] *De universo*, I, 3, 25 (*Mag. div.*, I, 793aA). The position William attacked was essentially the answer Anselm gave in the passages cited above, n. 3, and even more clearly in *De veritate*, 13 (Schmitt, I, 196–99).
[5] Immediately after the statement cited above in n. 4, William said: "Moreover, I shall show you the ways this error can be destroyed."
[6] *De universo*, I, 3, 25 (*Mag. div.*, I, 793aB).
[7] See *De universo*, I, 3, 25 (*Mag. div.*, I, 793aB and 794aH).
[8] This argument and those that follow all come from *De universo*, I, 3, 25 (*Mag. div.*, I, 793aB–793bD).

volved in propositions referring to future facts was an event
that had not yet occurred. Even the proposition itself was not
really a positive thing, nor did it represent real existence, for it
was, in his words, actually a division, separating present being
from a subject that was not yet. Consequently, in these instances there was no existing thing in the present in which
God or His effect could come to lie. Who would hold that
being could be in nonbeing? It was impossible, and there was
no way the views under consideration could account for truth
in such cases. In the same vein he argued that these views involved God in circumstances incompatible with His immutability. Many true statements were only temporarily or occasionally true, and it was unlikely that the Divine Truth would
dart in and out of them, or the reality to which they referred,
like a fugitive. There were further difficulties in explaining
statements of exclusive alternation or disjunction. They were
always true, but how could one work out the problem of where
Truth would reside in them and how it would move from one
side of the disjunction to the other?

After a short statement that these views of truth would
probably implicate God's will in the worst evils—for He would
stand as guarantor of truth even in the case of assertions about
criminal events—William turned to arguments pertaining
solely to the notion of truth as God's light.[9] He protested that
if truth were an influence from God, then it would be separable
from the divine essence. This would make it possible for God
to exist without truth, in which circumstance it would be true
there was no truth, a patent absurdity. Next he argued that
such an influence or light could also be separated from the true
thing upon which it fell, so that at least in theory one would
be able to understand any proposition whatsoever without
knowing whether it was true or not. Yet there were many cases
where this was impossible, such as with immediately evident
truths, like the disjunction, Socrates either disputes or does not
dispute. One could not comprehend such assertions without

---

[9] *De universo,* I, 3, 25 (*Mag. div.,* I, 794aE–G).

recognizing them as true. Finally, William argued that many things were true from eternity (*multa vera ab aeterno*) even though nothing but God had existed that long.[10] This meant that whatever truth accounted for these true things, it could not be a light from God. Any such light would have to be different from the divine essence, its existence, like that of all other created things, necessarily having a beginning in time. This argument is particularly interesting, since it is the first time William hinted that complex truth might not be related to being: many things were true from eternity but only one thing had existed that long.

William was satisfied that his arguments demonstrated the bankruptcy of any view holding God or His light to be the basis for truth in complex knowledge. Such notions were so far off the mark that he had nothing good to say for them. Even their way of approaching the problem was wrong. They all began with the assumption that truth was eternal and worked their way to a supernatural essence, either God or something directly from Him, upon which truth could rest. William, on the other hand, completely recast the question and in the process offered a radically different idea of truth. He began with a formal definition of truth in complex cognition and then considered the logical and ontological problems that arose in working out the details. Only then did he examine the broad metaphysical dilemmas out of which had arisen the theory of a divine basis for truth, and he took care to show how little metaphysical speculation was actually relevant to the issue. William thus broke dramatically with the tradition that had seen the question of truth as part of the theological problem of man's relation to God. In contrast, his emphasis lay on the truth as a problem primarily for logic and on a theory of truth as an instrument of reason, not as a way to confront the divine. He set out on his own to find a more critical notion of truth that would fit more easily with the new scientific aspirations of his time.

The sixth in William's list of the definitions of truth dealt

[10] *De universo,* I, 3, 25 (*Mag. div.,* I, 794aG-H).

with complex knowledge, and this definition was the one that interested him the most and to which he gave the greatest attention. According to him, the idea came from Avicenna, who said that the truth by which statements were said to be true was an accommodation of speech and reality: *adaequatio orationis et rerum.*[11] Another way William frequently described this condition was as a conformity (*convenientia*), or sometimes a harmony (*concordia*) or harmonizing (*concordantia*). Other words for the same thing were equation (*aequatio*), equality (*aequalitas*), similitude (*similtudo*), comparison (*comparatio*), and most important, a reference (*respectus*) or relation (*relatio*).[12] As for the two elements brought together by this accommodation, there was, on the one side, speech (*oratio*), which William identified specifically as a proposition (*enunciatio*), more frequently known by its function as either an affirmation (*affirmatio*) or a negation (*negatio*).[13] Here there was no question what he intended. By speech he meant simply the complex statements by which one made positive or negative assertions, and he indicated that as Avicenna had shown, such statements could be either exterior—that is, spoken and written asser-

---

[11] *De universo,* I, 3, 26 (*Mag. div.,* I, 795aB). Avicenna spoke in these terms in what was known in Latin translation as his *Metaphysics* (I, 9) (Avicenna, *Opera in lucem redacta* [Venice, 1508; repr. Frankfurt a. M., 1961], f. 74ra–b). For a discussion of the history of this definition in the thirteenth century and the erroneous attribution of it to Isaac Israeli, see J. T. Muckle, "Isaac Israeli's Definition of Truth," *Archives d'Histoire Doctrinale et Littéraire du Moyen Age* 8 (1933), 5–8; Henri Pouillon, "Le premier Traité des Propriétés transcendentales. La 'Summa de bono' du Chancelier Philippe," *Revue Néoscolastique de Philosophie* 42 (1939), 59; and Alexander Altmann and Samuel M. Stern, *Isaac Israeli. A Neoplatonic Philosopher of the Early Tenth Century* (Oxford, 1958), pp. 58–59.

[12] All these terms are found in *De universo,* I, 3, 26 (*Mag. div.,* I, 795a–796a). For *adaequatio,* see pp. 795aB (twice), 795aC, 795bB, and 796aE; for *convenientia* see pp. 795aC (twice), 795bB, 795bC (twice), 795bD (three times), and 796aE (twice); for *concordia,* p. 795aC; for *aequatio* and *similitudo,* pp. 796aB and 795aC; for *aequalitas,* pp. 795aB and 795bB; for *comparatio,* pp. 795aC (twice) and 795bB; for *respectus,* p. 795aC (twice); for *relatio,* pp. 795aC and 796aE.

[13] Again, all these terms are to be found in *De universo,* I, 3, 26. For *oratio,* see pp. 795aB (three times), 795aC, 795bC, and 795bD; for *enunciatio,* pp. 795aB, 795aC (twice), and 796aE; for *affirmatio* and *negatio,* pp. 795aB, 795aC (three times, for *negatio* alone), and 795bD.

tions—or spiritual and intellectual associations of concepts in the mind.[14] On the other side was reality, a category for which William used the most varied terms and which remained the most ambiguous element in his notion of truth. Sometimes he characterized this part of the accommodation as substantial reality, calling it things (*res*) or, to be more precise, the complex associations that held among them (*compositiones et divisiones rerum*). Occasionally he represented this side as whatever the assertions referred to: the things stated (*enunciata*) or what was signified (*significatum*) or affirmed (*affirmatum*). Most often he turned to the language of possibility and called it whatever was capable of being described by a statement—that is, the statable (*enunciabile*) or the affirmable (*affirmabile*) or negatable (*negabile*).[15] What united these names was that they all included the idea that this side of the accommodation of truth was the referent of a complex utterance—in William's words, what was signified or stated—but they differed in that some of them left open the question of where the referent was fixed in reality and even whether it actually had to exist at the time when the true statement was made.

Of all the ways William characterized the accommodation that made up the truth, the most general and the one that provided the key to his thought was the idea of relation. Upon this foundation he elaborated the formal qualities of complex truth, and by this means he solved the metaphysical dilemmas of his opponents. In his own words:

It is clear [according to the sixth meaning] that the truth and falsehood [of what is signified] are like references or comparisons of the compositions and divisions [of things] to their affirmations and negations and that the truth and falsehood of affirma-

[14] *De universo*, I, 3, 26 (*Mag. div.*, I, 795aB). Again, William did not seem to give priority of reference to either mental or external signs; both referred directly to the object. See above, Chapter II, n. 13.
[15] All these terms are found in *De universo*, I, 3, 26 (*Mag. div.*, I, 795a–796a). For *res*, see p. 795aB; for *compositiones et divisiones rerum*, p. 795aC (twice); for *enunciata*, pp. 795aB and 795bC; for *significatum*, p. 795bC; for *affirmatum*, p. 796aE (twice); for *enunciabile*, pp. 795aC (five times), 795bB, 795bD (three times), and 796aE; for *affirmabilia* and *negabilia*, pp. 795aC, 795aD, and 795bD.

tions and negations are comparisons or relations or references [of them] to the compositions and divisions of the things that they signify.[16]

Truth in complex knowledge consisted, therefore, in a particular type of relation between the two fundamental elements involved in man's complex cognition: the knowledge itself or an assertion representing it, on the one side, and the fact this knowledge referred to, on the other. Each term in the relation was complex. On the part of the knowledge what was involved was an aggregation of concepts or words arranged in a determinate way, which is to say in a proposition either formed internally and retained as a mental statement or delivered externally as a spoken or written assertion. On the part of the referent there was an association among objects, whether this be as simple as the association or dissociation of an essence or nature with its own being or as complex as a multiple arrangement of natures and qualities. In any case the referential correlative had to be more than just a simple essence or substance abstracted from any consideration of its existence or properties, for this was the object of simple cognition and did not allow one to make a statement asserting something. Truth had to deal with facts, complex situations; it confirmed or negated one's assertions about the conditions of things.

According to the terms of the definition, the relation that made complex knowledge true was one of agreement or conformity. If at times William used the words "equation" or "equality" to describe this conformity, he did not have in mind mathematical equality or even specific identity. He carefully pointed out that knowledge was generically and specifically different from the object it referred to and that the two could never be said to agree by any sort of essential similarity.[17] Yet at least since Aristotle there had been another way to explain agreement between assertions and facts, and this way led back to William's theory of the reference of simple terms. All concepts and words referred to a definite object, and except for

[16] *De universo,* I, 3, 26 (*Mag. div.,* I, 795aC).
[17] *De universo,* II, 2, 65 (*Mag. div.,* I, 914bH).

fantastic concepts and words and the special category of properties referring primarily to God, the object referred to was some
substance or quality of a substance in the created world. When
words or concepts were grouped together into propositions,
they implied a corresponding grouping among the substances
or qualities to which they referred. Here was where the notion
of agreement or conformity came in, for although every word
in a proposition might refer to a definite object, there was
nothing to say that these objects indeed related the way the
proposition maintained. When the configuration of things in
reality was actually the same as the statement held it to be,
there was agreement. When it was not, there was none. Truth,
William claimed, was properly defined as this agreement, the
condition that existed between an assertion and its complex
object when the fact that the assertion implied actually proved
to be the case among its referents in the real world.

Curiously enough, William held that the relation between
assertion and referent was symmetrical; it allowed either one of
these correlatives to be called true. A proposition was true
when what it stated to be actually was, or when what it stated
to have been or to be in the future actually had been or would
be.[18] Put negatively, this meant that no proposition was true
that affirmed or denied anything other, more or less, or in any
other manner than was the case with its referent.[19] A complex
referent, on the other hand, was true when it did not disagree
with or differ from its affirmation or negation, that is, the assertion by which it was described.[20] One could therefore speak
of the truth of either a proposition or a complex fact, and one
would be referring to the harmony that existed between them,
the fact that one was adequately reflected in the other. The

[18] *De universo,* I, 3, 26 (*Mag. div.,* I, 795aB). William's language
echoes that of Aristotle in *Metaphysics,* IV, 7 (1011b25–27) as well as
Anselm in *De veritate,* 2. For Aristotle, see the Latin "Translatio anon-
yma," also known as the "Translatio media," which would have been
available to William (*Metaphysica,* Aristoteles Latinus, XXV, 2, ed. Gudrun Vuillemin-Diem [Leiden, 1976], p. 80). For Anselm, see *Opera
omnia,* ed. Schmitt, I, 178.
[19] *De universo,* I 3, 26 (*Mag. div.,* I, 795aC).
[20] Ibid.

contrary of such a state or its absence (*privatio*) was known as the falsehood of each of the two.[21]

From the terms of the definition alone, it is evident how completely William had divorced himself from the search for an ideal and transcendent standard of truth, a higher Truth directly implicated in all the other truths known here below. He made the point doubly clear in a short discussion of the nature of relation in general. By his account, a relation neither added anything to nor subtracted anything from the elements it related, nor did it signify anything inherent to them. The fact that one thing was related to another did not say anything about its essence as such but rather indicated something about the attitude of another thing to it.[22] Consequently, a relation was no more nor less than the elements it brought together, each of which was essentially and qualitatively unchanged by being related. This meant that truth, formally defined as a relation, was not a separate thing in itself but just the two extremes of speech and referent it brought together; and given William's explanation of the normal referents for simple concepts or terms, it was clear that the conditions for truth could be fully satisfied without going beyond the created world. Those who set about looking for a real basis for truth anywhere else but in the mind and its substantial object were doomed to failure. Above all, there was no role for God or for any direct influence from Him in the normal apprehension of truth. Simple apprehension in the world provided all the information one needed to determine the truth of complex knowledge.

2. ETERNAL TRUTHS: PROBLEMS OF REFERENCE AND MEANING

William's formal explanation of complex truth, eliminating the need to search for a standard outside of knowledge itself and the objects in the world to which it referred, constituted perhaps the most significant element in his radical reconstruc-

---

[21] Ibid.
[22] *De universo,* I, 3, 26 (*Mag. div.,* I, 795aD).

tion of the problem for thinkers of the thirteenth century. Yet if he were to succeed in persuading others to follow him, he had to show how his theory would meet the difficulties that had introduced him to the problem of complex truth in the first place, all of which difficulties could be subsumed under the larger and more fundamental issue of immutable truth. Resolving this larger issue was crucial if William's ideas were to provide a theoretical foundation for scientific thought, because science concerned itself exclusively with truths medieval thinkers recognized as immutable.

The problem of immutable truth arose from the difficulties of explaining how there could be such a thing in the face of the constantly changing nature of the real world and the human mind. It applied to three major sorts of knowledge. First, there were statements of universal truth, including both the principles of demonstrative thought and necessary propositions about the natures of things. An example of the former widely recognized by scholastic thinkers was the law of excluded middle, that every fact must be either affirmed or denied; an example of the latter, the universal truth that man is a rational animal. These were the truths that made up the substance of science, and a program of scientific thought would depend on some understanding of what it was that raised them above the level of ordinary statements of fact. Second came statements of nonexistence and many negative assertions, what medieval thinkers referred to as divisions, since they divided a subject and a predicate. Among such truths were propositions stating that some imaginary thing did not exist, that two different substances were not the same, or that a specific essence was incompatible with a specified quality. William himself gave two examples of this type of proposition: the assertion that a chimera did not exist and that man was not a jackass.[23] Since the validity of such statements did not seem to depend on the existence of anything, they appeared to be true regard-

[23] *De universo,* I, 3, 26 (*Mag. div.,* I, 796aE), and *De anima,* VII, 6 (*Mag. div.,* II supp., 211a).

less of conditions in the real world and therefore for all time. Finally, there were statements of future fact, both necessary and contingent. Although these were not strictly speaking immutable truths, since their truth-value would change when the event they predicted occurred, up until that time they shared the same characteristics as assertions of the first two categories. They were true as far back in time as one wanted to go and therefore seemed to be set apart from the temporal conditions of existence in the real world.

Before William's time, medieval thinkers commonly voiced the problem of immutable truth in terms of eternity. After all, the most salient characteristic of immutable truths was that they held over all time, and for scholars accustomed to speculating on the nature of God's existence it was easy to move from the idea of things that always held true to the idea of things whose truth was eternal or outside of time altogether. Given this point of view, the problem reduced to explaining how some truths were eternal. It is not surprising that once the issue had been set in these terms thinkers tended to see it as a matter to be resolved in metaphysics or ontology by showing how some aspects of human knowledge or objective reality incorporated or touched on eternal being. The traditional identification of truth with God encouraged such an attitude, since it suggested a simple solution: immutable truths were the way they were because they were founded in the invariable and eternal being of God Himself. Perhaps because it was so easy to explain immutable truths in this way, men did not question whether or not some such perduring reality was actually a necessary part of their nature. It seemed evident enough that the crux of the matter lay in showing how some special forms of knowledge possessed qualities properly attributed only to God and were therefore immediately derived from Him.

The way William handled the problem of immutable truth marked a radical break with this tradition. To a large extent the attitude he took was determined by strict adherence to his own formal definition of complex truth. He could not consistently have claimed that the foundation for immutable truth lay in

God and still held to his insistence that truth in human knowledge consisted solely in a correct relation between language or mind and its object in the created world. Yet William's new departure involved more than just rejecting the traditional resolution of the problem. Once he had come to see that God's eternal being was separable from the notion of immutable truth, he began to suspect that the problem itself had been misconstrued. For him the issue was not that of accounting for God's relation to the world or to man but merely that of explaining reference and time in certain special, seemingly atemporal kinds of complex truth. Despite the well-established custom of resolving the matter by having recourse to some special doctrine of ontology or metaphysics, he suggested that most of the peculiarities of immutable truth could be explained simply in epistemological or even logical terms.

For all its power, William's radical solution was not immediately apparent in his work. When he first came to the problem of immutable truth, he introduced it in strictly traditional terms, inquiring after the nature of eternal truth. As he noted, many truths did not hold at only one moment but rather over an extended period of time, in some cases all the way into eternity.[24] The problem was that he had already defined truth as a relation between real and linguistic elements in the world, and yet, like all Christian thinkers, he recognized that nothing but God possessed eternal existence.[25] It appeared he would be forced to concede that in the case of eternal truths there would be occasions when there was truth even though neither of the elements of the relation that made it up, either assertions or real objects, actually existed. William had to find some way of showing how this was possible.

One response would have been to turn to a modified version of the traditional view that immutable and thus eternal truth had its foundation in God, claiming that all possible assertions

---

[24] *De universo*, I, 3, 26 (*Mag. div.*, I, 795aB).
[25] The exclusive eternity of God had been the basis for some of William's arguments against the position that truths werre true by a divine light.

had in fact been made from eternity in God's word. This would mean that for every eternal truth there was a divine statement constituting one side of the relation in which that truth consisted, thereby giving it a basis in eternal existence.[26] William recognized that some thinkers might take this option, and he conceded that they were right in maintaining that God had indeed made all possible true assertions from eternity and that these assertions could have served as the linguistic terms for eternal truths. He denied, however, that this provided a solution to the problem at hand. Even if one accepted the premise that eternal truths consisted of accommodations made to divine assertions, one would still be only halfway to explaining how there could be truth on the occasion when nothing but God existed. After all, there was still the other, objective side of the relation of truth to account for. In William's own words:

This does not cut the knot of the question, since it does not set forth the truth concerning this sort of conformity or accommodation. And this is because it necessarily limps, not having anything on the side of the statable (*enunciabile*) where it could set its foot. For the reality signified (*res*), even though it be statable, would nevertheless not exist in the truth of being.[27]

This answer provided an existential basis for eternal truth on the side of the proposition, but it left the referent in an ontological limbo.

Yet William criticized this response not only because he thought it was incomplete but also because he believed that it totally missed the point of the issue and so there was no use in following it up. To maintain that God's eternal assertions made up one element of the relations constituting eternal truths might provide a partial explanation for eternal truth insofar as the problem applied to knowledge possessed by God. Yet he held it did nothing at all to explain the nature of knowledge available to the human mind. Human knowledge

---

[26] *De universo*, I, 3, 26 (*Mag. div.*, I, 795bD).
[27] *De universo*, I, 3, 26 (*Mag. div.*, I, 795bD–796aE).

referred directly to something in the world and not to some divine exemplar, and complex truth in human knowledge was defined as the proper relation between language or concepts and things in the world. To William, then, consistency demanded that if some of the truths humans knew were eternally true, he would have to account for this fact, and for their eternity, within the worldly parameters of his theory of reference and his formal definition of complex truth. He could not, at this point, have recourse to God.

Instead, William accounted for the phenomenon of eternal truth by means of a peculiar theory of relation. He had explained that in reality, relations did not stand for anything more than the extremes they related. Beyond this, however, he also maintained that many relations, like those involved in signification, apprehension, thought, and love, did not require the existence of all the real elements that they related and to which they referred. What he had in mind were relations that permitted passive predication (*denominatio passiva*).[28] In such instances one could predicate something of one of the elements of the relation without implying that the predicated quality or what accounted for it actually inhered in the subject. In the case of love, for example, the emotion that permitted one to call an object loved did not reside in the object itself but rather in something else from which it was directed toward the object.[29] This meant that something could be loved that did not exist or would never exist. Love was, to be sure, a real relation between lover and loved, but it did not require the existence of both of them. William insisted that truth was a relation of just this sort. As in the case of love there could be truth even at times when both of the elements it related did not actually exist.

William's principle could be applied separately to either of the two sides of the relation of truth. For example, statements

[28] *De universo*, I, 3, 26 (*Mag. div.*, I, 795aD-795bA).
[29] *De universo*, I, 3, 26 (*Mag. div.*, I, 795bA).

about future conditions could be true in the present even though there might well be no real object presently existing to which the subject or the predicate of the true proposition could refer. One reason for this was that truth, beyond being a relation of passive predication, was also one of a type of relation called a privation (*privatio*). There were many such relations to be found in the real world, comparisons drawn among objects not because of any actual thing they shared but because of something they lacked. All nonbeings were said to agree in nonbeing, all impossible things in impossibility, all blind men in blindness, and so on, and yet in none of these cases was the quality shared a positive trait of the objects that shared it. Indeed, although the privative relation itself was real, it did not necessarily posit anything real in existence.[30] In the case of truth the privative nature of the relation was revealed in the definition William had given before: that a true statement was one that asserted nothing more or less, other or otherwise, than was contained in its referent.[31] In these terms truth did not so much imply something positive about being as refrain from indicating what was not the case. An assertion could be true even if there were no referent already existing in the world so long as it did not imply something about reality that was not so.[32] Statements of future fact could therefore be true without having to be related to some presently existing object. Technically, they met the terms of the definition so long as they did not refer to anything more than would come to be.

Likewise, there could be truth even when there was no exist-

---

[30] See the whole column in *De universo,* I, 3, 26 (*Mag. div.,* I, 795b).
[31] See above, n. 19.
[32] William's theory here reveals affinities with the doctrine of Abelard, as described by Jean Jolivet, that necessary propositions in effect signified nothing real at all. See Jean Jolivet, "Comparaison des théories du langage chez Abélard et chez les Nominalistes du XIVe siècle," in *Peter Abelard,* ed. E. M. Buytaert (Louvain, 1974), p. 174. Note, however, that behind Abelard's doctrine lay an ultimate appeal to the divine ideas as the basis for necessary truth (Jolivet, p. 175). William avoided such realism and thereby made full use of the doctrine, the significance of which Abelard had only partially realized.

ing assertion. Here the argument depended on the idea of possibility. As William said:

When statables are said to be true—that is, conforming or accommodated to their affirmations or negations—this is not to be understood of their affirmations and negations as actually existing (*secundum actum*) but rather as possible (*secundum potentiam*). And this is to say that I do not intend [them to be accommodated] to affirmations or negations which they have in the present—that is, by which they are presently or actually signified—but rather to those by which it is possible that they be affirmed or negated.[33]

In other words, for a relation of truth to hold, it was enough that an assertion could be made that would adequately reflect the conditions of the factual referent. This was the reason William frequently used words incorporating an element of possibility when he talked about the object side of the relation of truth. Terms like "statable," "affirmable," and "negatable" indicated that the referent had to be capable of being expressed by an assertion adequate to it, without implying, however, that such an assertion had actually been made. So long as the mere possibility remained, a statable condition could be true, even from eternity, although there was no accompanying eternal assertion.[34]

Yet William wanted to say more than that the relation of truth could hold when either one or the other of its two relatable elements did not exist. In his concluding statement on privative relations he remarked that since truth was a privation, one could find times when true things were true by a truth that did not exist, in the same way one had to admit that blind men were blind by a blindness that was not a real existent but rather the absence of sight.[35] Here, then, he was willing to extend the possibility of nonexistence to the very relation itself without undermining the validity of the predicate "true." The applicability to the problem of eternal truth was clear. One could, in-

[33] *De universo*, I, 3, 26 (*Mag. div.*, I, 795bD).
[34] Ibid.
[35] *De universo*, I, 3, 26 (*Mag. div.*, I, 795bC).

deed, hold that there were many things true from eternity and
not be forced to concede that there were many real things
called "truths" that actually had eternal existence.[36] In other
words, the problem of eternal truth could be separated from
the question of eternal existence. One could abandon the language of eternal truths and talk instead about things that were
eternally true. This was why William was able to reject any
implication that the truth as humans knew it, even where it
was eternally valid, necessarily relied on some divine foundation. The problem of eternal truth did not challenge his definition of complex truth, even when this definition was construed
so strictly as to apply only to things in the created world of the
human mind and its normal objects.

For all the echoes of tradition that remain in William's
language, he had, quite clearly, transformed the problem with
which he was dealing. As he said in his own words, one could
say something was true by a truth that did not exist at some
point or another because the truth he was considering did not
primarily have to do with being but was rather a rational or
logical truth (*veritas rationalis, sive logica*), having to do with
the appropriateness of propositions.[37] In short, although he
continued to speak in terms of "eternal truth," he had actually
come to see the question as the problem of immutable truth,
one divorced of most of the traditional trappings of ontology
and natural theology, finding its solution more in theories of
logic and language.

Yet if William had come to see the importance of a new way
of viewing the question of unchanging truth, he did not work
out all the problems his proposed solution to the issue implied.
The most successful aspect of his efforts concerned the asser-

---

[36] *De universo*, I, 3, 26 (*Mag. div.*, I, 795bD). This had been William's
original dilemma.

[37] ". . . sic non est mirum, si aliquid est verum veritate, quae non est,
maxime cum veritas hujusmodi, veritas rationalis, sive logica, sit, et convenientia enunciationum, quae non magis exigit res esse, quam non esse,
et econverso, nec magis est ad entia, quam ad non entia." *De universo*, I,
3, 26 (*Mag. div.*, I, 796aE).

tion side of relations of immutable or eternal truth. William had said that when a fact was called eternally true this was because it was always possible to make a true statement about it, not because there was always an actual proposition relating to it. In effect, he substituted the notion of possibility for that of time as a way of ensuring the immutability implied in the word eternal. In this way, the words "eternally true" did not mean "true by a real relation at all times," but rather "always possible of being true by a real relation." It was here that William most fully demonstrated the logical aspect of truth at the expense of metaphysical considerations.

When it came to applying his theory of immutable truth to the referential side of such relations, however, William did not hold so well to his fundamental insight. For each of the three sorts of proposition whose truth could be called immutable, he would have to show how it made sense to talk about truth even when no real referent existed. William's discussion of the problem with regard to statements of future fact has already been examined, and it has been shown how he explained that particular issue in specific terms by seeing truth as a privation. So long as a statement posited nothing more than was or would eventually be the case in the real world, it was true. Negative assertions, the second sort of immutable truth, could be handled in the same way, and indeed, when William touched on the problem of eternal truths in a passage in *De anima* he explicitly said as much. As an example, he offered the proposition, it is not possible for a man to be a jackass.[38] He said that such a statement was eternally true and this did not require the actual eternal existence of the objects to which it referred. In fact, the statement was eternally true even if neither a man nor a jackass had ever existed or ever would exist. The reason, he said, was that such a statement was pure negation—that is, a kind of absolute privation—and for a discussion of the matter he referred the reader back to *De universo,* the very section that has just been examined above.

[38] *De anima,* VII, 6 (*Mag. div.,* II supp., 211a).

The problem was, however, more difficult with regard to immutable truths of the first category, statements of universal truth, and they constituted the most important case, making up the very substance of scientific thought. Because universal truths typically made positive assertions about real natures, it would seem that their immutability could not have been shielded from questions concerning the existence of their referents simply by having recourse to the notion of truth as a privative relation, as William had done in the case of negative assertions or statements of future fact. Nevertheless, it appears he believed he could do just that. The passage in *De anima* where he gave the example about man and jackass was ostensibly about all principles of knowledge, by which he meant to include the most fundamental universal truths, and so he must have intended his general solution, analyzing such truths as pure negations or absolute privations, to work for them all.[39] In fact, two examples of the first principles of science that William cited in the passage—the law of excluded middle, that every fact must be either affirmed or denied; and the law of noncontradiction, that the same thing cannot be both affirmed and denied of a single subject—might have encouraged him to think he had found the solution. Both of these propositions included a kind of negativity in their predicate, so that one could have been led to maintain that when no referent actually existed for either of them, their truth reduced to that of a simple negative. Yet even if one agreed it was possible to account for the immutability of some of the principles of science this way, it is not clear how one could have applied the notion of truth as a privation to positive assertions about the natures of things, by far the larger proportion of statements of universal truth. According to William's views on reference, propositions of this sort necessarily referred to something real in the world, and so it would seem that for them to be true there would at the same time have to be some actual fact to which they could be related. The only example of such a truth William mentioned in the passage in *De anima* came from Aristotle: the law

---

[39] See above, n. 38.

that the diagonal of a square was incommensurate with any one of the sides. William asserted that the law was always true.[40] And yet, interpreted in terms of eternity, this meant that there would have been a time—or to be more precise, there would have been some occasion outside of time—when the law was true even though no real referent for it actually existed.

To resolve this problem William would have had to go back to his general assertion that the apparent difficulty in such a situation lay not with the nature of being, which was, for all creation, unquestionably not eternal, but rather in the proper understanding of language and logic. He would have had to show explicitly how the question could be restated in logical, or epistemological, terms that permitted its solution. This would have brought him to an examination of the nature of universals, the question of their existential import and of the exact way their reference related to their meaning. Later scholastic thinkers were to do this, and even William's contemporary, Robert Grosseteste, began to chart the way, but William did not. Indeed, he never really answered the problem at all, and it remains one of the most significant gaps in his theory of truth. Moreover, it is hard to see how, even if he had sensed this deficiency in his thought and tried to find a remedy, he could have done so without being forced to rethink some of his other arguments about the nature of complex truth. William consistently used the notion of privation to explain why it was not necessary for all truth to involve an actually existing referent, but clearly something else was needed here. This suggests, of course, that William's explanation of the referential conditions in immutable truth was inadequate or incomplete. In the end, it seems he grasped the theoretical point that the problem of immutable truth had to be approached with more

---

[40] See above, n. 38. In fact, William claimed Aristotle held that this law "always was" (*semper est*). Although Aristotle frequently referred to the incommensurability of the diagonal with the side of a square as an example of a mathematical truth, there does not seem to be any place where he specifically stated that it was "always" or was "always" true.

logical concerns in mind, but he did not discover a complete philosophical language and apparatus suitable to the task.

For all its difficulties, however, William's discussion of immutable truth marked an important stage in the development of medieval thought, and its significance must not be overlooked. He and his contemporary, Robert Grosseteste, were among the first thinkers in the medieval West to come to see how much the problem of truth depended on logic rather than metaphysics, so that it could be separated more radically from theoretical questions of being and the nature of existence in the created world and viewed independently of the issue concerning the relation of the mind and creation to God.[41] He was one of the first to put this realization into words. If his understanding of the problem was not without ambiguities and if he had not worked out a solution that applied to every case, he had nevertheless taken an important step toward a notion of truth and a theory of reference that would be fully elaborated only in later scholastic thought.

3. THE WAY TO KNOWLEDGE OF COMPLEX TRUTH

In addition to investigating the formal nature of truth in complex knowledge William also undertook to examine how the mind could attain such truth. His answer to this problem depended on the terms of his definition of truth and constituted in fact its ultimate extension into epistemology and noetics, establishing the conditions under which the human intellect could meet the requirements for certain understanding in this life and identifying the evidence upon which it would have to rely. This was the practical side of the question of truth and the one most immediately relevant to the scientific aspirations of thirteenth-century thinkers.

---

[41] Although Abelard had begun to work out a way of explaining immutable truth in logical terms, he still held to the notion that the real guarantors of such truth were the ideas in the mind of God (see above, n. 32). William made the radical break of eliminating altogether any question of an eternal ontological base.

In its most general form the question applied to knowledge of both universal propositions and statements of particular fact. Among the latter, where there was no place for demonstrative reasoning or any formal process of inference, the matter reduced to explaining the immediate knowledge of the truth of particular propositions. Such knowledge formed an analogue, on the side of particular cognition, to knowledge of the principles of science in universal knowledge, both being a kind of uninferred evident cognition. William himself recognized this when he held that there were two fundamental elements to human knowledge—he called them *extrema prima*—which were universal principles and sensible singulars.[42] The latter, when combined into assertions, constituted statements of particular fact, and they formed a class of propositional knowledge just as primary or immediate as any universal principle of science.

Although William never actually addressed the question of how the mind came to know the truth of such complex particulars, there can be no doubt how he would have answered it, given all he said about knowledge of particulars in his general account of simple cognition. The simplest way to judge the truth of a statement was to compare it with its complex referent in order to see if the two agreed in the way prescribed in the formal definition of complex truth. In the case of particular knowledge about everything except God Himself, the referents were individual objects in the created world, to which the mind had ready access even if it could reach them only indirectly in this life, through the senses. Consequently, the mind had merely to be exposed to the objective referents of any particular statement in order to be able to judge immediately whether it was true or false. This is what it meant to say that such propositions were primary. In each case where a referent actually existed and could be exposed to the sensory scrutiny of the intelligent subject, the particular truth of a statement was immediately evident. As for the way the mind came to know

---

[42] William referred to these two in *De bono et malo*, p. 283.

the statement in the first place, before it tested its truth, this was a routine matter of simple cognition, for the terms from which such statements were composed were normally acquired in the processes of everyday cognition. In short, the problem of the way to knowledge of the complex truth on the level of singular fact was trivial, merely an extension of William's theory of knowledge.

William took an interest in the problem of the way to knowledge of complex truth only when it came to necessary and universal truth, the kind of knowledge upon which scientific thought depended, and this is in itself yet another indication of his overriding concern for the issues of science and demonstrative certitude. On this level a full explanation of how the mind came to know truth would have had to refer to the knowledge of complex conclusions as well as to the principles of science. In the case of conclusions this would have entailed a return to the fundamental rules of logic. Aristotle had held— and scholars of the thirteenth century followed him on this score—that one could regard a conclusion as certain or scientific only if it came at the end of a demonstrative syllogism. Therefore, any account of the way men drew true conclusions would necessarily have involved an account of demonstrative logic, and any attempt to justify the results of this method would have had to entail a justification of the logical process itself. William was not a logician, and he felt under no obligation to cover the rules of syllogistic reasoning. Like his colleagues, he had been thoroughly trained in logic, and he assumed that his readers would know what constituted a conclusive, which is to say a demonstrative, argument and what did not. Furthermore, he saw no need to try to underwrite the general confidence in the demonstrative method. For him the problem would have been to understand how anyone could have doubted what seemed like unassailable rules of the mind.

Instead of discussing the truth of scientific conclusions as a problem, therefore, William merely expressed his full reliance in the syllogistic process. As he said:

When [the principles of science] have been ordered in a syllogistic arrangement and fitted to their conclusions, that is to those that follow necessarily and immediately from them, they introduce such conclusions into the receptive mind and are therefore the cause of the conclusions. Consequently it is clear that certain knowledge (*scientia sive cognitio*) of [principles] is the cause of certain knowledge of conclusions.[43]

In fact, the intellect was not free to doubt a conclusion once it had been shown how the conclusion could be demonstrated from accepted principles.[44] By its very nature the mind was compelled to assent to logical argument. Indeed, it would have made no sense to try to support such argument with another reason on a different level, for logic was its own justification. Put in metaphorical terms, this meant that principles were lights to the intellect. Just as the light of the sun revealed other objects to the eyes, so principles, by their own light, revealed conclusions accommodated to them, making these conclusions shine to the mind. In this way alone was the knowledge of conclusions available to the human intellect; without the light of their demonstrative premises they would remain shrouded in an intellectual night.[45]

It is interesting to note that William's comments on the incontrovertible evidence of syllogistic reasoning revealed a fundamental belief in the metaphysical realism of logic. He thought the relations that held in reality between the referents of principles and the referents of conclusions were immediately and accurately reflected in the logical relations between propositions in a demonstrative proof. As he explained it, it was because principles, or their objective reality, caused the condition described by the conclusion that knowledge of the principles was sufficient to account for knowledge of the conclusion.[46] Since it was by means of the syllogism that the mind went

<hr />

[43] *De anima,* VII, 4 (*Mag. div.,* II supp., 209b).
[44] *De virtutibus,* IX (*Mag. div.,* I, 102aH). See also *De anima,* VII, 4 (*Mag. div.,* II supp., 209b).
[45] *De anima,* VII, 5 (*Mag. div.,* II supp., 210b).
[46] *De anima,* VII, 4 (*Mag. div.,* II supp., 209b).

from principles to conclusion, this implied that the syllogism itself was a logical expression of external causality. It was more than just a dialectical mechanism that enabled the intellect to achieve certitude; it was a kind of map that directed the mind in a spiritual movement from concept to concept, paralleling the connection among natures in the real world.

By reasoning along these lines William was able to bring into relief the realistic element in Aristotle's distinction between a dialectical syllogism, capable of leading only to opinion, and the demonstrative argument of scientific proof. The former, weaker instance arose not only where men had not discovered sufficient reasons for phenomena, cases where their imperfect understanding was at fault, but also when connections in nature could not support any more than a dialectical argument. If the relation among real things was not necessary, then the best one could draw from a syllogism about them was a defensible opinion. Only when the causal nexus among things was necessary could necessary arguments be made, ones that permitted syllogizing to a certain conclusion.[47] In short, the variations of reliability within a single form of logical argument faithfully represented conditions in the world; logic was a true mirror of reality.

These few comments were all William had to say about the way to arrive at true conclusions. When it came to the knowledge of principles, however, he took the opportunity to air his views more completely. This should come as no surprise, since the principles of science stood in the crucial position of providing the foundation for all scientific thought and it was with them that the formal definition of truth would find its most immediate application to the concerns of demonstrative certitude. William derived his views on the cognitive function of principles directly from Aristotle. Quoting from the *Posterior Analytics,* he declared that all learning and teaching came from some pre-existing knowledge and that in the case of the sciences this precedent cognition consisted in knowledge of the

---

[47] *De anima,* VII, 8 (*Mag. div.,* II supp., 213b).

principles of science, those universal propositions recognized as true without the aid of syllogistic reasoning.[48] It was from these principles that men drew the conclusions out of which they constructed the whole edifice of systematic reasoning. He added that Aristotle himself gave exemplary confirmation of the procedure in his *Physics,* where he not only stated his intention of working solely from principles, including the causes and elements of things, but also succeeded in carrying out his plan for a large part of natural science.[49]

William's answer to the question of how men recognized the truth of the principles of knowledge was remarkably simple. He said that the principles were lights to the human mind and so were in themselves capable of revealing their own truth.[50] In fact, it was impossible for the intellect not to accede to their truth, much less contradict it, for they constituted a spiritual light (*lux spiritualis*) that always had access to the innermost reaches of the mind.[51] This was presumably the same light William spoke of on another occasion as being natural to the human intellective power. In that instance he identified the light as truth itself and added that it was what underlay all intelligibility.[52] If one puts these statements together, they indicate that he thought the principles themselves were identical with their truth, which is to say that they were assertions that carried their own evidence with them. This was, of course, precisely what made them immediately evident propositions. In less metaphorical terms, one could say that the proper relation among the terms of a principal proposition, the relation that made the proposition true, was evident to the knower in the

---

[48] *De anima,* VII, 5 (*Mag. div.,* II supp., 210a). William's quotation came from *Posterior Analytics,* I, 1 (71a1-2). See the translation by James of Venice (Aristoteles Latinus, IV, 1-4, ed. Minio-Paluello and Dod, p. 5).

[49] *De anima,* VII, 5 (*Mag. div.,* II supp., 210a). In speaking of Aristotle's intentions, William was referring to what Aristotle says in the very first paragraph of the first book of the *Physics* (184a9-15).

[50] See above, n. 45.

[51] *De anima,* VII, 5 (*Mag. div.,* II supp., 210b).

[52] *De anima,* VII, 7 (*Mag. div.,* II supp., 212b).

very knowledge of the separate terms themselves. William explained that principles were composed of abstract universals referring to real things.[53] Knowing the truth of principles, therefore, came down to knowing the meaning of the universal terms of which they were composed. If one could understand what a principle signified, then by that fact one had to concede its truth.[54]

For William, therefore, the critical question was not how men came to know the principles of science as true but rather how they came to formulate or comprehend the principles in themselves. There was no question here of a judgment or even, for the most part, of an ordering of terms. All that was necessary was to explain how the intellect came upon the simple terms of its principal knowledge, for then the evident nature of their relation would account for the procedure of arranging them into a true proposition. In Aristotelian language, the problem was to discover what impressed on the mind the intelligible forms that went into principles as they were formulated in the mind and to which corresponded the words by which they were expressed. As William said in his own words: "Moreover, since it is not possible for the soul to know (*intelligere*) without a mental image, and I mean without a sign or an intelligible form. . . , therefore, it is asked with good reason where those signs or forms have come from into the intellect. And this same question applies to the understanding or intellection of the principles of science."[55]

In William's view, science could be divided into two major categories. On the one hand there was the knowledge of the natural sciences (*scientiae naturales*); on the other that of the mathematical sciences, which he also called doctrinal, or sometimes disciplined (*scientiae doctrinales, disciplinales*). The distinc-

---

[53] *De anima*, VII, 5 (*Mag. div.*, II supp., 210b).

[54] As shown below, this general rule had to be stretched a bit to account for the principles of natural science. For them, knowledge of the correct positioning of the terms was not absolutely immediate but involved some nondemonstrative inference.

[55] *De anima*, VII, 6 (*Mag. div.*, II supp., 211a).

tion was based on the traditional three-part division of speculative science into natural, mathematical, and divine.[56] It was the
principles of the two purely human fields of speculation that
interested William. These were what he had in mind when he
gave the definition that principles were abstract universals arranged so as to reflect the truth.[57]

Although William never formally drew any other distinction among principles, the lines of his thought suggest a further subdivision into three types that cut across the separation
into mathematical and natural sectors. William's contemporary, Robert Grosseteste, would in fact make explicit a division
that followed much the same pattern, a fact that reveals how
much the thought of both men depended on fundamentals
drawn from Aristotle, whose view of science suggested discrim-
inating among principles in just this way. First of all there were
the first principles of science, common to all fields of certain
reasoning. They comprised the basic rules of demonstrative

[56] See *De virtutibus*, IX (*Mag. div.*, I, 124bE), and also n. 48, above.
William's language is not entirely clear on this score, but the best interpretation seems to be that he used *"doctrinalis"* and *"disciplinalis"* synon-
ymously to mean "mathematical." At any rate there can be no doubt
about his general intention to divide the sciences into two fields, natural
and mathematical.

The Western tradition of the tripartite division went back to
Boethius, who in his *De Trinitate* divided speculative science into *naturalis, mathematica,* and *theologica* or *divina* (see James A. Weisheipl,
"Classification of the Sciences in Medieval Thought," *Mediaeval Studies*
27 [1965], 60–61, and Boethius, *De Trinitate*, 2 [PL 64, 1250B]). Of
course, the ultimate written origin can be found in Aristotle's *Metaphysics,* VI, 1 [1026a18–19] [Aristoteles Latinus, XXV, 2, ed. Vuillemin-
Diem, pp. 117–18].) Boethius held that the method of the mathematical
sciences was disciplinary (*disciplinaliter*). When William called them also
"doctrinal," he may have had in mind the description of the same general division given by Avicenna in his *Metaphysics,* I, 1: "Et diximus quod
speculative comprehenduntur in tres partes, in naturales scilicet et doctrinales et divinas." *Opera,* f. 70ra.

For the tradition associating *disciplina* with the mathematical sciences,
see Henri-Irénée Marrou, " 'Doctrina' et 'disciplina' dans la langue des
Pères de l'Englise," *Bulletin du Cange* 10 (1934), 5–25, and Marie-
Dominique Chenu, "Notes de lexicographie philosophique médiévale:
Disciplina," *Revue des Sciences Philosophiques et Théologiques* 25 (1936),
686–92.

[57] See above, n. 53.

thought, such as the law of excluded middle and the principle of noncontradiction. Second came all other immediately evident universal truths, making up most of the principles proper to one science or another. These were propositions analyzing the essential nature of the subjects of the sciences—an example was the essential truth that man is a rational animal. Finally, there were those principles of science that were not truly immediately evident but had to be arrived at by some process of inference, although not by demonstration. These principles were to be found in the natural sciences, like astronomy and physics, where one could not normally attain the evidential clarity of the more abstract fields like mathematics. Instead of analyzing the essence of something, they made statements about efficient or final causation. This did not mean, however, that they were not principles, for they still provided the premises out of which many of the demonstrations of science could be formulated. Examples of principles of this sort would be the rule, accepted in the thirteenth century, that light from a distant object twinkled, or the statement that a lunar eclipse was caused by the interposition of the earth between the moon and the sun. Of the three types, William gave special attention to the first and third.[58] Yet they were all important, and to understand William's views on the origins of knowledge of the principles of science, each one must be considered in turn.

The problem with accounting for the knowledge of principles was, according to William, that no universal was in itself capable of action. Since universal principles were comprised solely of universal terms, they could not themselves be what caused the presence of intelligible forms in the intellect.[59] It should not be assumed here that William was repudiating his earlier statements on the process of human cognition, whereby he held that the specific essence of each thing was identical

[58] For Grosseteste, these were the complex principles proper, as opposed to statements drawn from the subjects of a science, which corresponded to the second category mentioned here.
[59] *De anima,* VII, 6 (*Mag. div.,* II supp., 211a–b).

with its individual substance and provided the occasion for universal as well as particular knowledge. When he denied that universals accounted for the knowledge of principles, he did not mean to say that the foundation for universal cognition did not lie in created reality. The target William was aiming at was Platonism, a system of thought he continually attacked, and in particular the doctrine that there were separate universals from which the mind could receive the forms that permitted its own formulation of principles. He wanted to make it clear that neither the principles nor the terms that made them up had some separate universal being that could be the cause of their cognitive presence in the mind. Like Aristotle, he thought this was pure nonsense. Yet he differed with Aristotle, too, and refused to have recourse to an agent-intellect.[60] According to William, it was necessary to find some other nonuniversal source for the forms of complex, principal cognition.

William thought that his model of the human mind on the border between two worlds—God above, sensible creation below—provided a way out of the dilemma. On the one hand God Himself served as a living book and a mirror full of forms for the intellect. The mind looked on this book and took from it the impressions of intelligible signs that could be combined into complex, evident truths.[61] Yet God was not the only source for intellectual principles. The other side of the mind's vision, into the lower world of the sensibles, also furnished the occasion for immediate cognition, after the manner William had described in his analysis of simple apprehension.[62] From

[60] De anima, VII, 6 (Mag. div., II supp., 211b).
[61] Ibid.
[62] De anima, VII, 7 (Mag. div., II supp., 213a). See the passage given below in Appendix A. Since this text is separated from the statement that God is a source of principles by a long discussion about how God is the ultimate object of the intellect, it might seem at first glance that it is not part of William's account of the knowledge of principles. In fact, however, the intervening passage is merely a digression, subsidiary to the claim that God can serve as a mirror for some primary forms and attempting to demonstrate that there is nothing unnatural or extraordinary about this. As soon as William has made this secondary point, he returns to the question of principles and reviews the role of the lower world in revealing them.

this world came intelligible forms that the intellect could shape into propositions just as evident as anything it saw in the divinity. There can be no doubt that William considered both worlds to be necessary for the acquisition of science—that is, that each legitimately provided some of the immediate propositions that underlay systematic thought. This is doubly clear in a passage where he examined the reasons for differences in intellectual achievement among men.[63] Part of the responsibility lay with God, who revealed more of the principles of science to some men than to others. Since the truths involved here seemed to arise from deep within the confines of the mind, this cause for diversity could be somewhat loosely attributed to a quality in the mind itself, to what in modern parlance would be called aptitude. But external factors also played a role. Different men were exposed to different schooling and experience (*doctrinae et experientiae*), and variation in these circumstances explained a good deal of the unequal distribution of scientific expertise. This could happen only if external circumstances, too, accounted for the knowledge of principles. In many cases, the mind would have to depend on sensation and the created world for the primary elements of its thought.

Given the fact that both God and sensible creation supplied forms for the understanding of principles, the next question to ask was what principles came from which world. William said the mind learned directly from God all the rules of truth (*regulae veritatis*), that is, those that were primary (*primae*) and known per se; the rules of right living (*regulae honestatis*); and a whole world of hidden knowledge (*universitas absconditorum scibilium*), made manifest only by the gift and grace of divine revelation.[64] Without yet determining precisely what William intended to include in each of these categories, one can see that he had generally in mind, first of all, fundamental speculative rules; second, basic moral precepts, perhaps the elements of a natural law; and finally, all God's mysteries. In the precise terms in which William had posed the problem of the origin of

[63] *De anima*, VII, 6 (*Mag. div.*, II supp., 212a).
[64] *De anima*, VII, 6 (*Mag. div.*, II supp., 211b).

knowledge of principles, this meant that the intellect took the mental terms it used to formulate such rules and secrets immediately from God.

It is possible at the outset to eliminate from consideration the third category, divine mysteries. William showed clearly enough that what he was thinking of here were the revealed articles of faith, directly perceived only by the prophets and the apostles, held by the rest of believers on authority alone.[65] Truths known in this way clearly constituted a special case and did not enter into the normal processes of cognition. Indeed, William himself felt compelled to point out that no matter how common some other forms of divine intervention might be in human knowledge, the direct communication of these hidden knowables was rare and very unusual. God was a living book to the mind, but He contained uncountable pages, and it was completely in His power to show as many or as few as He wanted to any viewer.[66] The articles of faith He revealed directly only to a tiny number of the chosen few. In addition to this category of knowables direct from God it is also possible to ignore the second group, basic moral precepts. They had to do with right living, but did not bear on the question of speculative truth. That leaves only the category of fundamental speculative rules. They are the ones to be examined in order to determine exactly what primary propositions William thought came directly from God.

As shown above, William first called these propositions the primary rules of truth, known per se. What he meant by per se was explained earlier in the same work.[67] It signified, simply, "not by any other"—which is to say that such rules of truth were the most immediately evident of the elements of primary cognition. William noted that the philosophers had called them first impressions, a name he often used himself to describe them. They were also known as the per se principles of

[65] *De anima*, VII, 6 (*Mag. div.*, II supp., 211b).
[66] *De anima*, VII, 6 (*Mag. div.*, II supp., 211b–212a).
[67] *De anima*, VII, 4 (*Mag. div.*, II supp., 209b).

the sciences (*principia scientiarum nota per semetipsa*), or more specifically *dignitates, maximae propositiones,* or the common conceptions of the mind (*communes animarum conceptiones*)—all terms used in scholastic Latin to refer to axioms, unproved principles of thought.[68] In one of the passages where William called them first impressions he added that the knowledge of nothing else preceded them in the intellect and that not only was it impossible to doubt that they were true but no intelligent being was capable of not knowing them. Here he adduced two examples from among what he identified as the principles of mathematical (*doctrinalis*) science: the law of excluded middle and the rule that the whole is always greater than any part.[69] In another place he called them the first principles of philosophy (*principia prima philosophiae*), and there he added another example, the fundamental logical law of noncontradiction.[70]

Clearly, what William had in mind when he spoke of the rules of truth revealed to men directly by God were those propositions that stood in the place of axioms in Aristotle's scheme of certain thought, what Aristotle specifically called the common principles of demonstrative science.[71] These were the principles comprising the first of the three categories set out at the beginning of this discussion, those basic laws and assumptions that lay at the foundation of all certain reasoning. Not limited to any particular type or genus of existing being, they

[68] William used all these terms in the passage cited above, n. 67. See also *De virtutibus,* IX (*Mag. div.,* I, 120aH). James of Venice, in his translation of Aristotle's *Posterior Analytics,* had used the terms *"dignitas"* and *"maxima propositio"* to refer to the axioms of science. See *Posterior Analytics,* I, 2 (72a17) (Aristoteles Latinus, IV, 1–4, ed. Minio-Paluello and Dod, p. 9). John of Salisbury spoke of the *communes conceptiones animi* as the very first concepts known to the mind. They were universal and known by all. See his *Metalogicon,* IV, 8 (ed. Webb, pp. 172–73). It was perhaps Boethius who coined the phrase *communis animi conceptio,* and he used it to refer to the axioms. See *Quomodo substantiae* (PL, 64, 1311).

[69] *De anima,* V, 15 (*Mag. div.,* II supp., 137a). See also *De universo,* II, 2, 49 (*Mag. div.,* I, 891aA).

[70] *De anima,* I, 3 (*Mag. div.,* II supp., 66b–67a).

[71] See *Posterior Analytics,* I, 10 (76a37–40).

could be used to analyze the whole breadth of creation, even divinity itself, and in fact every logical process began with them, whether they were explicitly introduced or not. They were the rules from which demonstration took its start, and in some cases, such as the philosophical principles of noncontradiction and the law of excluded middle, they were so fundamental as to give to syllogism its basic form. It is easy to see why William referred to them as the rules of truth, for the mind had to recognize them as invariably true before it could proceed to use the logic that made possible the expansion of knowledge into its various fields.

As for the way the mind received the knowledge of these principles, it is important to remember that William did not hold that they were impressed on the intellect as integral propositions. Instead, the mind took up separately the forms corresponding to each term. This meant that beyond the initial reception there had to be some kind of arrangement before one could speak of complex cognition. Since God provided only the plain concepts, the impetus for such an arrangement could not be attributed to Him. Nor did it come rightly from the mental faculty itself, as if some act of reasoning were involved by which the mind worked its way to an understanding of how the terms related. As noted before, William laid the burden for this ordering back on the simple concepts themselves. Once understood, they themselves compelled the mind to see that they fit together in a particular, predetermined way. This was in fact a further reason William spoke of these principal truths as known per se. God took care that all minds were familiar with the concepts; no further cause was required to explain the complex knowledge that arose out of them.

Because of the place these first principles occupied in the whole scheme of William's thought, marking a signal instance of divine intervention in ordinary human cognition, it is important to speculate on where the universal concepts or terms of which they were composed fit into his account of simple knowledge. He never actually addressed the issue, but it seems that the concepts or words he had in mind were precisely those he had said referred primarily to God or to some aspect of His essence and only secondarily to things in this world. These were, after all, the only ones in ordinary human discourse that William thought had a direct connection to God.

Once one makes this assumption, it becomes easier to understand what he said about those special simple concepts when he spoke about the imposition of terms. First of all, one can see exactly what William intended to include in this special category. If the words referring primarily to God were in fact the same as those that went into the common principles of science, they would have to be ones whose meaning was not limited to any genus, as were nouns like plant, animal, or star, but rather applicable to every entity in the world. The examples William gave in his discussion of simple cognition included words like "powerful," "good," "true," and "creature," but now the list can be expanded to embrace a host of other nongeneric terms, words such as "whole," "part," "equal," "odd," and all the fundamental concepts of rational thought. They were, as William called them, the first intelligibles, by which he presumably meant those concepts most immediately known and most basic to all further reasoning.[72] They would make up the common language of all scientific endeavor. Second, it now becomes evident how William thought such concepts were introduced into the mind. Although he never said so when talking specifically about the simple words themselves, it is clear that they must have come through a direct, although absolutely commonplace, revelation from God. In addition, if the basic terms of the first principles of science were these simple concepts that referred directly to God, then the principles themselves would have to refer primarily to a divine reality. The truth of these complex principles was then necessarily and strictly speaking an accommodation between an assertion and the corresponding ideas in the mind of God.

Knowledge of the first principles of science was the only occasion where William conceded a place to divine intervention

---

[72] See *De anima*, VII, 6 (*Mag. div.*, II supp., 211b).

in the normal complex operations of the mind. Yet it was a significant concession. Although he had completely eliminated any illumationist language from his formal definition of truth, this purely epistemological doctrine reintroduced a divine role at the very foundation of scientific thought. It constituted, in the midst of a predominantly scientific scheme, a throwback to the more traditional notions of truth. Understandably enough, William found a place here for the vocabulary of Platonic and Neoplatonic thought. He said that the knowledge of first principles was as if it were innate or naturally implanted in the intellect.[73] And he explained why such knowledge could be called natural, using terms that consciously echoed the words of Augustine. Not being acquired externally by either teaching or special revelation, it seemed to arise from within the soul and to be born in the very deepest recesses of the mind.[74]

Yet William's theory of divine intervention accounted for only a portion of the complex principles men knew—all the common laws of logic, metaphysics, mathematics, and natural philosophy. Most of the principles that served as a basis for scientific demonstration were, on the other hand, not common but rather proper to the specific sciences. To explain how they came to be known, William had to offer a more worldly theory. It was here that he turned to the other half of man's intellectual vision, that into the created world below.

The proper principles of science, which made up the second and third categories mentioned before, were both immediately evident and inferred. Immediately evident proper principles constituted the second category; they consisted primarily of statements about the generic or specific natures of things. Nowhere in his *Magisterium* did William ever explain how the mind derived such propositions, except to say that they came from schooling and experience.[75] Given his epistemology, however, it is easy to see how he would have resolved the problem

---

[73] See above, n. 69.
[74] *De virtutibus,* IX (*Mag. div.,* I, 124aG).
[75] See above, n. 63.

had he been called upon to do so. The concepts and words that went into the evident universal propositions making up the second category were universals themselves, terms like man, horse, and jackass. Although William's account of simple cognition never fully clarified the process of abstraction, he definitely insisted that the origin of universal concepts lay in particular substances in the world, and he argued that the mind alone, working according to the method imposed on it after the Fall, was able to cull from this origin all that it knew about the universal natures of things. Consequently, the concepts and words for all the immediately evident proper principles of science came directly from sensation, via the active power of the mind. Beyond this point William's theory of immediate truth sufficed to account for their ordering into true propositions. Since these principles were immediately evident, their complex form and their truth arose immediately from knowledge of the simple elements of which they were comprised. Universal natures that were fully understood revealed their own mutual relations to the cognizant mind.

It was not so easy to explain how men came to know the proper principles that made up the third of the categories, those having to do with efficient and final causation in natural phenomena. Although just as in the case of the second category the mind took the simple concepts for this third kind of principle from the sensible world here below, this time the form of the principles themselves—the order and relation of terms that made them true—was not immediately evident once one knew the meaning of the words of which they were to be composed. Instead, this form or order had to be inferred. An example William gave for this type of principle was the scientific explanation or definition of an eclipse of the moon.[76] What he meant was not the conclusion of a deductive argument showing how an eclipse occurred, which would not have been a form of principle cognition, but rather the grasp of a connection between an eclipse and the relative positions of the

[76] See *De anima,* VII, 8 (*Mag. div.,* II supp., 213b).

earth, moon, and sun upon which a deductive argument could rest. The knowledge made available by such propositions was crucial for science—although admittedly thinkers of the thirteenth century made few new discoveries in this area—for such knowledge put flesh on the skeleton of first principles and universal statements about the natures of things and thereby filled out the structure of demonstrative thought.

William suggested that the key to the formulation of principles of this sort lay in the classical Aristotelian problem of the discovery of middle terms (*inventio mediorum*).[77] The task in understanding natural phenomena was to find out how to relate objects in the external world in a way that would reveal the lines of natural causation. In the language of logic, if one could find a concept that would serve as a middle term to connect major and minor terms, representing objects one already knew but whose relation one was seeking to determine, then one could formulate a proposition that would explain the phenomenon and permit the construction of a demonstrative syllogism embodying this explanation. For an eclipse one presumably had to discover the idea of "interposition of the earth"—that is, a notion of proper place—that would mediate between the ideas of "eclipse" and "earth, moon, and sun" so as to indicate the cause.

The process by which the mind came to find the middle was, according to William, primarily a matter for simple cognition. He discussed it under the third of the ways he gave for how the mind acquired simple knowledge in its normal workings in the world, the way that worked by following the natural connections among things.[78] At the outset William explained the objective foundation for this way of coming to know. As he saw it, the relation between an efficient cause and its effect came down to a real connection or bond in the world (*colligatio, connexio,* or *concomitantia*).[79] Such bonds were ontologically so tight—indeed, in the case of necessary causality, one of the re-

[77] Ibid.
[78] See above, Chapter II, n. 93.
[79] Ibid.

lated objects could not exist without the other—that William thought it was only reasonable that one of the objects could not be known without the other. In other words, the connections were not only real, they had the epistemological effect of leading the mind from one of the connected substances to its correlative.[80] William explained that the related substances acted something like two physical bodies tied together. If one of them were moved within range of the mind, it would necessarily pull the other along with it.[81] Another way he described the same phenomenon was to say that the two were signs for each other, so that if one substance were made known to the mind it would reveal the remaining one.[82] Although it might have seemed puzzling how one thing could be a sign for something essentially different, William defended himself by pointing out that not all signs were similitudes of the things they signified, as was indeed evident in the case of the names of things and their real referents.[83]

The intellect, having been led to one of the related objects by knowing the other, was thereby in possession of the middle it was looking for. From this point on, it was a simple matter for it to formulate the relation between the two in terms of a proposition explaining cause and effect. It merely had to state the configuration of objects it had come upon. In doing so it "discovered" the principle relating major and minor, through a middle term, in a way productive of demonstrative knowledge. Of course, stating the relation correctly meant that the intellect had to be able not only to see the two objects but also to read the nature of the bond between them, so that the two stood to each other in the proposition as they did in nature. Apparently, this knowledge was provided in the very act by which the mind was led from one to the other. What is more, the mind could read the connection no matter which term it started with—the cause could reveal the effect or the effect the cause. In this way William thought he could account for the

---

[80] *De anima*, VII, 8 (*Mag. div.*, II supp., 213b).
[81] *De anima*, VII, 8 (*Mag. div.*, II supp., 215a).
[82] *De anima*, VII, 9 (*Mag. div.*, II supp., 216a).
[83] *De anima*, VII, 8 (*Mag. div.*, II supp., 215a).

two basic types of scientific knowledge: a priori and a posteriori. Translations of Aristotle sometimes suggested that these two were the same as science of the reasoned fact (*propter quid*) and science of the fact (*quia*), and William himself employed the latter term to denote knowledge of the cause through the effect, also calling it indicative science.[84]

Given all this, William could have ended by saying that the process of discovering the middle term and formulating the third kind of principle was a simple effect of the ability of the mind to reflect the character of the real world. Yet he was not satisfied that his explanation had solved all the problems. For him it still did not fully account for the workings of the mind. In particular he wanted to know what effectively produced knowledge of a connected substance once its correlative was known and what made clear the nature of the connection; he wanted to penetrate more deeply into the matter of causation.[85] His questions were analogous to the ones that had arisen earlier when considering simple cognition. If the origin of knowledge lay in the external world, then would it not be necessary for physical objects to act on the mind in order for there to be cognition? Was it not the referent of the major or minor that caused knowledge of the middle in the mind? As before, William denied that any corporeal being could be the efficient cause of something that happened in the mind. External objects could be, at the most, occasions for intellectual acts.[86] The operation by which the mind followed the connections among things had to be attributed primarily to the mind itself. It was, therefore, the mind's own active power that performed the task and thereby accounted for knowledge of the third category of principle. Turning to the same language he

---

[84] See *De anima*, VII, 8 (*Mag. div.,* II supp., 213b). In fact, these two terms referred more properly, in the strict sense in which Aristotle had used them, to the form of the syllogism than to the method of discovery. Once the minor proposition had been found, whether from a cause or effect, it was a matter of arranging the terms to produce a demonstration *quia* or *propter quid.*

[85] William posed the question of efficient causality explicitly in *De anima*, VII, 8 (*Mag. div.,* II supp., 213b and 214a).

[86] *De anima*, VII, 8 (*Mag. div.,* II supp., 213b).

had used when solving the problem of simple cognition from sensation, William explained that the mind was born to be led from knowledge of one connected substance to knowledge of another; the capacity to follow the connection lay within it. Even the examples he used to clarify the process were the same as those he had employed before: Aristotle's model of the money-changer and his own of the spider and his web.[87] The situation was only slightly more complicated in this instance, for he held to his law that knowledge of the external world came by means of signs, so that the mind's perception of each of the connected substances had to be by separate intelligible forms. This meant that knowledge of the first, itself through a sign, did not immediately introduce the second substance to the mind but rather revealed another sign, by which its correlative was understood.[88]

The difficulty for William lay in describing the nature of this immanent act of the mind as it followed the connections among things. It was in the example of the spider that he found the metaphor most congenial to his thought. He said the spider reacted to the vibration of its web through custom (*mos*). As he explained, the custom that allowed the mind to follow the connection from one term to another was a most prompt potential or a *habitus*.[89] This same word appeared in the analysis of simple cognition, and indeed the many parallels between William's explanation of this sort of complex understanding and his account of simple knowledge led Gilson to conclude that everything William said here about the origin and operation of *habitus* applied directly to every act of cognition, simple or complex. Since Gilson thought the *habitus* must be specially infused into the mind by God, he read William to mean that an infused habit was the necessary prerequisite and foundation for all acts of the mind.[90]

[87] Ibid.
[88] *De anima*, VII, 9 (*Mag. div.*, II supp., 215a–b).
[89] *De anima*, VII, 8 (*Mag. div.*, II supp., 213b–214a).
[90] See above, Chapter II, 2, and Gilson, "Pourquoi saint Thomas," p. 75.

Besides the fact that Gilson's interpretation presumes too much of a direct role for God, it also takes William's use of the word *habitus* too rigidly. As Aristotle made clear in the *Categories,* habits were among a constellation of qualities explaining various conditions of substantial objects, primarily those conditions that had to do with the ability to perform a specified act or elicit a specified response. If the condition were more or less permanent, it could be described as a habit, in the strict sense of the word, but if it were transitory or easily displaced, it should be called a disposition. Another quality related to these was an innate capacity or incapacity.[91] William's use of *habitus* oscillated among these three senses. In a general sense, of course, it always served for him the function of underlining the capacity of the intellect to act on its own, to produce an immanent act. In the case of simple cognition, for example, the word *habitus* was little more than a suggestion of the ability of the mind to perform in a certain way. Yet when it came to complex cognition, specifically the production of principles of the third sort, the idea of *habitus* took on more analytically specific applications. Here, after all, the mind did produce habits in the strong Aristotelian sense of the term, the scientific habits that amounted to what the trained mind carried with it after it had learned some of the principles and conclusions of science. One must therefore be very careful in attending to William's language in this part of his work.

The primary and most basic way William used the term *habitus* to explain the process behind the discovery of principles was to refer to the initial knowledge of the correlative itself, which introduced into the mind the second term, or middle, through which the intellect came to understand the causal fact. The *habitus* was, he said, the intelligible form of the first of the related objects in the mind, and it acted like custom (*mos*) in the spider to lead the mind to knowledge of the cause or effect

[91] Aristotle, *Categories,* 8 (8b25–9a27). See *Categoriae vel praedicamenta,* Aristoteles Latinus, I, 1–5, ed. Lorenzo Minio-Paluello (Bruges, 1961), pp. 23–24.

related to it.[92] In other words, the potential knowledge of the second term, the middle, was something actually inhering in the intellect as soon as it knew its major or minor correlative. It was, as it were, a disposition, ready to realize itself in act, and in real terms this disposition could be sufficiently described as the form itself of the first term resting in the mind.

By speaking of the *habitus* in this way, as the simple source of an immanent act, resting in the intellect, William managed to separate the active from the receptive aspects of the generation and understanding of the middle term. This was important to him, for in fine Aristotelian fashion he insisted that the same power could not, at one and the same time and with respect to the same action, be both active and passive, giving and receiving.[93] With his theory he could now claim that it was the *habitus,* technically distinct from the mind itself, that accounted for the production of the intelligible form of the middle term, while it was the mind out of its own aptitude that received this knowledge.[94] In this way the *habitus* made the soul, in one of William's favorite expressions, an overflowing and most full fountain (*fons inundantissimus, et copiosissimus*), pouring out knowledge into itself, the principal actor (*eductor, adjutor*) remaining the habit itself by which the mind was made full.[95] To use another image, it was the mind, impregnated by the *habitus,* that drew on the *habitus*'s fullness to bring forth the forms of its actual knowledge.[96]

Yet there was a second way William spoke of *habitus* in connection with the following of causal bonds and the discovery of principles, even though this in effect conflicted with the first use, whereby the *habitus* were the intelligible forms themselves.

---

[92] *De anima,* VII, 8 (*Mag. div.,* II supp., 213b–214a). The text reads "tanquam mors in anima araneae" for "tanquam mos in anima araneae."
[93] *De anima,* VII, 8 (*Mag. div.,* II supp., 214a).
[94] *De anima,* VII, 8 (*Mag. div.,* II supp., 214b).
[95] *De anima,* VII, 8 (*Mag. div.,* II supp., 214a). See also *De anima,* VII, 9 (*Mag. div.,* II supp., 216a).
[96] *De anima,* VII, 8 (*Mag. div.,* II supp., 214b). The image of the intellect as the womb of science (*matrix quaedam scientiae vel sapientiae*) reappears in *De Trinitate,* 15 (ed. Switalski, p. 95).

At times he actually spoke of the *habitus* as if it were a faculty of the mind itself.[97] The intellect, capable of scientific knowledge, was the *habitus,* prompt and ready to understand.[98] Or perhaps the *habitus* was an innate ability of the intellect. William once called it the quick wit (*sol[l]ertia*) that Aristotle had talked about, that inborn mental facility or quickness at discovering the middle term.[99] Authentic Latin words for this quality were *ingenium* and *ingeniositas,* and when referring to them William noted that not all men possessed this trait, for some were decidedly slow at grasping middle terms or even demonstrative proofs.[100] Naturally, speaking of *habitus* in this way obscured William's previous point, that the mind itself was not both active and passive with respect to the same act. Yet it did make clear that the efficient cause of knowledge of the middle was not something outside the mind but rather the very power of the mind itself, its own ability to know reality. This was a constant theme of William's and one, in fact, that his notion of a *mos* or custom in the mind was principally intended to defend.

Finally, and within the bonds of this same discussion, William even referred to the *habitus* as if they were true Aristotelian habits, the scientific habits that were the mark of the learned mind. Often he spoke of the *habitus scientiales vel sapientiales* as if they were the real object of his examination and

---

[97] A similar ambiguity or oscillation in meaning between a faculty and a disposition can be found with reference to Aristotle himself. Jonathan Barnes has pointed out that commentators on Aristotle's *Posterior Analytics* differ as to whether he intended *nous* to refer to a disposition of mind or to a faculty or method for finding principles (see Barnes's translation of Aristotle's *Posterior Analytics* [Oxford, 1975], pp. 256-57). The situation is essentially analogous to what we find in William on the matter of the discovery of middle terms, although where in William's case the ambiguity can be attributed to the author himself, Barnes would say that in Aristotle it is a problem critics have read into the text.

[98] *De anima,* VII, 8 (*Mag. div.,* II supp., 214a).

[99] *De anima,* VII, 8 (*Mag. div.,* II supp., 213b). Aristotle introduced the notion of this power of the mind in his *Posterior Analytics,* I, 34 (89b10-20). See also above, Chapter II, n. 75.

[100] *De anima,* VII, 8 (*Mag. div.,* II supp., 215a).

not the process by which the mind came to discover a middle term. Indeed, he even took time to explain the difference between *habitus* in this sense and in the sense with which he had previously been concerned. Scientific habits brought forth the knowledge of old things (*vetera*)—that is, propositions that had been formulated and whose truth had been known before—and insofar as they were potencies to know, they lay in the treasury of the memory (*thesaurus memoriae*). The *habitus* that brought forth original knowledge of the principles, or perhaps more correctly, knowledge of the middle from which the principle was fashioned, did not have to do with memory but rather were productive of new things (*nova*). They were what operated in the actual acquisition or formation of scientific knowledge (*scientiae actuales*).[101] The two processes were related, for the *habitus* out of which original knowledge of the principles arose laid the foundations for the habitual regeneration of the same principles in the mind that was characteristic of scientific habit; yet they were not technically the same.

William's use of *habitus,* therefore, covered the whole spectrum; it spanned the range of those meanings that in Aristotle had been clustered around this special word. Perhaps it was this very openness to varied meanings that made the term so attractive to him, for it allowed him to talk about a number of different qualities or activities of the mind, all the while emphasizing a common factor they shared. No matter what its specific application, the term *habitus* stressed the active capability of the intellect, its power to act without any efficient cause outside itself. It was this independence, this self-realizing power of the mind, that concerned William most of all. But the idea of *habitus* also allowed him to show that there was some change, and some response on the part of the mind to what lay outside. *Habitus* were among those qualities most closely tied to the essence of the subject, implying a condition that could not be

---

[101] Ibid. See also *De anima,* VII, 8 and 9 (*Mag. div.,* II supp., 214b and 216b). In *De Trinitate,* 15 (ed. Switalski, p. 94), William even described the habits in terms he elsewhere reserved for the intellect itself, as "fountains" and "wombs" of knowledge.

described as an alteration but yet was not completely identifiable with the substance as such. They thereby characterized a potential for which the subject already possessed some essential basis, although they would eventuate in something quite new to the subject and might well need the further stimulus of contact with an object different from the subject itself. In the case of *habitus* in the first sense alone, dispositions explaining discovery of the middle, it should be clear how much such an idea suited the meaning William wanted to convey. Such *habitus* were related to, even identifiable with, the received intelligible forms of the first of causally connected terms, yet they were in some way more than these forms, for they included some element of the active power of the intellect into which the forms had been received. *Habitus* provided perhaps the only available term to describe a process that divided the active power to understand in so subtle a way between the mind and the reality of the external world.

There were, therefore, gradations of meaning, even ambiguities in the way William described and analyzed the *habitus* of the mind. Nevertheless, throughout the whole discussion he left no doubt that the origin of the knowledge with which he was concerned, its objective basis, lay in the world, even if the effective power to know came from the mind. And this applied whether he was speaking of the disposition to discover the second of two related objects through knowledge of the first or of the complex habits of science, stored somehow in the memory and capable of being released into actuality. In fact, the similarity between the two kinds of *habitus,* the fact that one was the preliminary basis for the other, made the question of their real origin one and the same. It is instructive, therefore, to take a last look at what William had to say when he was speaking of the origin of scientific habits alone, habits in the most proper and strict sense of the word.

For all his insistence that the active power behind the generation of scientific knowledge came from the mind, he expressly stated that the habits of science were acquired. One last time he posed the question of where they were acquired.

Again, he turned to his model of the two worlds. There were two origins. Some of the acquired *habitus* came from God, and these were more properly called infused or superinfused. Others, however, derived from the lower world of created reality.[102] As always, only the latter were involved in the normal processes of cognition. William insisted that the *habitus* from above were special, available only by the revelation of God. They constituted the foundation of what he called the contemplative sciences and apparently were the exclusive possession of saints and prophets.[103] It was the *habitus* the mind gleaned from below that contributed to the formation of speculative knowledge. In *De Trinitate* William stated the point even more explicitly, saying that the fertility of the *habitus* permit-

---

[102] "Fons autem inundativus earum [scientiarum], generativus earum in effectu est [virtus intellectiva] per habitum acquisitum: acquisitum autem intelligo superinfusum, qualis fuit sapientia regis illius sapientissimi, atque incliti Hebraeorum quae eidem a Deo altissimo infusa est. Doctrina etiam et experientia sapientiales, et scientiales habitus, sicut tibi manifestum est, saepissime acquiruntur." *De anima*, VII, 8 (*Mag. div.*, II supp., 214a). Because of the importance of this passage, it has been quoted here verbatim. It would be very easy to overlook the fact that William was speaking of two origins for scientific habits. Yet as he indicated even more clearly in *De anima*, VII, 9 (see below, n. 103), by *doctrina et experientia* he meant a way of acquisition different from infusion from God; he meant acquisition from the created world. Masnovo seriously misinterpreted William on this score. First of all he did not recognize that these *habitus* accounted not only for the mind's knowledge of the connection between cause and effect, but also for its initial perception of the second of the two terms. Second, he did not see that for the most part, according to William, these *habitus* did not come from God but rather from schooling and experience. See Masnovo, *Da Guglielmo d'Auvergne*, III, 70-71 and 82-84.

[103] Again, it seems important here to quote the original Latin text: "Declaravi etiam tibi quod possibile est ut fontes isti de inundatione primi ac universalis fontis veniant atque scateant, sicut apparent in scientiis quae per revelationem Dei altissimi fiunt, quales sunt scientiae contemplativae, quibus dignatione sua illustrat, et replet intellectus virorum sanctorum, tales sunt, et prophetici spendores. Nihilominus autem, et aliunde, videlicet doctrinis, et investigationibus philosophicis repletur vis intellectiva, ita ut efficiatur fontes multi sive scaturigines scientiarum actualium. Accidit et hoc sibi de memoriis, et experimentis juxta sermonem Aristotelis in suo libro metaphysicorum." *De anima*, VII, 9 (*Mag. div.*, II supp., 216b).

ting scientific speculation came to mind through the knowledge it had gained via the senses, from the perception of things and their forms in the external world.[104] As for how the mind acquired these *habitus* from below, William noted there were two ways. It was by means of schooling and experience (*doctrina et experientia*) that the mind derived the fundamental ability to follow the connections among substances.[105] Both were, as William pointed out, dependent on sensation.[106]

All this was little more than William had said before. Yet there were two instances where, in speaking about the origin of scientific habits, he gave the hint of something greater—that at least so far as the derivation of scientific habits from sensible experience was concerned, he had in mind some sort of inductive procedure. At one point he claimed that the intellect was made a fountain of scientific knowledge through schooling and philosophical investigation. By the latter term, he explained, he meant what Aristotle had been speaking about in his *Metaphysics* when he proposed that all science and all art came from memories and experience.[107] In this work Aristotle had introduced his thoughts on the cognitive progression from sensible object to universal through the intermediate states of comparison and gathering into what he named *memoria* and *experimenta*. This served as a brief but classic exposition of the process of induction, and it is reasonable to assume William intended his citation to be a kind of shorthand reference to the same procedure. Yet there is even more conclusive evidence that William was thinking of induction. Just after he claimed that, under normal circumstances, the *habitus* were engendered by schooling and experience, he tried to explain what he meant by drawing an analogy between the mind and a mirror.[108] A plain mirror could receive images but could not produce them

---

[104] *De Trinitate,* 15 (ed. Switalski, pp. 93–94).

[105] See above, nn. 102 and 103.

[106] *De Trinitate,* 15 (ed. Switalski, p. 95).

[107] See above, n. 103. The passage in Aristotle comes at the very beginning of his *Metaphysics,* bk. I, chap. I (980b28–981a3).

[108] *De anima,* VII, 8 (*Mag. div.,* II supp., 214a).

on its own. If, however, through some special dispensation, frequent reflection of the same image made it possible for the mirror to generate its own images, without the aid of an object, then it could be said to be not only a mirror (*speculum*) but also full of forms (*speciosum*). This was, indeed, the status of the intellective power once it had received the *habitus* making it a fountain of scientific knowledge. If William's analogy was to hold, then it was repetition of the same cognitive experience that induced the *habitus* and thus led the mind to follow the connection. In short, the *habitus* was nothing more than the end product of a process of induction leading immediately to knowledge of the middle term and its relation to the major or minor. Nowhere is the inductive origin of the *habitus* more clearly revealed.

With this final theory William was able to cap his account of the mind's formation of the three major categories of the principles of science. There were difficulties and ambiguities in his views, most especially in the case of the third category, inferred principles, but the basic outline of his thought remains clear. Here again, one can see the novel direction he took concerning the problem of truth. Admittedly, he did keep some place for the traditional view that God was the origin of human knowledge of the truth, for he held that the formation of the first category, the first principles of science, was the result of God's active intervention in the workings of the mind. What is important to recognize, however, is that he totally eliminated this divine influence for the two remaining categories of scientific principles, whose origin he placed securely in the created world. It was there, and not in some transcendent world, that the mind had to look for the evidence of their truth. As with his formal definitions of truth this, too, represented a major step toward a more critical and scientific theory of truth in the thirteenth century.

I V

Conclusion

===

WILLIAM'S EFFORTS to come to grips with the problem of truth in human knowledge constituted a remarkable achievement. They marked him as one of the foremost thinkers of his time, whose ideas, paralleled among his contemporaries only by those of Robert Grosseteste, foreshadowed the intellectual development of the rest of the century. His theory of truth was imperfect, to be sure. There were areas where he did not have the analytical tools to work out his views to perfection, and it seems that in some cases the weight of traditional language prevented him from realizing all the implications of his own thought. He left some questions crucial to a complete understanding of the problem untouched, while to others he gave so perfunctory an answer that the reader must surmise what he actually had in mind. Finally, he retained a place for the traditional explanation of the nature of truth, even though it seems to have been at variance with the rest of his thought on the matter. Yet these more hesitant aspects of his work cannot overshadow the innovative character of his theory taken as a whole. First of all, he elaborated an explicit theory of reference for simple cognition that directed the mind immediately to the world, in most cases without any need to appeal to divine ideas or God's intelligible light even for absolute certitude. Second, he made it clear that the problem of the truth of knowledge was a matter of complex, not simple, cognition. He thereby isolated the problem of truth as it pertained to scientific thought and indicated where thinkers would have to focus their energies if they were going to elaborate a theory adequate to their aspiration systematically to apply the scientific model. Third, he went a long way toward emphasizing the logical aspects of the problem of reference in complex knowledge, especially universal knowledge, all at the expense of metaphysical and theological notions that had tended to dominate before. Here was the beginning of a solution to the vexing question of immutable truth that would allow scholars to justify their efforts to establish true knowledge relying solely on their natural capacities in the created world. In addition to these general accomplishments, associated with a change in the way the problem itself was viewed, William also started working out the particulars of a new theory. Perhaps most important of all, he began to construct the critical language subsequent thinkers would have to use in continuing his efforts. In all this he, along with Grosseteste, introduced to the scholastic world, even to the schools of theology, a notion of intellectual endeavor further from the currents traditionally associated with Augustine's vision of truth and much more sympathetic to Aristotle and logical disputation.

Accepting the novel nature of William's theory of truth does not mean, however, that one must overlook aspects of his thought more in line with the intellectual attitudes of preceding centuries. Such aspects are there, and it will not do to dismiss them all as accidental holdovers from the past. What is important to recognize is that when William retained views about truth previously established in the medieval West, he assigned them a place they had not held in the thought of the thinkers from whom they derived, a place that made them clearly secondary to his own novel, critical ideas whenever it came to explaining cognition in the world. Thus, he often used conventional concepts and language, but in a manner that largely transformed their significance. This is apparent in two ways. First of all, William sometimes selected isolated doctrines from earlier discussions of truth and used them in a manner that strictly limited their scope and, more important, their formal implications. It has been shown how he incorporated some doctrines of illumination into his description of knowledge of the truth here on earth, using them to account for knowledge of the truth of some first principles and the terms that made them up. Truth, as William defined it, depended on the referents of knowledge, which constituted one leg of a true relation; and in the case of some first principles, God or His qualities were the primary object to which knowledge referred. In these instances a higher illumination was necessary for men to know the truth. Yet the fact that God entered into the determination of what was true in these cases was not due to the formal terms of William's theory of truth, which did not explicitly implicate God, but rather to certain peculiarities of his theory of reference. This meant that although there was still a trace of the traditional doctrines in his thought on some issues, he was free to develop a formal theory of truth that totally escaped the older, less critical attitude about its nature and that would serve as the foundation for later movement toward an even more worldly notion of human cognition.

The second way William used old concepts while transforming their significance was by making a sharp division between normal and supernatural or beatific processes of thought. In this way he could preserve earlier attitudes about truth, indeed adopt the full schema of the traditional notion of divine illumination, so long as he limited its applicability to special occasions. God intervened as a constant force to generate knowledge and directly underwrite truth only in the ages of man before the Fall and after the Resurrection. To make this point William accepted the familiar model of the mind on the boundary of two worlds, higher and lower, but changed its meaning by distributing the ability to see into each world, for the most part, according to different stages in the soul's immortal career. The lower vision worked for the wayfarer in the world of sin, the higher for the innocent and the blessed. By this means William was able to retain for the old doctrines much of their force, even though they did not infringe on his more worldly theory of knowledge here below. He turned the horizon between the mind's two universes into a breach of formidable proportions and left the intellect to work its way to knowledge practically without God in a world of created, evident truths.

In the end, however, beyond all his epistemological theorizing William wanted to avoid making the cleavage between the two mental worlds too complete. The danger that this might happen was already apparent in his occasional tendency to disparage the value of knowledge in this world, especially when compared with what could be expected in the world beyond. If the gap between these worlds were to become too great, one might well come to look on man's activity here below, both moral and intellectual, as absolutely fruitless. Why make an effort here when it was necessary to wait until after the Resurrection for the power adequate to accomplish any of the acts for which man was actually created?

At one point William actually tried to span the gap and explain how the two intellectual worlds did connect. Although this attempt was not of any significance for his formal theory of truth in the created world, it is not without interest for what it reveals about the full nature of his intellectual vision. Perhaps even more important, an understanding of William on this point may shed light on the general intellectual currents with which he was associated, for a similar pattern can be observed in the thought of several scholastic apologists for science in the thirteenth century, beginning with Grosseteste himself.

William's attempt to bring together the worldly and divine spheres of intellectual vision came in a passage where his immediate purpose was to show how God could be an object for the mind; indeed, He would be the primary one for the souls of the blessed.[1] Although William cited numerous Biblical authorities to prove that this was so, he added that for the sake of unbelievers he wanted to introduce arguments dependent solely on reason. In his words: "Since incredulous men do not believe the words of the wise or even the divine oracles, I shall lead you to know this as I have been accustomed to do, and that is

---

[1] *De anima,* VII, 7 (*Mag. div.,* II supp., 212a–13a).

to say, by means of demonstrative certitude."[2] His opening argument began with the assertion that the intellective and higher motive powers of man—that is, mind and will—revolved around and inclined naturally toward truth, on the one hand, and goodness, on the other. After a glance at the relation between goodness and will he turned to truth and the intellect, the matters with which he was primarily concerned. He said that since beatitude consisted in the perfect fulfillment of man's natural capacities and since only direct knowledge of the divine essence, the First Truth, was capable of fully satisfying the intellect, it was clear that the perfection of the mind consisted in full illumination by the light of God.[3]

This first argument could have settled the matter, but in fact it was only a preparation for a fuller statement. William wanted to show not only that God was the final object of the intellect, its perfection, but also that He was an object in some way natural to it as well. To this purpose he devoted the longer, more complex discussion that followed. It actually consisted of two identical arguments, one at the beginning and one at the end, framing a series of statements about the relation of truth to the mind.[4] Everything depended on a notion of truth oblivious of the distinctions William usually drew, such as that between complex and simple truth, the truth of knowledge and truth in the world. Instead, here he used truth to mean something so general that it could encompass all the definitions in his explanation of worldly cognition and also God Himself, a notion of truth that clearly had its roots in the Neoplatonic traditions William was often careful to avoid. His series of statements about truth and the mind all elaborated the basic point that truth in this most general sense was purely and simply the object of the intellect. This fact was put in various ways: the true (*verum*) was the proper knowable object (*proprium cognoscibile*) of the intellect as well as its natural light

[2] *De anima,* VII, 6 (*Mag. div.,* II supp., 212a).
[3] *De anima,* VII, 7 (*Mag. div.,* II supp., 212a–b).
[4] *De anima,* VII, 7 (*Mag. div.,* II supp., 212b–13a).

(*naturaliter lumen*), and the same could be said of truth (*veritas*) itself. On these grounds William built his fundamental claim: that the intellect was intended from creation (*natus est ad*) to see the light of truth—that is, truth was its natural object.[5]

At this point William made a crucial jump. What he did was to turn from the notion of a natural object to that of an inclination toward an end. By this simple maneuver he transformed an otherwise static scheme into one that was dynamic. He apparently felt that the shift required no justification, although grounds for a similar theoretical connection between objects and ends could have been found in Aristotle.[6] William merely restated things so that what the intellect was created to see (*natus ad*) was also that toward which it had a natural inclination. Once he had reformulated the relation of mind to object in these terms, it was a simple matter to begin talking about ultimate ends. His argument ran that if the intellect was naturally inclined toward truth, then because every inclination implied and required an end, the inclination would have to be toward some specific and determinate truth or true thing and not toward unspecified and universal truth. Of all single truths there was only one that could properly serve as such an end— that is, as a truth in which the mind could find peace and fulfillment—and that was the brightest and most powerful truth,

---

[5] *De anima*, VII, 7 (*Mag. div.*, II supp., 213a).

[6] Duns Scotus, for example, recognized that Aristotle's *Nicomachean Ethics*, X, 4 (1174b14-23), provided justification for identifying the best of the natural objects of a power with its natural end. See Duns's *Quaestiones in primum librum Sententiarum (Ordinatio)*, prologue, q. 1 [*Opera omina*, Vivès (Paris, 1893), VIII, 20-21]. This does not mean, however, that William drew his ideas directly from Aristotle or was familiar with the *Nicomachean Ethics*. Grosseteste's translation of the *Ethics*, the first translation widely circulated in the Latin West to go as far as the tenth book, dates from no earlier than 1246-47. See Daniel A. Callus, "The Date of Grosseteste's Translations and Commentaries on Pseudo-Dionysius and the Nicomachean Ethics," *Recherches de Théologie Ancienne et Médiévale* 14 (1947), 207-8, and René A.Gauthier in the "Praefatio" to Aristoteles, *Ethica Nicomachea*, Aristotieles Latinus, XXVI, 1-3, fasc. 1 (Leiden, 1974), p. CCI.

God Himself. Consequently, God was the end of the intellect's inclination. He was the most radiant truth to the intellect, and in Him all intelligence found its beatitude. Furthermore, it was fully reasonable that this should be so; all intelligence, including the human mind, was capable of being illuminated and informed by God—every intellect was a mirror to the divine.[7]

This conclusion came back again to what William had been aiming to prove. But there was an idea in his longer and more rambling discussion that had not been clear in the first, concise argument he gave. In addition to demonstrating that the intellect would in the end come to the vision of God, William had now also succeeded in showing along the way that God was the end into which the mind was *naturally* inclined—He was the end of its natural inclination (*naturalis inclinatio sive intentio*). It could even be said that God Himself was the natural light of the intellect, so long as it was remembered that He was not the only light natural to it.[8] And the reason for all this was that God was truth, even if He was truth of a much more elevated sort than that which the intellect normally pursued; and truth was, after all, the proper object of the mind. In short, man's intellectual striving in the world was continuous, at least as seen from the most general point of view, with the vision of First Truth promised to the blessed. The efforts after truth in the lower intellectual sphere during this life were therefore not totally divorced from those the mind would be able to make in the higher sphere after the Resurrection, for even if they were

---

[7] *De anima,* VII, 7 (*Mag. div.,* II supp., 213a).

[8] *De anima,* VII, 7 (*Mag. div.,* II supp., 212b). William did not intend his readers to take God as the only natural object, or even one that could be attained in his life, and so he carefully explained that saying God was the natural light of the intellect had to be understood in the sense that it was toward God the mind was led by its naturl inclination.

See also *De bono et malo,* p. 278. Here again, emphasis must be laid on the terms by which William said such knowledge of the divine was possible. By its nature or essence the mind had the power of attaining God most easily of all intelligible objects. Yet in this world the essential powers of the mind were so corrupted that they could not operate as originally designed, and therefore men could not aspire to any vision of God or his attributes without some special grace.

on different levels, they were still two forms of the same activity. The beatific state Christians looked forward to was not some unnatural transformation of their nature but rather the proper, if superhuman, fulfillment and full realization of innate human capacities.

In the end, then, William managed to suggest that there was harmony between intellectual activity in this world and in the world beyond, despite all he had said previously about the unworthiness of cognition here below. Coming to know truth in the created world admittedly did not approach the glory of the vision of God as Truth in the sphere of divine intelligibles, but the two phenomena were at least in a broad sense one and the same activity: knowing the truth. Just searching for truth on earth was evidence of a natural inclination that would, in the final days, bind men to God. Such considerations may have helped William to justify his evident interest in worldly theories of truth and knowledge. On the other hand, they also permitted him freely to eliminate most of the traditional views of divine illumination or intervention from his theory of human knowledge of the truth on earth without fear of having thereby forsaken such views entirely, especially insofar as concerned the functions they had served in Augustine's thought to make clear God's special relation to man and to guarantee the final, beatific vision. William could still call God the light of the intellect and so emphasize that the soul was, from its origin, naturally ordained to enjoy the intellectual vision of the divine. He expected his readers to understand that the potential for this vision would not normally be realized so long as the soul lived in the world of sin. Only in its natural—that is, original—health, liberty, and purity (*naturalis sanitas, libertas et puritas*) would the mind be capable of perceiving God in Himself.[9]

By this subtle means William was able to take advantage of the theological potential of the language of illumination without being required to adopt this language exclusively for his

[9] *De anima*, V, 15 (*Mag. div.*, II supp., 139a).

own epistemology or even to accept the epistemology with which it had traditionally been associated. William could, therefore, sometimes sound like a traditionalist. Yet even where he appeared most traditional, what he was doing was full of promise for the future. He was, in effect, carving out a new field of epistemology, logic, and truth and consigning the old epistemological language to the limited role of being the repository solely for the theological verities it had long been used to support. He was beginning to isolate the critical problem of truth from the theological issues with which it had been entwined so long. Later thinkers would follow his lead.

PART TWO

Robert Grosseteste

WILLIAM OF AUVERGNE and Robert Grosseteste were almost exact contemporaries, and the period of their greatest literary activity in the areas of philosophy and speculative theology neatly coincided.[1] Together, they laid the foundations for the invasion of theology by the methods of demonstrative science from the middle of the thirteenth century on. Yet to pass from William to Robert is to move from a man who, though profoundly influenced by the ideal of knowledge he had found in Aristotle, was content to suggest the importance of the new ideal in writings that were otherwise traditional in their style and orientation, to one who, for nearly two decades of his life, made it his business to propound the ideal of the new science and make it available in a way that challenged thinkers to reconsider their own methods and transform the nature of their work. It is to move from a world of suggestion, where profound ruminations on the new ideal have to be chiseled out of a work in which they often seem out of place or only half formed, to a world where the problems of knowledge are confronted head-on, abstracted from most of the more general concerns of theology, and followed up almost systematically in an effort to establish a complete solution.

More is known about the career of Robert Grosseteste than about that of William, although here again there are many matters about which scholars can only speculate.[2] Grosseteste

[1] Although the precise dates of the major works of William examined in this study seem to place them after the commentaries of Grosseteste, the versions we have of William's compositions most probably represent a polishing of ideas worked out in the 1220s. This fact, along with the chronological ambiguities surrounding the writings of both of these men, mean that it is safest to consider their ideas as if they were elaborated simultaneously. Since there are no apparent references in the works of either to those of the other, any more precise chronology or theory of dependence is, at least for the present, impossible.
[2] The conclusions of an early work on Grosseteste's life, Francis S. Stevenson, *Robert Grosseteste, Bishop of London* (London, 1899), have been superseded by more recent studies. For the recent views, see Josiah C.

was born in England, probably in the county of Suffolk, sometime around the year 1168. Early in his career he served as a
clerk and most likely as master of arts at the episcopal sees of
Lincoln and Hereford. Although no one knows where Grosseteste received his training in the arts, it is generally assumed he
studied either at Oxford or at Paris, and most scholars believe
that he returned to Oxford to teach in the faculty of arts during the first decade of the thirteenth century. It was at this
time that he made his first commentaries on the logical works
of Aristotle. During the dispersion of masters and scholars at
Oxford from 1209 to 1214 Grosseteste probably followed the
example of many other English scholars and went to Paris to
study theology. At any rate, he clearly attended some school of
theology in the second decade of the thirteenth century, and
there is good reason to think that it was at Paris. Grosseteste's
later letters show that he was on terms of friendship with several eminent figures of the school of theology at Paris, including William of Auvergne and the Dominican master, John of
St. Gilles, and it seems most likely he established these ties as a
fellow student with these men early in the thirteenth century.
Sometime between 1214 and the mid-1220s Grosseteste came

Russell, "Richard of Bardney's Account of Robert Grosseteste's Early
and Middle Life," *Medievalia et Humanistica* 2 (1944), 45-54; "Phases of
Grosseteste's Intellectual Life," *Harvard Theological Review* 43 (1950),
93-116; and "Some Notes Upon the Career of Robert Grosseteste,"
Harvard Theological Review 48 (1955), 197-211; Alistair C. Crombie,
Robert Grosseteste and the Origins of Experimental Science, 1100-1700 (Oxford, 1953); Daniel A. Callus, "The Oxford Career of Robert Grosseteste," *Oxoniensia* 10 (1945), 42-72; and "Robert Grosseteste as Scholar,"
in *Robert Grosseteste, Scholar and Bishop*, ed. Daniel A. Callus (Oxford,
1955), pp. 1-69; and Richard C. Dales's introduction to his edition of
Grosseteste's *Commentarius in VIII libros Physicorum Aristotelis* (Boulder,
Colo., 1963). A complete bibliography of works on Grosseteste published up through 1969 can be found in Servus Gieben, "Bibliographia
universa Roberti Grosseteste ab an. 1473 ad an. 1969," *Collectanea
Franciscana* 39 (1969), 362-418.

The reader should note that by the time the present book is published,
another major work of Grosseteste's will have appeared in a critical edition. See Richard C. Dales and Servus Gieben, eds., *Robert Grosseteste on
the Creation (Hexaëmeron)*, to be published in 1982 by Oxford University
Press.

back to England to teach theology at Oxford, where he became either the first or one of the earliest chancellors of the university. In 1229 and 1230 he assumed the position of first lecturer to the newly installed Franciscans at Oxford, an office he relinquished only in 1235 when he was named bishop of Lincoln. He died in 1253.

Grosseteste's activity as a philosopher and natural scientist came during his years as a master in the schools of arts and theology; after he became bishop he devoted himself almost exclusively to administration and the translation of classical and Christian works from the Greek.[3] The present study will therefore concern itself only with works composed before 1235. Among these, however, it is necessary to distinguish two different sets. The first set consists of a number of short treatises cast in the form of questions on subjects in theology and philosophy. Those of importance for this study are his *Quaestiones theologicae, De veritate, De veritate propositionis,* and *De scientia Dei.*[4] Although it was once thought that Grosseteste wrote these works rather late in his career, it is now believed that they date from much earlier.[5] Daniel Callus has argued that they are

---

[3] See Daniel A.Callus, "Robert Grosseteste's Place in the History of Philosophy," *Actes du XIe Congrès International de Philosophie,* Brussels, 20–26 August 1953 (Amsterdam, 1953), XII, 161, and "Robert Grosseteste as Scholar," p. 12.

[4] The *Quaestiones theologicae* exist in a manuscript at Exeter College, Oxford, and Daniel A. Callus has published them in his article "The *summa theologiae* of Robert Grosseteste," in *Studies in Medieval History Presented to Frederick Maurice Powicke* (Oxford, 1948), pp. 180–208. All other treatises appear in a single volume edited by Ludwig Baur: *Die philosophischen Werke des Robert Grosseteste, Bischofs von Lincoln,* Beiträge, IX (Münster, 1912), henceforth referred to as *Phil. Werke.*

[5] Baur tentatively dated the treatises to around 1939 (*Phil. Werke,* p. 104*), while Samuel H. Thomson, in *The Writings of Robert Grosseteste, Bishop of Lincoln, 1235–1253* (Cambridge, 1940), p. 120, preferred a date around 1225. More recently Daniel Callus has settled on an even earlier date. See his "Oxford Career," pp. 53–54; *"Summa theologiae,"* p. 194; and "Robert Grosseteste as Scholar," p. 29. Pietro Rossi, in the introduction to his edition of Grosseteste's *Commentarius in Posteriorum analyticorum libros* (Florence, 1981), p. 10, seems to have misinterpreted Callus, and this explains why he places the writing of *De veritate* and *De scientia Dei* at about the same time as the composition of the commentary on the *Physics*—that is, sometime around 1230.

fragments from a larger work Grosseteste intended to write—a kind of *summa* of collected questions arranged topically follow-ing the pattern of the *Sentences* of Peter Lombard—and he at-tributes them to the early years of Grosseteste's career as a teacher at the university, most likely the time when he was en-gaged in the study of theology.[6] This would mean that Grosse-teste composed these treatises sometime around the first half of the second decade of the thirteenth century. Together with a letter known under the title *De unica forma omnium* they con-stitute a corpus of works representing the scholar's first pub-lished thoughts on the questions of truth and certain knowl-edge.[7] Callus feels that they savor of late twelfth- and early thirteenth-century theology, and in this study they will be ex-amined independently and carefully set against Grosseteste's later works, where he elaborated more fully, and in a different vein, his views on the same questions.[8]

The second set of works to be considered in this study con-sists of Grosseteste's explicit statements on science and the na-ture of scientific thought, his commentaries on Aristotle's *Pos-terior Analytics* and on his *Physics*.[9] It used to be thought that Grosseteste worked out his method in theoretical treatises such as these early in his career and only later applied it in specific works on the sciences, but there is now reason to believe that he developed his methodology concurrently with his substan-tive scientific investigations.[10] Grosseteste's scientific career ran

---

[6] See Callus, *"Summa theologiae,"* especially pp. 193–94.

[7] This letter is included in Baur's edition of the philosophical works. Baur assigned it a date before 1210 (*Phil. Werke,* p. 95*).

[8] See Callus, "Robert Grosseteste as Scholar," p. 29.

[9] The text of the *Commentary on the Posterior Analytics* used in the pre-sent study is the recent critical edition by Pietro Rossi, *Commentarius in Posteriorum analyticorum libros* (Florence, 1981). Citations to this edition will be abbreviated as *Comm. Post. an.* The text of the *Commentary on the Physics* is the edition by Richard C. Dales, *Commentarius in VIII libros Physicorum Aristotelis.*

[10] Callus, in "Robert Grosseteste as Scholar," p. 12, placed the compo-sition of the *Commentary on the Posterior Analytics* early in Grosseteste's career, prior to 1209 and long before his other scientific works. Crombie, in *Robert Grosseteste,* pp. 46–47, came to essentially the same conclusion,

from about 1220 to the time when he became bishop, and the composition of his two commentaries on Aristotle seems to fall right in the middle of those years. Although Grosseteste probably wrote some form of a commentary on the *Posterior Analytics* before 1209, while he was still master of arts, the version that was associated with his name in the Middle Ages and has come down to modern times was composed after 1220 and more than likely dates from around the year 1228.[11] As for his *Commentary on the Physics,* it is nearly certain that it was written between the years of 1228 and 1231.[12] These works constituted Grosseteste's response to the increasing desire for an investigation of the theoretical bases of scientific reasoning, and they testify to the enormous debt early thirteenth-century advances in this area of speculation owed to the inspiration provided by

---

even though he recognized that the final version of the *Commentary* must have been written after 1217-20. He continued to maintain that this final version still predated most of the other scientific works. Richard Dales, on the other hand, after a close examination of all of Grosseteste's scientific writings, feels that they belong to a period from 1220 to 1235 and holds that the theory was developed concurrently with the practical investigations. See Dales, "Robert Grosseteste's Scientific Works," *Isis* 52 (1961), 382 and 401. Dales's views on dating are accepted in the present study. It should be noted that Pietro Rossi, in "Per l'edizione del *Commentarius in Posteriorum Analyticorum Libros* di Roberto Grossatesta," *Rivista di Filosofia Neo-Scolastica* 67 (1975), 494-98, has stated that he does not regard Dales's arguments as conclusive, and in the introduction of his edition of Grosseteste's *Commentarius,* pp. 13-21, he reaffirms his view that any statements concerning the dating of the *Commentary* must remain hypothetical. Yet James McEvoy, in an article to appear in *Speculum,* comes close to settling the issue once and for all. McEvoy's study, "The Chronology of Robert Grosseteste's Writings on Nature and Natural Philosophy," is the most exhaustive to follow that of Dales, and it leaves little alternative but to accept for the *Commentary* a date of composition between 1228 and 1230.

[11] Nicholas Trivet said of Grosseteste that he wrote on the *Posterior Analytics* while he was still a master of arts, but Richard Dales has shown that the final version of the *Commentary* must have been composed much later. See Dales, "Robert Grosseteste's *Commentarius in Octo Libros Physicorum Aristotelis,*" *Medievalia et Humanistica* 11 (1957), 13; "Robert Grosseteste's Scientific Works," pp. 395 and 401; and the introduction to his edition of the *Commentarius in VIII libros Physicorum,* p. xi. See also McEvoy's forthcoming article in *Speculum.*

[12] See Dales, "Robert Grosseteste's Scientific Works," p. 401.

Aristotle.[13] It was in these commentaries that Grosseteste elaborated his fundamental response to the problems raised by the ideal of a systematic arrangement of human thought. They represent his mature opinions on the nature of knowledge and truth.

It is important to note that both phases of Grosseteste's speculation about truth, that associated with his theological treatises and that of his later logical and scientific commentaries, exerted considerable influence on scholars at Paris as well as at his own university of Oxford. The incisiveness and originality of his thought as well as the fact that he maintained close contact with theologians all over Europe ensured him a widespread audience eager to follow the progress of his work. Even during his lifetime Grosseteste's early ideas on truth were taken up by a Franciscan theologian at Paris, Guibert of Tournai, who inserted verbatim several pages from Grosseteste's treatise *De veritate* into his own work, the *Rudimentum doctrinae,* and generally assimilated his own views to those of the English master.[14] Through Guibert, Grosseteste's influence spread among subsequent Franciscans at Paris and even left its mark on the work of Bonaventure.[15] Grosseteste's commentaries needed no such intermediary, for they appealed directly to the scientific aspirations of the time. His work on the *Posterior Analytics* represented the first major attempt in the medieval West at a commentary on this difficult and abstruse work, whose clear interpretation had been awaited at least since the days of John of Salisbury.[16] This commentary drew attention

[13] Pietro Rossi, in "Un contributo all storia della scienza nel Medioevo," *Rivista di Filosofia Neo-Scolastica* 67 (1975), 107, has also drawn attention to the influence of Euclid on Grosseteste's *Commentary on the Posterior Analytics.*

[14] See Camille Bérubé and Servus Gieben, "Guibert de Tournai et Robert Grosseteste," in *S. Bonaventura, 1274-1974* (Grottaferrata, 1973), II, 630. This article also contains an edition of several chapters from the *Rudimentum.*

[15] Bérubé and Gieben, "Guibert de Tournai," p. 631.

[16] See Callus, "Robert Grosseteste as Scholar," pp. 12-13, on the need medieval thinkers felt for an interpretation of this work. He notes that John of Salisbury explained how few masters dared teach so difficult a text.

both in England and on the Continent shortly after its composition, and it was used frequently in the schools up to the end of the Middle Ages.[17] Along with his *Commentary on the Physics* it served as a conduit through which Grosseteste's mature ideas on truth were passed on to the later thirteenth century, where they had a profound if generally unacknowledged effect.

[17] Callus, "Robert Grosseteste's Place," p. 161. See also Rossi, "Per l'edizione del *Commentarius,*" p. 489.

V

Truth in Simple Knowledge
According to Grosseteste's
Early Works

===

THE THEOLOGICAL treaties of Grosseteste's early years represented a less elaborate and complete investigation of the problem of truth than was to be found in his commentaries on
Aristotle, but more important than this, they struck a philosophical tone quite different from that of his later works. It
should hardly be surprising that this was the case, since as
much as fifteen years may have intervened between the composition of the two sets of works, and they were years of great intellectual ferment both at Oxford and at the University of
Paris. Nevertheless, the shift in Grosseteste's views has been
virtually overlooked in modern expositions of his thought.[1] Its

---

[1] The major works on Grosseteste's philosophy are Ludwig Baur, *Die
Philosophie des Robert Grosseteste, Bischofs von Lincoln,* Beiträge XVIII, 4–6
(Münster, 1917); Crombie, *Robert Grosseteste;* and Callus, "Robert Grosse-
teste as Scholar." (An interesting critique of Crombie can be found in
Alexandre Koyré, "The Origins of Modern Science: A New Interpreta-
tion," *Diogenes* 16 [1956], 1–22.) Three more recent publications of considerable importance for the subject of the present study are Bruce S.
Eastwood, "Medieval Empiricism: The Case of Grosseteste's Optics,"
Speculum 43 (1968), 306–21; William A. Wallace, *Causality and Scientific
Explanation,* I: Medieval and Early Classical Science (Ann Arbor, 1972);
and Eileen F. Serene, "Robert Grosseteste on Induction and Demonstra-
tive Science," *Synthese* 40 (1979), 97–115. On Grosseteste's thought in
general, see also Ludwig Baur, "Das Licht in der Naturphilosophie des
Robert Grosseteste," in *Festgabe zum 70. Geburtstag Georg Freiherrn von
Hertling* (Freiburg im Br., 1931), pp. 41–55; Dorothea E. Sharp, *Francis-*

importance for a study of this sort cannot be stressed too much.

The key to the difference between the two sets of works is that only in the latter did Grosseteste come to espouse the scientific ideal of knowledge and to take an interest in formulating an explicit set of criteria upon which to establish it. His earlier writings were free of these concerns, and in them he could speculate about truth without any of the constraints they imposed. Among other things this meant that in his theological treatises he could pass over the whole question of the truth of complex knowledge—knowledge that lay at the heart of science—with only a comment. For Grosseteste's views on the nature of complex truth it is necessary to turn to his later works, where he indeed devoted most of his attention to that aspect of the problem. The case of truth in simple cognition was a different matter, and Grosseteste gave a full account of his ideas on this aspect of the problem of truth in both his early and his later writings. An examination of these accounts reveals that in the years between the composition of the two sets of works, Grosseteste radically altered his vision of the nature of simple truth and man's knowledge of it. In order to

---

can Philosophy at Oxford in the Thirteenth Century (Oxford, 1930), pp. 7–46; Alistair C. Crombie, "Robert Grosseteste on the Logic of Science," Actes du XIe Congrès International de Philosophie, Brussels, 22–26 August 1953 (Amsterdam, 1953), XII, 171–73; and "Grosseteste's Position in the History of Science," in Robert Grosseteste, Scholar and Bishop, pp. 98–120; and Rossi, "Un contributo." Other studies of Grosseteste's thought, in particular his epistemology, are Johannes Beumer, "Robert Grosseteste von Lincoln der angebliche Begründer der Franziskanerschule," Franziskanische Studien 57 (1975), 183–95; Lawrence E. Lynch, "The Doctrine of Divine Ideas and Illumination in Robert Grosseteste, Bishop of Lindoln," Mediaeval Studies 3 (1941), 161–73; V. Miano, "La teoria della conoscenza in Roberto Grossatesta," Giornale di Metafisica 9 (1954), 60–88; and Robert J. Palma, "Robert Grosseteste's Understanding of Truth," The Irish Theological Quarterly 42 (1975), 300–306; and "Grosseteste's Ordering of Scientia," The New Scholasticism 50 (1976), 447–63. An interesting recent work that interprets Grosseteste differently from the present study, particularly on the issue of divine illumination, is James McEvoy, "La connaissance intellectuelle selon Robert Grosseteste," Revue Philosophique de Louvain 75 (1977), 5–48.

understand him it is necessary to keep these two accounts separate and to realize that for all the points of comparison between them, they represent the two poles of a development that was of critical importance in his thought.

Grosseteste, like William of Auvergne, followed Aristotle in holding that of the two types of knowledge, simple and complex, only the latter could be qualified by the notions of truth and falsehood. He maintained that the truth of knowledge was a measure of the value of a proposition or statement and not of a simple idea.[2] Indeed, it made no sense to talk of the truth of a simple concept or to speak of a true idea. Every concept or idea referred to something, whether that thing itself truly existed or not, and so each concept or idea had its own validity outside of any judgmental considerations. This was not to say that the problem of truth had nothing to do with the problem of simple cognition, and Grosseteste, again like William of Auvergne, made a large place for the idea of truth on that cognitive level. The kind of truth that entered into simple knowledge did not attach to the knowledge itself but rather to the object understood; it belonged in the extramental world as something toward which the intellect was directed.

For his primary definition of simple truth in the early treatise *De veritate,* Grosseteste went back to Anselm, who in his own *De veritate* had maintained that truth was first and foremost a rightness (*rectitudo*).[3] The adoption of such a definition shows how traditional Grosseteste's thought still was when he wrote his theological treatises and contrasts sharply with the identification of simple truth and being that would appear later in William of Auvergne's *Magisterium divinale* or in Grosseteste's own mature speculation on truth. Grosseteste glossed Anselm's definition by explaining that being right involved conforming

---

[2] *De veritate* (*Phil. Werke,* p. 134). Grosseteste's language here echoes that of Anselm in *De veritate,* 2 (Schmitt, ed., *Opera omnia,* I, 177).

[3] "Possumus igitur, nisi fallor, definire quia veritas est rectitudo mente sola perceptibilis." Anselm, *De veritate,* 11 (Schmitt, ed., *Opera omnia,* I, 191). Grosseteste quoted this passage in his *De veritate* (*Phil. Werke,* p. 135).

to a rule that revealed what ought to be.[4] In the case of simple truth the rule was the divine word itself, and so the truth of things could be defined quite plainly as their conformity to God's eternal word.[5] In more precise terms, this meant conforming to an idea (*ratio*) in the mind of God, for the divine ideas were the exemplars or standards by which His word created all things in the universe.[6]

By casting his definition the way he did Grosseteste made it clear that simple truth was an attribute of created things. Defined as a relation attached to real objects in the world, it was involved in human cognition only as it became known. Thus, while it made no sense to speak of the truth of simple knowledge, it was perfectly reasonable to talk about knowledge of the simple truth, and so to explain the place of truth in simple cognition was not so much a matter of the logical analysis of the form of thought or expression as a question of noetics. It was necessary to describe the process of simple cognition by which simple truth was perceived.

Grosseteste realized this and devoted a section of his *De veritate* to a discussion of just such noetic concerns. It is, however, difficult to make an absolutely unambiguous analysis of this work. Although Grosseteste spoke as if he were giving a perfectly straightforward exposition of a single epistemological procedure, in fact he offered two different descriptions of the way the mind came to know simple truth, each one dependent on a model not fully compatible with the other.

The terms of the formal definition of simple truth in *De veritate* made it necessary to explain human knowledge of such truth as dependent on some sort of Godly intervention, and it was only natural that Grosseteste should have turned to the traditional way of explaining such a process, the notion of divine illumination. As he said at the beginning of his discussion: "Since the truth of each thing is its conformity to its ex-

---

[4] *De veritate* (*Phil. Werke,* pp. 134–35).
[5] *De veritate* (*Phil. Werke,* p. 135). Grosseteste's account was consonant with the ideas Anselm himself propounded in *De veritate,* 7.
[6] See *De veritate* (*Phil Werke,* pp. 137 and 139).

emplar (*ratio*) in the eternal Word, it is clear that every created truth is perceived only in the light of the Highest Truth."[7] Yet even though Grosseteste introduced his subject by referring to God's role in terms of light, he cast his first account of knowledge of simple truth in language that did not make use of this image. Instead, he built this account on a model derived directly from the formal definition, by which truth was the conformity of thing to idea. He maintained that one could perceive the conformity of one thing to another only if one could see that other thing to which the first object should conform. Likewise, one could not know a thing as right (*rectificata*) or know its rightness (*rectitudo*) unless one knew the rule or standard (*regula*) by which it was judged to be so. In the case of simple truth, of course, the rule or idea lay in God Himself, so that knowledge of the truth depended on seeing the true object and at the same time having a mental vision of the divine idea that made it true. By comparing one to the other the mind came to perceive truth itself.[8]

Immediately after this first description Grosseteste offered a second one. It was not, however, completely congruent with what he had just said. In this second account he returned to the image of light.[9] As he characterized things, there were three elements, besides the mind, that had to do with the process he was examining: they were the light of divine Truth (*lux summae veritatis*), created truth (*creata veritas*), and *id, quod est*. The light of divine Truth needs no explanation. The created truth Grosseteste had in mind was the simple truth in the world he had been speaking of all along, that special relationship between a created thing and its divine exemplar. This is evident from the fact that he substituted for the term "created truth" the term "truth of the thing" (*veritas rei*), which he later defined as a conformity along exactly the same

---

[7] *De veritate* (*Phil. Werke*, p. 137).
[8] Ibid.
[9] Ibid.

lines as his formal definition of simple truth.[10] *Id, quod est* was, as has been shown above, a term principally associated with a much-debated text from the works of Boethius. As Boethius had used it, the term referred to the complete substance of a real thing, and Grosseteste held to essentially the same definition, alternating the term with an equivalent form, "the true thing" (*res vera*).[11]

The way these three elements cooperated in knowledge of the simple truth was relatively uncomplicated. Drawing on a phrase of Augustine's, Grosseteste maintained that created truth revealed the substance of a thing (*id, quod est*), which was to say the existing substance (*res vera*).[12] It could not, however, do this on its own, without relying on the Highest Truth, God Himself. Grosseteste compared the workings of the three basic elements in the process to that of light, color, and body in sensory vision. Just as color indicated the colored body, but only in the presence of light, so created truth revealed an existing substance, but only in the light of the First Truth.[13] Another way Grosseteste described the process was to say that the divine Truth illuminated created truth, which then showed the mind the true thing.[14] In any case primary efficacy in revealing existing substance lay with God, the First Truth; created truth was the secondary and more immediate cause. In Grosseteste's words: "The light of the Highest Truth alone reveals substance (*id, quod est*) first and completely on its own,

---

[10] The term *"veritas rei"* appears as an equivalent for *"creata veritas"* in *De veritate* (*Phil. Werke*, p. 138). In *De veritate* (*Phil. Werke*, p. 139), Grosseteste defined *veritas rei* as the conformity of a thing to divine idea. It is essentially the same as the *veritas essentiae rerum* or *veritas rerum* Anselm spoke of in his *De veritate*, 7. See above, Chapter II, n. 14.

[11] Grosseteste cited several occasions where Augustine had spoken of *id, quod est*. (See below, nn. 12 and 21.) Augustine's meaning was, however, perfectly compatible with the way the term was later used by Boethius.

[12] "Veritas igitur etiam creata ostendit id, quod est...." *De veritate* (*Phil. Werke*, p. 137). Grosseteste attributed this formula to Augustine (see *De veritate* [*Phil. Werke*, p. 132]). It came from *De vera religione*, 36.

[13] *De veritate* (*Phil. Werke*, pp. 137 and 138).

[14] *De veritate* (*Phil. Werke*, p. 137).

just as light alone reveals bodies. Yet through this light the truth of a thing (*veritas rei*) also reveals substance (*id, quod est*), just as color reveals bodies through the light of the sun."[15]

From this simple exposition alone it is clear how different Grosseteste's two descriptions appear when subjected to close analysis. He not only employed a different model in each case, he even changed the basic nature of the process he was trying to explain. In the first of the two cases, the true thing along with the Highest Truth made it possible for the mind to see simple truth in the world. In the second, it was created simple truth, along with the Highest Truth, that revealed the true thing. The role of instrument and final object had been reversed.

Yet surely Grosseteste intended his two accounts to be compatible, and he had no reason to believe they would be read in any other way. The whole tradition surrounding the notion of divine illumination, going back at least as far as Augustine, had contained a similar imprecision concerning the exact role of the divinity, providing an umbrella wide enough to cover both of the descriptions Grosseteste gave. In fact, Augustine's language about truth and human knowledge of it would never have survived the kind of critical scrutiny being applied here. His ideas had not been intended to meet the scientific standards that began to be demanded in the schools of the West over the course of the thirteenth century. But the ambivalent theoretical model Grosseteste used not only had a long history, it also had strengths, ones deriving in large part from the ambivalence itself. The body of images associated with divine illumination, because of its two-faced nature, could serve two somewhat different functions at the same time. On the one hand, those elements emphasizing a comparison of exemplars explained how the formal definition of truth as a rectitude could be applied to the objects of human intellection. On the other hand, the literal image of a divine light shining over the intellective process, in some way generating it, made more

[15] *De veritate* (*Phil. Werke,* pp. 137–38).

plausible the role of divine intervention in the business of understanding, although at the expense of some formal clarity.
The fact that each specific explanation had its own drawbacks
makes it easier to understand why no one was in any hurry to
settle the difference between the two for the sake of consistency
alone. Grosseteste's language did, therefore, purchase a certain
philosophical advantage, if at the cost of imprecision and ambivalence. So long as he was not concerned with close analysis,
he could use this language without hesitation.

The way Grosseteste drew on the strengths and skirted the
weaknesses is clear enough. His first description of the knowledge of simple truth focused in the nature of the objects of
that knowledge—that is, on the exact referential conditions
that had to obtain. According to his formal definition, simple
truth in the world was the conformity of a real thing to its divine exemplar. In order for the mind to recognize this truth,
therefore, it had to make a comparison between the two elements, and this implied that it had to be able in some way to
see them both. The first description translated this requirement
literally into the terms of cognitive object. In effect, it stipulated that there were two referents in human knowledge of the
simple truth, one a created thing and the other a divine idea.

Yet there was a problem with Grosseteste's first description
of knowledge of simple truth, and it stemmed from the very
fact that he stuck so literally to the terms of his formal definition. By insisting that there was a divine object as well as a
created one in human knowledge of the truth, Grosseteste implied that knowing the truth involved in some way knowing
or seeing God in the literal sense of having some vision of the
ideas in His mind.[16] Common sense alone seemed to require as

---

[16] When describing knowledge of the truth in this first way, Grosseteste was explicit about the need to see the exemplar itself: "Aut qualiter
cognoscetur, quod res est, ut esse debet, nisi videatur ratio, secundum
quam sic esse debet?" *De veritate* (*Phil. Werke*, p. 137). It was a commonplace of medieval thought that the divine ideas were one with the
divine essence, so that seeing the ideas inevitably implied seeing at least
some aspect of God's essence.

much, since if one were going to compare a standard with the object it was designed to measure, then one had to see the standard in itself. Any less straightforward access to the standard, in this case to the divine essence, would have appeared to make a mockery of the formal definition of simple truth. The problem was that on every other occasion throughout his early works, Grosseteste maintained that in the world the mind could not have any direct intellectual vision of the divine essence or the exemplary forms inhering in it.[17] To say differently would come dangerously close to bringing the beatific vision down to earth.

It was probably Grosseteste's appreciation of this shortcoming of his first model that prompted him to give it so little attention and to turn instead to his second model, which offered an escape from his dilemma. In lieu of analyzing the exact makeup of the object of knowledge of the simple truth, this model focused more on the process by which such knowledge was attained. The key lay in drawing an analogy between sensory sight and intellectual vision. The eyes were capable of seeing only in an atmosphere of light, and the same was true, on a more spiritual level, when it came to the sight of the mind. The point was that for most cases of vision, whether sensible or intellectual, there were two sorts of agent, one proximate and the other primary and fundamental. In sensory vision both color and light were necessary for the eyes to see an object. On the level of the intellect these two agents were replaced by simple truth in the world and the light of God's Truth, and both

---

[17] At the end of *De veritate,* Grosseteste stated that the mind's eye, when it was healthy, had the power to see God in Himself, and in Him all the things he had created (*De veritate* [*Phil. Werke,* p. 142]). This was the same sort of vision or knowledge which, in his *Quaestiones theologicae,* Grosseteste had reserved for God alone (see Callus, "Summa theologiae," p. 195). The only way to reconcile these two passages is to assume, as must surely be the case, that when in *De veritate* Grosseteste spoke of the healthy mind's eye he was referring to the intellect before the Fall or after the Resurrection, so that when in the *Quaestiones* he limited knowledge of the divine exemplars to God alone he was simply contrasting God's powers with those man could exercise here on earth.

were necessary for human knowledge. Although truth in the world might be the proximate cause of knowledge of true things, it could work only if aided by the Highest Truth.

This second description avoided the difficulties of the first. God retained a fundamental role in the process of knowing the truth, but since this role was to act as a light in which perception of the true object took place, it was possible to say that man could know the truth without having any direct knowledge of God or the exemplars in His mind. Grosseteste explained how this was so by following out his analogy with sensory vision:

Just as the weak eyes of the body cannot see colored bodies except as they are enveloped in the light of the sun, and nevertheless they do not see the light of the sun in itself but only as it envelops colored bodies, so the weak eyes of the mind do not perceive true things except in the light of the Highest Truth, even though they are not able to perceive this Highest Truth in itself but only in a kind of conjunction with those true things it envelops.[18]

The crucial distinction lay between seeing the First Truth in itself and seeing other things in its light. Since it was only in the latter way that the mind perceived true objects and hence the truth, knowing the simple truth did not imply directly and consciously knowing God's Truth itself. Nevertheless, Grosseteste insisted that the terms of this process, even if they allowed knowledge of the truth without a direct vision of God, did show that whoever recognized the truth, whether he was the worst of sinners, in some meager way made contact with God.[19] The fact that few men realized this was no argument that it was not so. Just as someone who spent his time looking only at colored things in the world would not know of the sun until he raised his eyes to see it or was told about it by someone else, so the mind might spend its worldly days discovering

---

[18] *De veritate* (*Phil. Werke*, p. 138). Note how close Grosseteste's metaphor was to Augustine's in the *Soliloquia*, I, 6, 16, quoted above in the general Introduction, n. 14.

[19] *De veritate* (*Phil. Werke*, p. 138).

truths without ever knowing it was depending on God's light.[20] Since only the blessed could see God in Himself, and only the wise understood the process of divine illumination, most men never had any occasion to know that their perception of the truth in some way participated in the Highest Truth. In short, Grossseteste's second model allowed him in his early works to maintain God's role in the everyday cognition of simple truth without sacrificing the uniqueness of the blessed vision.

Yet there were problems with the second model, too. While the first model risked attributing a power to the human mind that might be theologically embarrassing, the second obscured the formal nature of truth itself. To a great extent the difficulty rested on an ambiguity. The second account was based, after all, on an analogy drawn with sensible cognition. Unfortunately, the analogy did not exactly fit the terms to which it was meant to apply. It was easy enough to compare the sun's light with God's Truth, given the traditions of Neoplatonic thought, and a corporeal substance with a true object; but it was practically impossible to see how color had anything in common with the created truth. Comparing the latter two elements did, to be sure, drive home the lesson that created truth was the secondary agent in knowledge of true things, but it only made it harder to understand what created truth actually was. Up to this point in *De veritate,* Grosseteste had consistently described created truth as a relation, but if it were to be comparable to color, it would have to be described as something like a simple quality of the object to which it adhered. Whatever this colorlike truth was, it could hardly have come very close to the formal definition Grosseteste gave in this work. What sense would it have made to say that God's light had to shine on truth, which in turn revealed the real object, if that truth were in fact the relation between God and thing? Of course, the visual analogy could have been read as a loose metaphor for the process explained by means of the first model as a comparing of exemplars, but that would have then denuded it of its value and contradicted Grosseteste's explicit statement that it was because God was involved in human cognition as a light, and not as a direct object, that the mind could be said to have some access to Him in the world.

In short, the terms of Grosseteste's second description threatened to undermine his formal definition of simple truth as a conformity, implying instead that it was a simple objective quality that revealed existing things to the mind. It is interesting to note that on a few occasions in *De veritate* Grosseteste actually described the truth of things as something simple. It was, so he maintained, the same as the being (*esse*) or *id, quod est* of a thing—that is to say, its existing reality as an object in the world.[21] In this way he conflated the last two elements of his second description: created truth and the true thing. The logical manifestation of this simple truth was the thing's definition, and in fact it was even possible to say, although only in a manner of speaking, that the truth of a thing was the definition itself.[22] Whichever way one described it, truth according to this new and secondary notion was something complete in

---

[21] *De veritate* (*Phil. Werke*, p. 141). Compare *De veritate* (*Phil. Werke*, p. 135). As an authority for his identification of truth and *id, quod est*, Grosseteste cited Augustine. In his *Soliloquia*, II, 5, 8 (PL, 32, 889), Augustine did define truth as *id, quod est*, although he offered other, incompatible definitions for truth in the same work. He was, however, not interested in the definitions as such but rather hoped that while juggling several different notions of truth at the same time he could ultimately make the point that truth was inextinguishable and that therefore the soul, the seat of truth, was immortal.

Another medieval source that defined truth similarly—as *quod est res*—was the Latin translation of Isaac Israeli's *Book of Definitions* (J. T. Muckle, ed., "Isaac Israeli: *Liber de definicionibus*," *Archives d'Histoire Doctrinale et Littéraire du Moyen Age*, 12–13 [1937–38], 322). See also the discussion in Altmann and Stern, *Isaac Israeli*, pp. 58–59.

By identifying truth (*veritas*) with *id, quod est*, Grosseteste broke down the distinction he otherwise maintained in *De veritate* between *veritas rei* and *id, quod est* or *res vera*. He thereby momentarily abandoned Anselm's definition of simple truth. What is more, when he made *esse* equivalent to *id, quod est*, he forsook the meaning Boethius had given to these two terms, much in the way William of Auvergne would do. Grosseteste's language was, however, more explicit than William's, who never went so far as to declare in so many words that *esse* and *id, quod est* could be seen as the same thing.

[22] *De veritate* (*Phil. Werke*, p. 142).

itself and did not formally involve a comparison between thing and divine idea. To this extent Grosseteste anticipated the position that William of Auvergne would take in his *Magisterium divinale* and that he himself would fully adopt in his *Commentary on the Posterior Analytics*.

The view of truth as a simple quality or substance was, however, an exception to the rule in Grosseteste's early works. For the most part he adhered to his original formal definition, whereby simple truth consisted in the conformity of a thing to its divine exemplar. And he continued to see this definition as a perfectly logical part of the traditional notion of divine illumination. The ambiguities of this tradition—so interesting to the modern historian concerned with the development of the notion of truth in general and of God's role in human cognition in particular—although in some way already apparent in his struggles to explain how the process worked, did not yet bother him sufficiently to drive him to look for a new solution. This alone shows how much he still held to a traditional, uncritical view of the problem and how far he was from the scientific aspirations of his later years. Grosseteste's allegiance in his early works lay firmly with a definition of simple truth that explicitly implicated God and with an explanation of the process by which this truth was known that gave the divine Truth a fundamental role. The central theme around which all his discussions of truth in the theological treatises turned was that God was instrumental to man's knowledge of simple truth.

VI

Truth in Simple Knowledge
According to Grosseteste's Commentaries
on Aristotle

===

I. THE NATURE OF SIMPLE TRUTH

When Grosseteste came to write his *Commentary on the Posterior Analytics,* at the peak of his academic career, he had changed his mind about the nature of simple truth. Although he continued to hold, as he had before, that the truth pertaining to simple cognition was a truth that had to do with the object of understanding and was not a quality applying directly to knowledge itself, there was no longer any trace of the old definition from *De veritate* by which truth consisted in the conformity of a created essence to the divine reason. Furthermore, in speaking of simple truth in his *Commentary* he made no mention of rightness (*rectitudo*) or of things as they ought to be. Nor did he speak of truth according to the Augustinian formula he had used earlier when sketching his doctrine of divine illumination, whereby truth was that which revealed the existing substance of a thing (*ostendit id, quod est*). In fact, he had by this time totally excised any mention of God or a conformity to some ideal exemplar from his formal definition of simple truth. Instead, he now saw simple truth as itself a simple element of reality. He now adopted fully the definition only hinted at it *De veritate.* Throughout the *Commentary,* Grosseteste defined simple truth as the substance itself of a real thing (*illud quod est*), which he interpreted as equivalent to the being (*esse*) of the thing, and he saw knowledge of the simple truth as knowledge of whatever existed.[1]

Naturally, there is no way to be certain of Grosseteste's motives for making this change. Perhaps he had become uncomfortable with the ambiguities attendant on his old definition of truth as a conformity or relation, or perhaps he was responding to a shift in the type of speculation in which he was engaged. He was, we must remember, now writing works explicitly concerned with the criteria for scientific thought, whereas his earlier ideas on truth were contained in theological compositions whose primary aim was to speculate on man's relation to God. Given the different nature of the genre, it might seem only natural that he should change his approach to the problem of truth. Yet there is good reason to believe that Grosseteste's change of mind represented a shift in his philosophy of an even profounder sort, a development of which the change in genre appears to be just one aspect. Grosseteste's emphasis in the latter half of the 1220s on the criteriological aspects of human knowledge, as well as on a critical examination of the question of truth, constituted a milestone in his thought. His return to the theoretical problems posed by the science of Aristotle, whose logical works he had first taught when he was a master of arts, and his decision to publish an elaborate commentary on a work that sought to establish the bases for systematic thought, culminated a decade of efforts spent largely on scientific research. The new, more critical tenor of his ideas and the breadth with which he dealt with problems treated so cursorily in *De veritate* reflected new insights and a novel attitude toward the whole problem of truth. Grosseteste himself was now

---

[1] "Cum autem veritas sit illud quod est et comprehensio veritatis sit comprehensio eius quod est. . . ." *Comm. Post. an.,* I, 2 (p. 99, ll. 16-18). That Grosseteste considered *id, quod est* to be equivalent to *esse* is shown by the fact that in his continuation of this train of thought he used the word *esse* in those places where his intention was clearly the same as *id, quod est.*

working fully in the spirit aroused by the prospect of demonstrative science sketched out by Aristotle. It is no accident
that in abandoning his old definition of truth he had settled
upon a new one much more suitable to the construction of
a theory of noetics and epistemology open to close critical
analysis.

The result of all this was that what had been a secondary and
essentially anomalous notion of truth in the theological treatises was now the primary way Grosseteste viewed simple
truth. Accordingly, he gave a greater indication of what he
meant by this definition. Not only did he continue to identify
the simple truth constituted by the substance of things (*id,
quod est*) with their being (*esse*)—an association, made earlier in
De veritate, that marked a departure from the strict Boethian
use of these two terms.[2] He now made it clear that he also
thought this substantial truth was the same as the essence of
things, so that the truth of the essence could be contrasted to
the inconstancy of material accidents, upon which could be
founded only an uncertain opinion.[3] It is clear, therefore, that
Grosseteste held to the view also found in the works of William of Auvergne that the essence, substance, and being of existing things were identical. The reality that these three stood
for, the ontological core that determined the immutable or specific characteristics of the thing as opposed to the fleeting qualities of its material conditions, was what he recognized as the
simple truth.[4] Equally important, he also maintained, like William of Auvergne, that this substantial ontological reality was
the basis not only for the specific nature of a thing but for its
individuality as well. If the human mind had remained in the
state of perfection, it would have been able to grasp the essence
of things immediately and in this one simple act know things
as both universal and particular.[5] Grosseteste called his simple

---

[2] See above, Chapter V, n. 21.
[3] *Comm. Post. an.,* I, 19 (pp. 283-84, ll. 136-39).
[4] See *Comm. Post. an.,* I, 19 (p. 285, ll. 164-67).
[5] See *Comm. Post. an.,* I, 14 (pp. 212-13, ll. 217-35). Grosseteste held
that this was the way God knew things at all times.

truth, the substance of an existing thing, the true thing itself.[6] Everything pertinent to the existence of a thing was contained in its truth. An object was, by its existence, true, and every true substance constituted a different simple truth.

Since simple truth was the substance of a thing existing in the world, the way it related to cognition was through human knowledge of real objects. Grosseteste explained that the formal means by which one came to knowledge of the simple truth, as well as the verbal manifestation of such knowledge, was the definition of a thing. The definition revealed the essence of a thing and made it known.[7] Another way of putting it was that the definition made known the substance of an object.[8] The definition was the logical correlative to a simple concept in the mind, and Grosseteste compared the mind's comprehension of a definition to the sensory vision of a single visible object or the hearing of one unconfused word.[9] In short, the definition was the hallmark of simple cognition, the sign of knowledge of a simple thing (*res incomplexa*).[10] In contrast to the demonstrations of complex knowledge, which revealed the fact of a thing's existence (*quia est*), the definition simply indicated what a thing was (*quid est res*).[11] This was, in the end, what knowledge of the simple truth came down to.

Clearly, Grosseteste had moved far from the notion of simple truth he had expounded in his theological treatises. No longer did he give any place to God or the divine reasons in his formal definition. Instead, he founded simple truth completely in the

---

[6] Grosseteste first made the identification of substance (*id, quod est*) with the *res vera* in his *De veritate*. His language in the *Commentary* showed that he continued to see the two as identical (see *Comm. Post. an.,* I, 19 (p. 285, ll. 167–72). Because Grosseteste had by this time come to define simple truth as the substance or *id, quod est,* he could now speak as if simple truth and the true thing were the same.

[7] *Comm. Post. an.,* II, 2 (p. 305, ll. 43–44).

[8] *Comm. Post. an.,* II, 2 (p. 306, ll. 67–68). Also see below, n. 12.

[9] *Comm. Post. an.,* I, 8 (p. 159, ll. 297–305). Rossi's text, l. 303, has *"in sensu visus,"* but the correct reading must certainly be *"in sensu auditus."*

[10] *Comm. Post. an.,* II, 2 (pp. 303, ll. 10–14, and pp. 343–44, ll. 841–43).

[11] *Comm. Post. an.,* II, 2 (pp. 307, ll. 83–84; 308–9, ll. 113–17 and 133–37; and 344, ll. 851–52).

existing world of created reality. What is more, he made this change without in any way disparaging the epistemological value of the simple true object. Where God had been the guarantor of knowledge of the simple truth in *De veritate,* in the *Commentary on the Posterior Analytics* the fact of an object's existence provided the mind with all it needed to know the truth. As he insisted, the definition was the vehicle for certain knowledge (*certa visio mentalis*) of the substance of things, and this meant, by the terms of his new notion of truth, for certain knowledge of the simple truth.[12]

2. REFERENCE IN KNOWLEDGE OF SIMPLE TRUTH

Once Grosseteste had eliminated the divine element from his definition of simple truth, the path lay open for him to explain human knowledge and the procedure by which men came to recognize the truth in a way that emphasized objects and powers in the created world. To do this he would have to discard or at least play down much of the epistemological language he had used in his earlier writings. Yet such a transformation would be possible only if he could find new theories to compensate for the loss of old ones. The exposition of knowledge of the truth in *De veritate* was in fact reducible to two different accounts: the first by means of a vision of and comparison to the divine reasons, the second less directly through an illumination by the light of divine Truth. For all the inconsistency between these two models there was more than just tradition to argue for using them both. Each model had its own virtue, and if one looks closely it is apparent that each worked to a different, but complementary, epistemological purpose. According to Grosseteste's early, more traditional views, the quality of epistemic reliability that could be characterized as truth was based directly on God. The first model explained this reliability in terms of the objects of knowledge; it showed how divinity entered into the conditions of reference. The second model fo-

----

[12] *Comm. Post. an.,* II, 4 (p. 379, ll. 324–28).

cused instead on the process of knowing. It showed how the means of knowing were reliable because they, too, implicated God. Any new approach to knowledge of simple truth would have to cover the same ground—that is, it would have to guarantee on both counts the reliability of truth, whether it directly involved God or not. In other words, it would have to advance its own theory of reference, including an explanation for the incorruptibility of universal cognition, and its own theory of the process by which simple truth was known. In fact, since the *Commentary on the Posterior Analytics* was more explicitly a work of formal analysis than were Grosseteste's earlier treatises, which were concerned primarily with the theological aspects of the questions he examined, it placed a greater burden on him to establish his theories fully, taking special care to avoid the sort of inconsistency he had tolerated before. His new doctrines had to be more explicit and more adequately defended than those he had previously held.

Of all the epistemological ramifications of Grosseteste's new notion of truth, his theory of reference would necessarily be the most intimately connected with his formal definition of truth. Simple truth was an object for knowledge, so the way it was defined determined the referential conditions that held whenever it was known. In *De veritate,* Grosseteste had maintained that simple truth was the accommodation between a created thing and its divine exemplar. Consequently, the real referent of knowledge of the simple truth according to that work consisted to two separate objects, both the created thing and an idea in the mind of God. Knowing the simple truth, therefore, involved in some way knowing God's essence itself. When, in his *Commentary on the Posterior Analytics,* Grosseteste turned away from his earlier definition of simple truth, he thereby committed himself to rejecting his previous theory of reference as well. Simple truth lay wholly in the world, and so, for the ordinary man, knowledge of the simple truth referred exclusively to objects in the world of created being. No longer was there any reference to God or to a standard inhering in Him. This omission constitutes one of the most striking indications of the change in Grosseteste's attitude about truth that accompanied his increasing commitment to the ideal of a scientific standard of thought.

In a sense, Grosseteste's answer to the question of reference did not have to go beyond this. Since he said in his *Commentary on the Posterior Analytics* that simple truth was identical with simple essence or substance, knowledge of simple truth plainly referred to simple essence existing in the world. Yet a full indication of how a notion of simple truth applied to the business of thought, especially in a scholarly atmosphere increasingly attuned to Aristotle's idea of science, would entail a more complex response. Most important, it would have to account for the difference between knowledge of particulars and knowledge of universals.

Grosseteste approached the issue by considering the nature of definitions. Among simple concepts, some were real and some were imaginary, but it was real concepts alone, those that stood for an actual essence in the external world, that had to do with truth. Now Grosseteste insisted that definitions, the logical manifestation of simple cognition, could be formed only for real concepts. There were no definitions, in the strict sense of the word, for imaginary ideas.[13] Thus, all definitions made reference to a real object, a simple truth, and so the problem of reference in knowledge of the simple truth could be restated as the problem of reference for definitions. The difficulty arose from the fact that pointing out some existing essence as the referent of a definition did not answer all questions about the way such a reference could be made. In Grosseteste's words, although the definition by itself explained the substance of its object, indicating its essential characteristics, it did not state that the object was this or that.[14] This was to say that a definition indicated that a certain sort of essence existed in the world, but it did not stipulate in exactly what way existence

[13] *Comm. Post. an.,* II, 2 (pp. 323–25).
[14] *Comm. Post. an.,* II, 2 (p. 307, ll. 78–80).

was meant. Two of the most important ways one could refer to existing essence were as a particular thing or as a universal nature, and Grosseteste held that the definition in itself was not determined one way or the other. Alone, it was neither universal nor particular.[15]

The point of all this was that each definition taken alone had a sort of general reference but no determinate one. In modern philosophical language one might say that a definition or real concept possessed or made sense, yet of itself it had no reference. The terminist grammarians and logicians of the later Middle Ages made the distinction between the signification (*significatio*) of a word—that is, its way of describing a nature—and its supposition (*suppositio*), which amounted to its indicating a specific referent in a definite context.[16] Interpreted according to this terminist language, what Grosseteste was saying about the definition was that by itself it had signification but no supposition, and in fact the evidence indicates that he had something like this terminist distinction in mind. For the terminist logicians a term (*terminus*) differed from a plain word (*vox, vocabulum, sermo*) by the fact that it occurred in the context of a proposition or sentence. A word became a term when it was used in a sentence, and this is what gave it supposition.[17] In a similar vein Grosseteste maintained that a definition or the concept it explained took on determinate reference only when it was used in a proposition.[18] He actually used the word *suppositio* and its verbal form, *supponere,* although not in exactly the same way as the terminists.[19] For Grosseteste,

---

[15] *Comm. Post. an.,* I, 8 (p. 159, ll. 305-6). This idea was related to Avicenna's claim that the essential nature in itself was neither universal nor individual, one nor many. See Avicenna, *Metaphysics,* V, 1 (in *Opera in lucem redacta,* ff. 86va–87ra).

[16] See Lambertus Marie de Rijk, *Logica modernorum* (Assen, 1967), II[1], 123–24.

[17] See de Rijk, *Logica modernorum,* II[1], 117, n. 1.

[18] See below, Chapter VII, nn. 107 and 108.

[19] There is one place in Grosseteste's works where he in fact used the words "supposition" and "signification" in just the way the terminists did. In his treatise *De veritate* he suggested that whenever the word "truth" was used to mean something in the world, supposition was to

it was *suppositio*—that is, inclusion in a statement or proposition—that gave a simple concept or definition its determinate reference.

One of the ways Grosseteste thought one could justify making a plain definition a term in a proposition, thereby giving it definite reference or, as the terminists would say, supposition, will be discussed below, for he held that some kinds of complex principles were merely hypothesized from definitions.[20] For the present, however, it is not important how Grosseteste thought one could explain moving from a simple definition to a definition with supposition; what counts is that he thought it was possible to do so and that indeed this was an inevitable part of the use of language. Once a definition or simple concept was used in a sentence, it had to be considered a real term, and this meant that its reference, previously indefinite, suddenly became determinate. Unlike definitions standing alone, definitions used as terms were therefore either universal or particular.

Given Grosseteste's view of essence, the matter of explaining how terms referred to particulars was trivial, and indeed he never explicitly elaborated his answer to this side of the question in his commentaries on Aristotle. For Grosseteste essence was identical with the substance or the being of a thing, and in each real case it was in and of itself individual.[21] Consequently, whenever a concept or definition was used to point to a single, determinate thing—that is, whenever it was used as a particular term—it simply referred to that one thing's essence or substance, which was already discrete enough to serve as an object for particular knowledge. The process of determining the precise reference of such a term was merely a matter of discovering

---

the particular truth of a created thing although in some way the eternal Truth of God was also signified. The precise terms Grosseteste employed were the verb *supponere* for supposition and the verb *significare* along with the noun *significatio* for signification. See *De veritate* (*Phil. Werke,* pp. 138–39).

[20] See below, Chapter VII, 4, B.
[21] See above, Chapter VI, 1.

which essence was indicated among the many individual essences that had the same nature, and here the propositional context of the term normally sufficed.[22] In sum, the precise reference of particular knowledge of simple truth was to the basic ontological unit of all reality, the substantial being of existing things.

When it came to knowledge of universals, however, the question of reference was not so easy to answer. Since all real terms referred to existing essence and since each existing essence was in itself particular, what could universal reference mean? Solving this problem was of crucial importance to Grosseteste in his *Commentary on the Posterior Analytics,* for he accepted without reservation Aristotle's view that universal knowledge was the exclusive basis for science. There was no scientific knowledge of particulars.[23]

In order to understand Grosseteste's solution it is necessary to begin by examining closely a long passage where he outlined the various ways he thought simple knowledge could be uni-

[22] Although the logical problem of the reference of particular terms was trivial for Grosseteste, the same could not be said for his explanation of the psychological and noetic foundations for particular cognition. Particular terms referred directly to the individual essence of the object, but in this life men could come to know this essence only indirectly. Grosseteste held, as had William of Auvergne, that knowledge of particulars was secondary for men in the world; it was acquired by adding perceptions of material accidents onto the more fundamental knowledge of universal natures. In purely mechanical terms this procedure sounds much like the indirect cognition of singulars Thomas Aquinas was later to advocate, but in their ontology the two theories were diametrically opposed. Thomas held that matter was in fact the basis for the individuality of a particular object. Grosseteste maintained in contrast that existing essences were individual in themselves. If men on earth had to know the individuality of things via a quality of matter—that is, material accidents—this was due to an imperfection in the intellectual apparatus of fallen man. In theory, individual essences could be known directly, without the accompanying knowledge of material conditions. Indeed, this was the way God knew particular essences and the way man had known them before the Fall and would come again to know them after the Resurrection.

[23] See *Comm. Post. an.;* I, 19 (p. 281, ll. 84-88).

versal.[24] Although Grosseteste himself did not speak expressly in terms of the reference of universals but rather said he would consider universals themselves insofar as they were *principia cognoscendi*—which was to say, as ways of knowing essence in its universal aspect—in fact what he proceeded to do was to identify the immediate object of the intellect in any simple knowledge of essence that could be called universal. This was, of course, precisely the problem of direct reference in universal cognition.

Grosseteste divided knowledge of universals into five different sorts. Apparently, the same universal concept could be known in each of the five ways, for the distinction among the sorts of universal knowledge lay not so much in the sense of the concept perceived under each as in its direct referent. The universals Grosseteste was concerned with were the genera and species commonly spoken of in scientific discourse, and the question he posed was: What, exactly, did the mind grasp in each case? According to him, there was no single answer. One had to take into account the different levels of understanding to which the human mind could aspire.

For the pure intellect, completely free from the obtrusive distraction of sensible images, it was possible to contemplate the First Light, which was God Himself, the first cause of all existence. In this case the mind could directly perceive the divine reasons, uncreated and existing from eternity in God's mind, and they would serve as the immediate referent for all universal knowledge. Grosseteste explained that in real terms these reasons were God's eternal perceptions (*cognitiones*) of the things he was going to create, so they could be described either in their cognitive function as the reasons of things (*rationes*

---

[24] *Comm. Post. an.*, I, 7 (pp. 139–41, ll. 96–145). It would seem necessary to amend the Rossi text to read, p. 140, l. 124: Iterum <in> virtutibus. . . ." I would also suggest accepting the variant reading of mss. 0a and W for l. 129 and taking the line to be: "sunt he causales rationes principia cognoscendi." The analysis that follows continuously refers back to this passage unless otherwise noted.

rerum creandarum) or in their practical, creative function as the formal exemplary causes (*cause formales exemplares*). They were what Plato had called the ideas and constituted his archetypal world. Since they were the bases for creation and the ultimate cause for the existence of all created things, they were principles not only of knowing but also of being (*principia tam essendi quam cognoscendi*). Whenever the mind perceived created objects through them, it knew these objects in the truest and clearest way possible.

If the intellect were not so completely purified that it could gaze immediately on the First Light, it still might receive illumination (*irradiatio*) from a higher created light, from an intelligence. This would mean it could see in the intelligence the forms (*forme*) or descriptions (*descriptiones*) of all those things that followed the intelligence in existence—which was to say, all those things below the intelligence and created after it—and these forms would then be the immediate referents of universals. Here Grosseteste noted that such forms were, in fact, the intelligence's perceptions (*cognitiones*) of the things that came after it. In formal terms, they could be called exemplary forms (*forme exemplares*) and created casual reasons (*rationes causales create*) of the things to be made after the intelligence, because the intelligence took some part in the generation of all things below it. It was through the aid (*ministerium*) of the intelligences, yet the power (*virtus*) of the First Cause, that corporeal things (*species corporales*) came into being. Even though these forms in the intelligences had a definite exemplary function in the production of corporeal being, however, Grosseteste apparently did not consider this function to be so great that such forms, like the divine ideas, should be thought of as foundations for the existence of things. He made no mention of them as principles of being but said only that they were the principles of understanding (*principia cognoscendi*) for any intellect illuminated by the intelligence.

A still lower level of universal cognition was available to an intellect that could not contemplate either the created or an uncreated incorruptible light in itself. This way lay open to the mind that knew how to gaze (*speculari*), with the proper appreciation, on the celestial bodies. In the stars and planets resided the causal reasons (*rationes causales*) of terrestrial species, which reasons were the incorruptible manifestation of the corruptible individuals to be found in each species on earth. If one accepts the reading of the text suggested above in note 24, then it can be said that Grosseteste denied these reasons any special status as ontological foundations for earthly things, just as he had done in the case of forms in the intelligences. They were, if perceived, principles of understanding (*principia cognoscendi*), but they were presumably not principles of being. At any rate, for the intellect that could attain them, they served as the immediate referents for universal knowledge of terrestrial objects.

Below knowledge in the celestial bodies was a fourth sort of universal cognition, knowledge of earthly things in their formal cause (*causa formalis*). In contrast to the higher exemplary forms or causal reasons, the formal cause proper was part of the existing thing itself that the universal concept ultimately signified; it was the form (*forma*) that entererd into the composition of a thing together with matter and that made a thing that which it was. In other words, the formal cause was the form according to the standard doctrine of hylomorphism. Although this form was literally only part of the whole thing, Grosseteste held that it was the principle for knowing both the thing and either of its constituent parts. Drawing an analogy with visible light, Grosseteste explained that the mind could see in the form the form itself, just as the eye could perceive light in itself; or it could see in the form the matter that went into a thing, presumably as the eye could sense material objects in the same sensible light. Yet in either of these cases, where the form offered the means of understanding only a part of the whole thing or essence, it could not be the referent of universal knowledge and would not serve as the basis for species or genera. Only when the form was the means of knowing the whole thing, a composite of matter and form, could it adequately represent the essential characteristics of a thing and thus provide universal knowledge. For the mind attaining the form in this way the form itself became the immediate referent for universal concepts. Grosseteste said that this was the sort of universal cognition Aristotle had in mind in his theory of abstraction ,and what he meant when he talked about the predication of species and genera. In contrast to the two previous levels of universal cognition, but much like the first, this sort came through an object that was the principle of being (*principium essendi*) as well as the principle of understanding (*principium cognoscendi*). Grosseteste, like many scholastic thinkers, believed that since the form made a thing what it was, it was the part of a thing primarily responsible for its being. It provided the formal counterpart to God, who was the efficient and final cause of all existence.

There were, finally, some intellects so weak they could not even rise to knowledge of forms. For such minds knowledge of things came only through perception of the accidents that followed upon essence. Here Grosseteste reminded the reader of his view that the simple truth of a thing was identical with its essence, for he described the essence, in contradistinction to the accidents attached to them, as true (*vera essentia*). It would seem therefore that knowledge by means of accidents would have fallen somewhat short of knowledge of the simple truth. Indeed, although Grosseteste maintained that accidents could act as direct referents for universal concepts, both genera and species, he also clearly stated that this kind of cognition did not attain to the level of knowledge of true genera and species (*non potest ascendere ad cognitionem horum verorum generum et specierum*). As could be expected, Grosseteste insisted that accidents served only a cognitive function: they were principles of understanding but not of being (*principia solum cognoscendi et non essendi*). Since only things whose accidents were perceptible to the mind could be known in this way, Grosseteste would probably have limited the range of this type of cognition to objects in the material world.

On the surface, Grosseteste's outline of the five sorts of universal cognition seems perfectly straightforward. There were, quite simply, five different kinds of object a concept could refer to in order to be considered universal. In fact, however, a careful reading of Grosseteste reveals that he did not intend all five ways to be available to human minds on earth. The key to interpreting the outline lies therefore in determining when and to what kinds of intellect he thought the various modes applied.

In a passage later in the *Commentary on the Posterior Analytics,* where Grosseteste dealt with the nature of predicates, he clearly indicated that he thought that the first of his five forms of universal knowledge had nothing to do with the reference of universals in normal human speech.[25] This is indeed what one would have expected, given the substance of his mature views about the nature of simple truth. He said that the separate forms Plato called genera and species, if they were held to be the referents of the universals used in predication, were monsters created by an erring mind, analogous to the occasional monsters nature produced by mistake. They were logical absurdities and should be rejected as completely unfounded. This did not mean that there was no archetypal world. He admitted that the divine ideas or reasons had existed from eternity in God's mind. According to what he said before in the passage on the five types of universal reference, he was willing to concede that if Plato had had these divine reasons in mind when he spoke of ideas, then he was right in placing them in a separate world. What Grosseteste denied was that such divine ideas had anything to do with the universal terms normally used in human discourse. As he said in his own words: "These ideas do not pertain at all to that rational process by which something is predicated of something. Of course, in themselves these ideas are not monsters, but when the intellect wants to make them predicable of things from which they are diverse and separate, then in this connection they are monsters."[26]

Grosseteste founded his argument on his often repeated

[25] See *Comm. Post. an.,* I, 15 (p. 224, ll. 142–52).
[26] *Comm. Post. an.,* I, 15 (p. 224, ll. 147–50).

claim that predication depended on the identity of subject and predicate. The universals men predicated of things in the world had to refer directly to the essenses of those things and not to some separate, ideal substance. Naturally, this contention struck not only at Plato but also at what can be said to have been Augustine's view of the reference of universals, if one is willing to allow that a theory of reference can be extrapolated from Augustine's ideas. Grosseteste plainly denied that the universals of human understanding made any reference at all to God or to something in Him, whether immediately or obliquely. There could be no more explicit refutation of the position on reference Grosseteste had once held in *De veritate*. God's ideas were not in any way objects in men's apprehension of universal, simple truth.

Of course, once Grosseteste had eliminated divine ideas from the specific referential conditions of human knowledge, he might still have retained for them a secondary role as the way to knowledge of some other, more appropriate referent outside God. After all, his exact words in introducing the five types of universal knowledge had been that he was examining the principles of cognition, a term that only partially coincides with the notion of referent. Yet there is evidence that Grosseteste rejected this weaker interpretation of the place of divine ideas as well. So much is clear from a short discussion in his early fragmentary work, the *Quaestiones theologicae.*[27] And this time it can be plainly seen that he meant to exclude from human

[27] Up until now the present study has maintained a distinction between the conclusions of Grosseteste's early works and those of the years when he was engaged in scientific investigation, and so it might be asked whether it is not incompatible with this principle to use the *Quaestiones* as evidence for what Grosseteste thought at the time he wrote his *Commentary on the Posterior Analytics*. In fact, there seems to be no reason why they cannot be used as such on this particular issue. Every indication is that over time Grosseteste reduced the importance of higher exemplars in his account of human knowledge, and therefore it would seem that a restriction on their role he had already made in the years when he was working on his theological treatises would have applied with equal if not greater force later when he was engaged in writing his commentaries on Aristotle.

knowledge in the world not only the first type of universal cognition but also the second and the third.

In the question *De scientia Dei* of the *Quaestiones,* Grosseteste maintained that all things had to be known by means of an immaterial species.[28] This was nothing more than the standard scholastic doctrine that there had to be some intelligible form, called a species in this special meaning of the word, through which the mind attained an object that was external to it. Grosseteste then went on to examine the nature of such species in general. He claimed that only rarely was the species identical with the object itself, by which he probably meant the object's proper form.[29] In most cases it was something different, a form either following the object or preceding it in existence. As he explained the doctrine: "For each creature there are two sorts of intelligible and immaterial species: one that is generated out of the creature through the power of a superior being, and another that does not depend on the creature in any way but rather is its cause, that is, its exemplary form."[30] If one interprets Grosseteste's fivefold distinction of universal cognition in the light of this earlier doctrine of noetics, it is clear that the first three types fell into the category of knowledge by a species that preceded the creature in existence, for in each of these three cases knowledge of a universal concept was obtained by knowing a form above the essence of the created object and existing before it, either as an exemplar or as a causal virtue. The last two types, on the other hand, constituted knowledge by means of a species following the existence of the created object, because here the intellect itself, a being superior to the object, drew from the object its knowledge of the universal concept. On the basis of its confrontation with the object or its material accidents the intellect was able to compose a species through which it came to know the universal.

Once the five sorts of universal cognition have been distrib-

[28] *Quaestiones theologicae* in Callus, *"Summa theologiae,"* pp. 194 and 195.
[29] Ibid.
[30] *Quaestiones theologicae* in Callus, *"Summa theologiae,"* p. 194. See also *Quaestiones theologicae,* pp. 195-96.

uted between the two categories of knowledge by species in this way, it is easy to see which of the five Grosseteste thought were available to mankind. In his *Quaestiones theologicae,* Grosseteste specifically stated that the human intellect knew things only by means of a species that followed the creature in existence. Knowledge by means of an exemplary species was reserved for God Himself.

It is by means of that immaterial species which follows a thing that a thing is known by a rational creature, either intellectually or sensibly. For when we know any form, we know it by means of a species generated from it. . . . It is, however, by means of the immaterial species of a creature that is its antecedent cause and exemplary form that the creature is known by God alone.[31]

By this account, the first three types of universal knowledge Grosseteste listed in his *Commentary on the Posterior Analytics* would have been completely above man's intellectual powers. To be precise, one would have to add that they were above the powers of the human intellect only as exercised here on earth after the Fall. In a critical passage toward the end of Chapter 14 of the first book of his *Commentary on the Posterior Analytics,* Grosseteste stipulated that before the Fall mankind had possessed the knowledge of the exemplars or forms above it that was denied to it in the world of sin and that men would regain this vision once death had released them from the weight of their material bodies.[32] For the duration of their lives in the world, however, their knowledge of universals had to be according to the terms of either of the last two types of universal cognition.

There may have been some exceptions to this rule. In the passage in Chapter 14, Book I, of the *Commentary,* Grosseteste suggested that some souls that were completely purged of any

---

[31] *Quaestiones theologicae* in Callus, *"Summa theologiae,"* pp. 194–95. The punctuation and sentence division of this translation differ from Callus's Latin text, but the changes made seem to be necessary to preserve the sense of the passage.
[32] See above, this chapter, n. 5.

inclination (*amor*) for material things and thereby freed from sensible phantasms might be able while in this life to look directly into the divine reasons, although he seemed uncertain about this possibility and said only that it was perhaps (*forte*) the case.[33] If this did sometimes happen, it would mean that there could have been some mystics who would have attained, at least concerning a number of objects, an understanding of simple substance far above that available to the rest of humankind. Apparently, Grosseteste had never achieved such knowledge himself or even known for sure of anyone else who had, but he kept the possibility open in concession to established Christian teachings on the contemplative life.[34] A second exception may have arisen concerning Grosseteste's third type of universal cognition, that by means of the causal reasons placed in the heavens. This would have held a special interest for Grosseteste, given his scientific interest in astronomy, and he may have thought that it was available to those on earth who were accomplished in studying the stars. The fact of the matter is, however, that this theory of universal knowledge does not appear anywhere else in his formal discussions of truth or human understanding, and he did not turn to it when he came to explaining the incorruptibility of the referents of universals.[35] If he did believe such knowledge was possible for men on earth, this was a second thought and one he never integrated into the rest of his teachings about truth.

On the whole, therefore, Grosseteste adhered to the rule that on earth man's universal knowledge of the simple truth could not refer to objects according to any of the ways he gave in his first three types of universal reference. This was true whether one interpreted these models in a strong sense, as pertaining

[33] See as above, n. 32.

[34] In his commentary on *De caelesti hierarchia* of Pseudo-Dionysius, Grosseteste suggested that the light of the divine essence may have revealed itself momentarily to Paul, Moses, and perhaps even the Virgin Mary. See Hyacinthe-François Dondaine, "L'objet et le 'medium' de la vision béatifique chez les théologiens du XIIIe siècle," *Recherches de Théologie Ancienne et Médiévale* 19 (1952), 125.

[35] See below, Chapter VI, 3.

to immediate reference, or weakly, as describing the species through which the mind came to know universals. If, in his *Commentary on the Posterior Analytics,* Grosseteste were going to establish a doctrine of science and a theory of truth that would work for men seeking knowledge in the world, he would have to explain knowledge of the truth without resorting to any of these three types.

This left only the last two kinds of universal cognition, knowledge in the form and knowledge in the accidents following upon essence. Both of them were fully in accord with his general stipulation about the reference of knowledge of the simple truth: that all such knowledge had to refer to something existing in the world. Yet Grosseteste did not intend to give each of the two ways equal weight. At the end of the first book of the *Commentary* he elaborated on Aristotle's distinction between science and opinion.[36] There were, he said, three ways one could speak of opinion: as the word was used most generally, as it was properly used, and as it was more properly used. It was the middle form, or opinion properly (*opinio proprie dicta*), that is relevant here.

Opinion properly so called is [that kind of] vision of the soul that, falling on intelligible and knowable objects, does not seize them in their purity but mixes with them the images of material, transmutable things. And from this mixture of images it begins to suspect that there is a possibility of change in those things that in truth are unchangeable.[37]

Such a mental act provided some kind of knowledge of the essential object, but only as mixed up with the material conditions of the thing.[38] Now material conditions were the most obvious kind of accident that followed upon essence. Since accidents following upon essence lay at the basis of the fifth sort of universal cognition, it is clear that in speaking of opinion

---

[36] Aristotle's discussion came in *Posterior Analytics,* I, 33.
[37] *Comm. Post. an.,* I, 19 (p. 280, ll. 49–53).
[38] *Comm. Post. an.,* I, 19 (p. 285, ll. 164–72).

proper, Grosseteste had in mind precisely knowledge of his fifth type.

According to the *Commentary,* opinion proper did not provide a wholly accurate picture of the object. Indeed, although opinion did, at least part of the time, lead to true knowledge, it did not in fact allow the mind to understand the intelligible object as it truly was—that is, essentially immutable.[39] In the same way, when speaking of the fifth type of universal knowledge, Grosseteste admitted that it, too, did not really lead to understanding of true universals.[40] It was a kind of surrogate universal knowledge. In short, Grosseteste's fifth type could not be taken as a proper description of reference in knowledge of universal simple truth. And beyond these simple definitions he actually took little note of it. Following Aristotle to the letter, he set the complex knowledge one could derive from opinion of this sort sharply against the certitude of scientific thought: in contrast to science, knowledge based on opinion always involved a slight fear or doubt that the contradictory position was true and the one believed to be true was actually false.[41] Such knowledge naturally was far from the epistemological ideal sketched out in the *Posterior Analytics.* It would seem that the only reason Grosseteste included it at all among his five types was to cover every possible way the mind could approach its simple object.

Real knowledge of universal simple truth for men on earth had to be according to the referential terms of Grosseteste's fourth kind of universal cognition, knowledge in the formal

---

[39] See *Comm. Post. an.,* I, 19 (p. 282, ll. 95-101, and p. 280, ll. 49-65).

[40] See *Comm. Post. an.,* I, 7 (p. 141, ll. 141-42). Another clear parallel between Grosseteste's description of opinion proper and his account of the fifth type of universal knowledge can be seen in his insistence that opinion proper did not allow the mind to see objects in the "truth" or "purity" of their essence (see *Comm. Post. an.,* I, 19 [p. 280, ll. 65-67, and p. 285, ll. 164-72]). In the same way he said the fifth sort of universal knowledge differed from the fourth in that it did not penetrate all the way to the "true essences" of things (see *Comm. Post. an.,* I, 7 [p. 141, ll. 142-43]).

[41] *Comm. Post. an.,* I, 19 (pp. 278-79, ll. 20-27).

cause. This was the one kind of simple knowledge available to the mind of fallen man that he was willing to call scientific. In the same passage where Grosseteste defined opinion, he claimed that what characterized science and set it off from opinion was that it was knowledge of things as they were in themselves (*sicut in se ipsis sunt*).[42] His words recall those he used to introduce the fourth kind of universal cognition—knowledge founded in that part of a thing that made it what it was (*a qua ipsa* [*res*] *est hoc quod est*).[43] This fourth level constituted, therefore, not only Aristotle's view of reference in universal terms, as Grosseteste had observed, but also his own, at least insofar as concerned man's knowledge on earth. Knowledge of universal simple truth referred to the essence of existing things as it was indicated in the form. In other words, the form was the immediate referent, standing for the existing substantial whole.

Yet every essence was, according to Grosseteste's ontology, particular in itself, and likewise so was every existing form. Consequently, this general theory of reference, for all its talk of knowing essence in the form, still did not show how universal knowledge differed from particular. It only reaffirmed that particular and universal cognition did not differ so much as to involve a different real referent; they both pointed to simple, existing essence.

In order to see how Grosseteste thought reference to particular essence through the form was compatible with the notion of universal knowledge, it is necessary to turn to several other passages in the *Commentary on the Posterior Analytics* where he spoke about universals in themselves. He clearly held that universals—or more precisely, the referents upon which they stood—were immanent in the particular world of created being. Indeed, he once went so far as to say that the units upon which scientific proof was founded, by which he apparently meant simple universals, were not wholly different from singu-

---

[42] *Comm. Post. an.,* I, 19 (p. 280, ll. 48-49).
[43] *Comm. Post. an.,* I, 7 (p. 141, ll. 131-32).

lars themselves. They were either part of the substance or, perhaps, the whole substance of which singulars were constituted.[44] In his description of the fourth kind of universal cognition he had used similar language to refer to the form itself, saying that although in itself the form was only part of the particular thing, taken as the basis for universal cognition it represented the substance in its entirety.[45] Later in the *Commentary* he would claim that Aristotle in fact equated simple universals with the forms found in the essences of particular beings.[46] Although it does not seem that Grosseteste, when he spoke of universals, had in mind the forms themselves, but rather something more like concepts in the intellect, he plainly thought that the relationship between universals and the forms of things was intimate, so close as to allow one to speak of the two as if they were almost identical.

Yet if Grosseteste was willing to say that universals were not entirely different from singulars, he also recognized that they were not exactly the same.[47] The problem was to find some middle ground. Early on in his *Commentary* he noted how Aristotle had shown that if the laws of demonstration and syllogism were to hold, it was not possible that universals be something apart from their subjects (*unum aliquid extra multa*). Instead, the universal was one thing from many and in many (*unum de multis et in multis*).[48] It was, in short, unity in multiplicity. The multiplicity in universals came from their reference to particulars. Unlike particular terms, each universal was predicable of many singulars and not just one particular thing. The difficulty arose in explaining how there could be unity in the face of such real referential multiplicity. Here lay the key to what made universals what they were. Grosseteste had to find an explanation that was compatible with his totally particularist theory of reference.

[44] *Comm. Post. an.,* I, 17 (p. 245, ll. 131–34).
[45] *Comm. Post. an.,* I, 7 (p. 141, ll. 132–38).
[46] *Comm. Post. an.,* I, 18 (p. 266, ll. 143–45).
[47] See above, n. 44.
[48] *Comm. Post. an.,* I, 8 (pp. 160–61, ll. 319–35).

In working out his views on this unity he tried to avoid the extremes of both exemplarism and nominalism. His rejection of the former was to be expected, given all he had said about the reference of human knowledge in the real world. Even in his early *Quaestiones theologicae* he recognized that the universals in human cognition, drawn as they were from created forms, did not possess the unity of exemplary forms in God's mind, which were indeed single and singular things standing apart from all those individuals they exemplified.[49] In contrast to such an exemplar, the universals that men knew had no objective reality outside the multitude of particular things to which each referred. Yet like Aristotle before him, Grosseteste was enough of a realist to reject the idea that the meaning of a universal was exhausted by an enumeration of its particular components. It had a unity that was greater than the collective unity of all its individual referents, a unity that made it different from just an aggregate of particulars.

Grosseteste gave an indication of what he meant in a passage ostensibly about complex knowledge but also related to the question of simple universals. He said that one could not claim that something pertained universally to all members of a class just because one had proved that it pertained to each existing member of individually. From the Aristotelian text he was commenting on, he drew as an example the law that the sum of the inside angles of a triangle is equal to two right angles. According to his argument, if one had proved this law separately of each particular triangle that existed, one still would not have demonstrative knowledge of its truth but only sophistical knowledge. The reason for this could be stated in terms of simple cognition. In order to have demonstrative knowledge of the law about the angles of a triangle, one had to know this fact about a triangle as triangle—in other words, about triangle as a universal. The universal for triangle was distributed over all triangles (*omne triangulum*) but was something other than all triangles at any particular time (*ut nunc*).

---

[49] *Quaestiones theologicae* in Callus, "*Summa theologiae*," p. 195.

Instead, it was all triangles taken simply (*simpliciter*). Taken simply, all triangles constituted a referential base—Grosseteste called the base universality (*universitas*)—that attached naturally to the universal term but could not be summed up in any specific listing of objects.[50] This was why the mere enumeration of all particular cases did not suffice to make a universal. In short, the unity of the universal was something special, lying somewhere below numerical unity and above that of many separate things taken together. It was more than the nominalists' unity of a name applied to many objects.

For Grosseteste, therefore, the unity of a universal, while not so complete as that of an exemplary form or a particular essence in itself, somehow included the idea of an essential nature outside the limits of any particular referential base. At times he seems to have been so interested in arguing for the real foundations of this special nature that he temporarily neglected the more particularist side of his thought. There are passages in the *Commentary on the Posterior Analytics* where he spoke in terms that plainly echo the Platonic or Neoplatonic assumptions of earlier attitudes toward cognition. He said that abstract things were by nature prior to concrete things and that universals could be said to have being to a greater degree (*magis ens*) than particulars.[51] Given all that has been said above about Grosseteste's views on universals, however, it should be clear that such language cannot be taken literally to mean that the unity of the universal came from its existing as a separate entity apart from its individual manifestations.

Only once did Grosseteste give any further indication what this unity might be. The occasion came when he tried to explain what it meant to say that the universal was being to a greater degree than the particular, a discussion that fell in the

---

[50] *Comm. Post. an.,* I, 5 (p. 126, ll. 206–17). The text may be corrupted in ll. 216–17, but the sense remains clear enough.

[51] See *Comm. Post. an.,* I, 17 (p. 257, ll. 374–75), and below, n. 53. It should be noted that Grosseteste's statement about universals being to a greater degree followed Aristotle's words very closely. See Aristotle, *Posterior Analytics,* I, 24 (85b15–18).

middle of an examination of the way Aristotle defended the superiority of scientific, which was to say universal, knowledge over knowledge of particulars.[52] Because of its uniqueness, and its obscurity, this passage deserves an explication all its own. It began with an explicit commentary on Aristotle's words but soon turned to a broader exposition of Grosseteste's own personal views.

To the second argument in opposition, Aristotle replies that the universal exists not to a lesser but rather to a greater degree than the particular. For as the universal is one and alone (*unicum*) and the basis for a single act of understanding (*intellectus unus*), it is necessary that it be one thing (*res una*), no matter where its unity comes from, whether from the intellect or from something else. Nevertheless, the universal in itself (*secundum se*) is neither one nor many, but it falls to it to be one and many. And I hold that the unity of the universal in many particulars is similar to the unity of light in light that generates and that is generated. For the light that is in the sun generates out of its substance the light in the air, and yet nothing new is created in order for there to be light in the air, but rather the light of the sun is multiplied and propagated. Admittedly, the light in the sun is different from the light in the air, yet they are not so completely different that there is not in some way an essential unity (*unitas essentie*) in the light that generates and the light that is generated. Otherwise, the light that is generated would be created totally anew and from nothing. Therefore, the universal is not just a mental fiction, but it is some one thing in many. And because it is more incorruptible than a particular, since it is more removed from the accidents of variable material and closer to First Being, it is being to a greater degree (*magis ens*).[53]

What strikes the reader first is the analogy drawn between universals and sensible light. Like William of Auvergne, Grosseteste, too, had his favorite analytical metaphors, and the exam-

---

[52] The full Aristotelian text appears in modern editions of Aristotle as *Posterior Analytics,* I, 24.

[53] *Comm. Post. an.,* I, 17 (pp. 244-45 ll. 109-24). Grosseteste's idea that the universal in itself was neither one nor many is related to a similar notion in Avicenna (see above, this chapter, n. 15).

ple of visible light was one he found especially congenial and significant. Yet it is extremely difficult to interpret such language on its own, especially in the present case, where the theoretical problem was extraordinarily difficult and the analogy subject to so many different readings. It is therefore necessary to begin with the more expository aspects of the passage, those places where Grosseteste spoke in a straightforward and technical way, before going on to explain the metaphor of light.

Since the arguments of Aristotle's opponents ran that universal cognition was inferior to particular because the universal was not a discrete and thereby fully intelligible entity, Aristotle, and Grosseteste along with him, responded that the universal did in fact have a kind of unity adequate to the needs of the mind. As evidence they pointed out that the mind grasped the universal in a single act of understanding. Consequently, Grosseteste continued, the universal could be said to be a unitary thing (*res una*) and not merely a mental fiction. Yet the universal was not one thing in the way that all particular objects were one thing. It was, as Grosseteste had said before, one thing in many (*unum in multis*), and this introduced complications. In fact, the unity of the universal did not belong to it in itself (*secundum se*), nor did its multiplicity. The universal in itself (*universale secundum se*) was neither one nor many, but these qualities fell to it (*accidit ei*) from outside. They were, so to speak, accidents of its being, given to it by the human intellect.[54]

[54] In the passage quoted above Grosseteste left it undecided whether the universal's unity came from the intellect or from something else. All that was certain was that it came from outside the universal and did not belong to it in itself. Yet it seems reasonably clear that Grosseteste held to the opinion that the intellect gave the universal its unity. The passage itself was intended to answer an argument that universal knowledge was inferior because the unity of the universal came from the mind and was not intrinsic (see *Comm. Post. an.,* I, 17 [pp. 242–43, ll. 78–84]). Grosseteste included the possibility that the universal received its unity from something other than the mind simply to remind the reader that his answer was directed to the broad formal question about the nature of the universal—whether or not the fact that the universal was not in itself one would make it an inferior kind of knowledge—and worked regardless of the way one settled the specific question of precisely how the universal arose in the mind.

If this was so, then the problem was to determine precisely what the universal in itself (*universale secundum se*) was. It was not the referent of universal knowledge, for this consisted of many real and particular forms existing in the world, through which the mind knew the essences of which they were a part.[55] It was not the universal concept in the mind, for that was one thing in itself, a mental entity just as real as any material object to which it referred. In fact, since the universal in itself was neither one nor many, it could be said in a strict sense not to be. All existing things, according to Grosseteste, had their unique substance, which was at once the sign of their being and the guarantor of their individuality.[56] In the real world there was no middle ground between substantial unity and multiplicity.

All this must mean that Grosseteste thought the universal in itself did not belong in the real world of existing things. Instead, it seems that he saw it as a logical entity, outside the bounds of substantial existence altogether. The key to this interpretation lies in what he said on other occasions about the use of mental and linguistic signs. Grosseteste had maintained that the definition was a simple thing, the linguistic equivalent of a single concept, and that it referred to the external world. On its own, however, it did not refer specifically either to one object or to many. It took on determinate reference only as it was used as a term in a proposition.[57] Apparently, for Grosse-

---

[55] Grosseteste would have found in works like Avicebron's *Fons vitae*, Thierry of Chartres's commentaries on Boethius (see *Commentaries on Boethius by Thierry of Chartres and his School,* ed. Nikolaus M. Häring [Toronto, 1971]), and even in his own earlier writings (see *De unica forma omnium* [*Phil. Werke,* pp. 109-10]) the theory that God was the form for all created things, a theory which, at least in Avicebron's case, implied that the form was a kind of supersubstance that flowed in and out of particular things but always maintained its essential oneness. This theory would not, however, have been available to Grosseteste to explain how the universal was both one and many when he sat down to write his *Commentary on the Posterior Analytics,* for by that time he had established that knowledge in God—that is, the first of his five kinds of universal reference—was not the way men knew universals here in this life.

[56] See above, Chapter VI, 1.

[57] See above, this chapter, nn. 15 and 18.

teste the universal in itself was such a term, or at least whatever logical entity such a term corresponded to, insofar as it was used to refer to many similar essences at once. In its context—that is, in the proposition—it was therefore both one and many, for it participated in the unity of the concept, definition, or word and it referred to or stood for many individual forms. In itself, however, the universal was neither the concept or definition nor its many referents but rather a kind of mediator between the two. Since it was the mind that brought the two together by deciding to use the term, the mind was in fact responsible for its being what it was. It gave this logical entity its elusive unity and multiplicity at the same time.

If this was indeed Grosseteste's view of univerals—and it appears almost certain that it was—then it becomes clear how one must interpret his metaphor comparing the universal to light. He claimed that the unity of the universal in many particulars was similar to the unity of light in a luminous source and in its resultant radiation. The theory of light Grosseteste had in mind was one that he had worked out at length in earlier works, such as *De luce,* and that served as a basis for what is often known as his metaphysics of light.[58] Of importance for

[58] The text of *De luce* can be found in Baur's edition of Grosseteste's philosophical treatises (*Phil. Werke,* pp. 51–59). For discussion of Grosseteste's metaphysics of light, see Baur, *Die Philosophie des Robert Grosseteste,* pp. 77–92, and "Das Licht in der Naturphilosophie des Robert Grosseteste." It was Clemens Baeumker, in *Witelo, ein Philosoph und Naturforscher des XIII. Jahrhunderts,* Beiträge, III, 2 (Münster, 1908), pp. 357–422, who first pointed out that there existed a tendency among several thinkers of the thirteenth century to explain many of the phenomena of metaphysics and natural philosophy by means of a doctrine of spiritual light and who coined the term "metaphysics of light" (*Lichtmetaphysik*) to describe this aspect of their thought. A recent discussion of the idea can be found in James McEvoy, "The Metaphysics of Light in the Middle Ages," *Philosophical Studies* (Ireland), 26 (1979), 126–45. One must not, however, assume—as many scholars have done, including Palma, McEvoy, and even Crombie—that Grosseteste always intended the terms of his own metaphysics of light to extend literally into his epistemology. In works like *De luce,* Grosseteste explained the formation of the cosmos and participation in the divine by means of a metaphysics of light, but he did not talk about human cognition and he spoke of the light of the cosmos in a way that clearly showed he had in

this particular application of the theory was Grosseteste's belief that light was infinitely expansible and could propagate itself without having to generate new substance. As he put it in this passage, the light of the sun generated out of its own substance the light in the air, in the process being multiplied but not creating anything substantially new. Despite the fact that the light in the air was different from the light in the sun, they were not so different that they did not share the same essence. According to the terms of the analogy, it was this essential unity (*unitas essentie*) that corresponded to the unity of the universal.

The point of the analogy was to indicate that there was a basis in reality for the unity of the universal. By saying that unity came to the universal from the mind, Grosseteste had opened the possibility that this unity sprang simply from the decision of the intellect to group many particular objects together under one rubric and represent them by a single concept or definition. In this way the coherence of the universal would derive solely from the unity of mental vision. Yet he had already insisted, to the contrary, that the unity of the universal arose from a deeper source, and his analogy with light helped to reveal precisely what this source was.[59] In the case of visible light the essential being of light in general was logically prior and ontologically fundamental to the varied existence of light in the sun and in the air. In the same way the unity of the uni-

---

mind visible light and not something that could be literally the same as the light of the mind. (On the light of the mind, see below, Chapter VI, section 4). Consequently, it is necessary to approach Grosseteste's epistemological references to light without any preconceived notion of how they fit in with his metaphysics. As mentioned in the Introduction, above, such references must be taken first of all as explanatory metaphors, and they must be compared both among themselves and with the rest of his epistemology in order to determine precisely what they mean. If one follows this procedure, one not only sees how little metaphysics is actually needed to understand Grosseteste's epistemology, one also avoids having to interpret his metaphysics of light in a manner that does violence to the way he himself used it in his own metaphysical and cosmological works.

[59] On the deeper source, see above, n. 50.

versal was logically independent of and essentially fundamental
to the separate and particular existence of its real referents. For
all their individual diversity there was an essential oneness to
them all. Since Grosseteste thought the essence of a thing was
the same as its individual substance, it is not possible that he
meant to imply that there was a single real and undifferentiated
essence underlying all the members of a universal category. He
must instead have been thinking of a sort of essential similarity
much in the way William of Auvergne conceived of it: as the
simple fact that the essences of individual things in the same
species were duplicates of one another and thereby specifically
the same. It was this that justified the mind in representing several numerically different but essentially identical objects with
the same definition or sign. Since simple concepts were derived
from and referred directly to the forms of existing things,
forms that in themselves were sufficient indicators of the essential nature of their subjects, they provided a natural and fully
justified basis for universal terms.

In the end, therefore, Grosseteste was able to work out a theory of reference for universal terms that fully met the conditions set by his theory of simple truth. The real basis for universal predication lay in the individual form, the difference
between universal and particular predication coming from
whether or not one regarded the form or the essence it stood
for as one single thing or as a general characteristic also possessed by other objects. Both universal and particular knowledge of simple truth referred, although in different ways, to
particular existing essence—in other words, directly to real
things in the created world. Perhaps the most curious aspect of
all this was that Grosseteste succeeded in coming to this understanding of universals despite the fact that he retained a
considerable amount of the language dependent on the Neoplatonic notions of exemplarism and the substantial unity of
universal form. He was able to do this only because he subjected this language to a process of interpretation that completely transformed its significance. What one sees in Grosseteste is a totally new theory of human knowledge—which at

least in the case of simple universals showed clear affinities with the terminist logic of his day—growing out of the very formulas that had long been associated with an entirely different attitude about the nature of understanding.

3. THE INCORRUPTIBILITY OF SIMPLE UNIVERSALS

Once Grosseteste had indicated the essentials of a theory of reference for simple cognition in this life, it remained for him to show how the universals of simple knowledge were incorruptible. This was a matter of considerable importance, since a theoretical defense of the new ideal of science depended upon its resolution. Scientific knowledge had to be at once universal and necessary, and according to Aristotle himself, incorruptibility was an essential part of both of these characteristics.[60]

Of course, in *De veritate* there had been an incorruptible element in human knowledge of the simple truth. It was provided by the second of the two exemplars the mind came to know, the divine idea. Yet in that work Grosseteste was still speaking about incorruptibility in terms of eternity, the traditional way for thinkers of the Middle Ages to approach the problem.[61] Since God alone was eternal, it was evident He should have some place in whatever was incorruptible about human thought. By the time Grosseteste came to write his *Commentary on the Posterior Analytics*, he had completely discarded this early approach. Perhaps he realized that his new views on reference, by fixing the object of knowledge solely in the created world, made it impossible to explain the incorruptibility involved in knowledge of simple universals in the old way. Perhaps he was merely being led by the vocabulary of the Aristotelian work

---

[60] See Aristotle, *Posterior Analytics,* I, 8 (75b21–26).
[61] See *De veritate* (*Phil. Werke,* p. 139). On incorruptibility as dependent on eternity, see above, Chapter III, 2. William of Auvergne posed the problem this way. It should be noted, however, that the question of the eternity or incorruptibility of knowledge of the truth arose for William only when he considered complex knowledge, while the problem here for Grosseteste had to do with knowledge of simple truth.

upon which he was commenting. At any rate, in the *Commentary,* Grosseteste dropped any mention of the eternity of universal truth. Instead, he spoke simply about the incorruptibility or, more precisely, the perpetuity (*perpetuitas*) of universals.[62] He noted that this was the quality Aristotle was thinking of when he said that somehow the universal always (*semper*) had to be.[63] With this neat transformation of the quesion he thereby secularized the terms of the search for universal truth. Unlike William of Auvergne, who in fact shared many of Grosseteste's ideas about the impropriety of a divine referent for human cognition and the need to emphasize the logical aspects of the problem of universality, he could thus avoid the tortuous attempts to accommodate a term like "eternal" when it did not really apply.

Grosseteste viewed the problem of the incorruptibility or perpetuity of universals as exclusively a question of reference. The issue was to locate some element of incorruptibility in the object known.[64] Given his theory of reference, however, a solution to the problem was not immediately evident, nor would it be easy to find. He held that all simple concepts, universal ones included, pointed directly to the individual forms of things and through them to individual essences. But most such individual things were transitory, at least those that existed on earth. How could any specific or generic group of them be described as incorruptible or perpetual?

It was at the end of the passage where he listed the five forms

---

[62] *Comm. Post. an.,* I, 7 (p. 139, ll. 89–97), and I, 18 (p. 266, ll. 142–43). The Latin version of Aristotle upon which Grosseteste was commenting used the word perpetual (*perpetuus*) to describe this special quality of universal knowledge. See *Posterior Analytics,* I, 8 (75b22) (Aristoteles Latinus, IV, 1–4, ed. Minio-Paluello and Dod, p. 20).

[63] *Comm. Post. an.,* I, 18 (p. 266, ll. 141–43). For the Aristotelian text, see *Posterior Analytics,* I, 31 (87b32) (Aristoteles Latinus, IV, 1–4, ed. Minio-Paluello and Dod, p. 62).

[64] Although common sense would lead one to believe that this is the only way to view the issue, throughout history there has frequently been some confusion as to whether the incorruptibility ought also to pertain in some way to the knowing subject. Aristotle himself was unclear on this point (see *De anima,* III, 5).

of universal cognition that Grosseteste directly confronted the issue. Indeed, he had introduced the five forms precisely to clarify this point: how the genera and species of predication could be said always to be.[65] Since his concern was to establish the incorruptibility relevant to human knowledge, he limited himself to considering only the last two types of universal cognition. Of course, the first three types would have posed no problem, for in each of those cases the referent of universal cognition was an object that naturally existed for all times; yet none of these three applied to human cognition in the world. It was the fourth and the fifth types—or, to speak properly of science, the fourth alone—that characterized the knowledge men had in this life.

From the outset Grosseteste admitted that the problem was a difficult one to resolve. He did, however, offer two solutions, and he said that one of them must necessarily be the right way. Since one of the solutions focused on the nature of the universal term in itself and the other considered the problem more ontologically, from the perspective of the reality of universal referents, they were theoretically compatible, and it is conceivable that Grosseteste accepted them both. His first argument, the briefer of the two, simply pointed out that universals in themselves were incorruptible and that they became corruptible only through their necessary identification in the real world with some corruptible base (*deferens corruptibile*). Clearly, he had in mind his own theory of the universal as a purely logical entity, a term used to refer to a multitude of particular things. It was the real, particular referents that constituted the "corruptible base," a set of things all of which were individual and transitory, determinate to a particular time. By its very logical nature, however, the universal in itself remained untouched by the transitoriness of these objects to which it re-

---

[65] Grosseteste's discussion of the five forms was discussed above, and the passage on the everlasting nature of the referent comes immediately after the text cited in this chapter, n. 24. See *Comm. Post. an.,* I, 7 (pp. 141–42, ll. 145–57). The analysis that follows depends completely on this passage.

ferred. In short, the corruptibility of reference at any moment did not entail the corruptibility of universal knowledge in itself. Naturally, this was more a negative defense than a positive explanation. Rather than argue specifically for permanence or perpetuity, it released the universal from the impermanence associated with the objects of knowledge in the real world. Yet despite its obliqueness, this first solution embodied, or at least implied, a most significant idea. Grosseteste was here beginning to suggest that the incorruptibility of the universal stemmed from its logical way of standing for things rather than being any objective thing in itself. Whether or not he realized the full implication of what he was saying, this was an idea that would become increasingly important in the scholastic world. With only a few words he had opened a path that would eventually lead to the work of William of Ockham himself.[66]

Grosseteste's second solution more directly addressed the question of the incorruptibility of each universal's referential base, accounting for the enduring existence of the universal in terms of the collective being of the individual objects to which it could refer. According to this view, universals were incorruptible because they were constantly maintained by the unbroken succession of individuals (*successio continua individuorum*) in each species or genus. As he explained it, this position rested on the principle that universality depended on the undiminished preservation of all of its parts, which was to say, of all its individual referents in the concrete world. He interpreted this to mean that the number of individual referents had to remain constant. Since it was clear that the number of members in a species or genus in any one place varied over

---

[66] For instance, Ockham used a similar argument to explain why there could be a science of corruptible things—that is, physics. See *Expositio super viii libros Physicorum* (prologue) in Ockham, *Philosophical Writings,* ed. and trans. Philotheus Boehner (Edinburgh, 1957), pp. 13-15. Pointing out the similarity is, however, not to deny that Ockham's theory of supposition and his notion of the object of knowledge was not only more elaborate but also more radically colored by terminist logic than anything to be found in Grosseteste.

time, however, Grosseteste was led to speculate that there was a kind of motion of species or genera over the face of the earth: "All species constantly move." He said that as some individuals were corrupted or passed away during the winter in one part of the world they were replaced by similar individuals in another part that was then having summer. Since there was always summer somewhere, the equilibrium could be maintained and a constant number of individual members in each species sustained. Presumably he thought that what was true of the corruption and generation due to the seasons applied by means of a less obvious but equally reliable rotation in the case of those things whose generation and corruption occurred according to a different schedule. It is interesting to note that had Grosseteste meant the "always" of universality to be truly "forever," then the validity of this position would have depended on holding the eternity of the world. It would seem, however, that he was able to avoid such an implication by taking it as a sufficient defense of perpetuity to hold that the universal referent was sustained by a process of constant generation throughout the time the world existed.[67]

After Grosseteste had indicated how it was possible to say that the universals of simple cognition were incorruptible in the proper sense that there was something perpetual about them or their conditions of reference, he turned to a second criterion he closely associated with this temporal incorruptibility—that is, ubiquity. Again, the idea came from Aristotle, who had said that what was universal was that which was always and everywhere (*semper et ubique*).[68] Having discussed the quality of being "always," it seemed incumbent upon Grosseteste to discuss that of being "everywhere," too.

As before, he gave two possible explanations, leaving it up to the reader to decide which was the most acceptable.[69] And again, the two explanations addressed different aspects of the

[67] See the discussion of perpetuity below, Chapter VII, 2, B.
[68] See above, n. 63.
[69] The analysis that follows in the present study is based on a single passage: *Comm. Post. an.,* I, 18 (pp. 266-67, ll. 143-62).

problem, although Grosseteste did not make precisely the same division he had made when examining perpetuity. One of the arguments, to be sure, did explain the ubiquity of the universal in ontological terms, but the other was not so much logical as psychological. It focused on the universal as a concept in the mind. Grosseteste made it plain from the start that these two accounts applied to his fourth type of universal cognition. He said he was examining universals the way Aristotle had defined them, as equivalent to the essential forms of particular things, and even though it does not seem that Grosseteste himself drew an exact equivalence between forms and universals, there can be no doubt that he associated Aristotle's view on universals with his own fourth type.[70] In short, just as had been the case with the problem of existing always, Grosseteste's handling of the ubiquity of universals was directed to the kind of knowledge available to men on earth.

According to Grosseteste's first explanation, the universal could be said to be everywhere because it existed in each one of its particular or individual manifestations. He justified this way of interpreting "to be everywhere" with a short argument. He said that for something to be everywhere (*ubique esse*) it had merely to be in every one of the places proper to it (*esse in quolibet suorum locorum*). Furthermore, he insisted that the places proper to universals (*loca universalium*) were the singulars themselves in which those universals were to be found—that is, all their existing referents. Consequently, to be everywhere it was enough for the universal to be wherever there was something the universal concept referred to. Seen in this way, Grosseteste's first explanation for ubiquity was merely a reaffirmation of his formal definition of a universal. A universal was everywhere just so long as it was a universal as Grosseteste had defined it: one in many.

The second reason a universal could be said to be everywhere was because it was located in the intellect. In this case the uni-

---

[70] See *Comm. Post. an.,* I, 7 (p. 141 ll. 140–41) and my discussion in Chapter VI, 2, at nn. 45 and 46.

versal would be the intellect, since it would participate in the intellect's substance, and being the intellect was, Grosseteste asserted, the same as being everywhere. Once again, Grosseteste had to justify his use of the word "everywhere." He proposed that the intellect was everywhere because it was present in a spiritual way (*per modum spiritualem ibi est*) wherever there was some object it understood. As an example of such a spiritual presence he cited the case of the lover, who could be said to be wherever there was something he loved. It is clear that although this second explanation was ostensibly concerned with the universal concept and, unlike the first, not with the referents of universal terms, in fact the two arguments were closely related. The mind, and consequently the universal, was everywhere in the sense that it could be said to be wherever it had an object. The spiritual location of each universal was, therefore, identical to the real location of all the particular substances to which that universal referred. As before, the ubiquity of the universal reduced to the normal spatial distribution of its referential base.

Grosseteste added that if the universal were taken to mean an idea in the mind of God, his first type of universal cognition, then it was everywhere in the way God was everywhere; and if it were taken as a causal virtue in a heavenly body, Grosseteste's third type, then it was everywhere in the way such virtues were found in all places. As these universals were not the universals of human discourse in the world, the explanations Grosseteste offered for their ubiquity were of little importance for his notion of scientific knowledge of the truth. It is interesting to remark, however, that Grosseteste did not feel he could rationally explain either of these ways of being everywhere or, for that matter, the second way he gave for human understanding of universal truth. He had to admit it was more than he could understand how a mind could be everywhere its object was or how God and the celestial virtues were in all places, but he believed that this was in fact the case and held his opinion to be absolutely reliable.

All in all, Grosseteste's account of the incorruptibility of simple universals was not without ambiguity. He never settled on a fixed doctrine, and he did not work out all the problems and implications of his thought. There can be no question, however, about the general direction in which he tended. He plainly believed that the incorruptibility behind man's knowledge of simple universal truth need have nothing to do with notions of eternity of God's supertemporal realm, and in accordance with this conviction he fully validated his theory that the simple truth men knew, even when it reached the level necessary for science, lay wholly in the created world.

4. THE WAY TO KNOWLEDGE OF SIMPLE TRUTH

Grosseteste's theory of reference in simple cognition, including his views on the nature and incorruptibility of simple universals, adequately elucidated the objective side of man's knowledge of simple truth in this life. Yet to justify fully his adoption of a notion of truth that focused exclusively on objects and powers in the created world, he also had to account for the reliability of the mental act involved in the process of simple cognition. In *De veritate,* Grosseteste had explained the validity of the cognitive process by turning to the notion of divine illumination. According to the second description of knowledge of simple truth given in that work, God did not act as a direct cognitive object or referent but rather in a more subtle and circuitous way. The radiance of God's Truth served as a light to the mind that allowed all other truths to be perceived, even though it was not seen in itself. Although, in his *Commentary on the Posterior Analytics,* Grosseteste had ruled out even an indirect place for God or the divine ideas in the reference of man's knowledge of simple truth, there still might have been some room for divine intervention in the process of simple human cognition along these lines. One of the virtues of the image of divine light was, after all, to make God's intervention logically independent of the precise formal arrangements of reference.

In fact, there are places in the *Commentary* where Grosseteste spoke of a light in which truth must be seen, and the language he used on such occasions sometimes recalls that of *De veritate*. These passages have suggested to most scholars that even in his efforts to come to grips with Aristotle, Grosseteste continued to hold to his early views on the place of divine illumination in man's knowledge of simple truth.[71] One of the most striking instances of this use of the image of light occurs in the middle of a discussion of the various ways one can measure knowledge. After examining the qualities of goodness and dignity, Grosseteste came to consider certitude, and here he paused to survey the factors that contributed to knowledge of simple truth.

Things are said to be certain according to the relation they have to knowledge or to mental vision. So I say that there is a spiritual light (*lux spiritualis*) that floods over intelligible objects (*res intelligibiles*) and over the mind's eye (*oculus mentis*) and that stands to the interior eye (*oculus interior*) and to intelligible objects as the corporeal sun stands to the bodily eye and to visible corporeal objects. Therefore, intelligible objects that are more receptive of this spiritual light are more visible to the interior eye. And those [objects] that are more similar to the nature of this light are more receptive of it. And so objects that are more receptive of this light are more perfectly penetrated by the power of the mind (*acies mentis*), which is likewise a spiritual light (*irradiatio spiritualis*). And this more perfect penetration [brings] greater certitude.[72]

Another example, one that makes the point perhaps even more forcefully, can be found in the course of a lengthy examination

[71] Every historian who has written about Grosseteste's thought has assumed that his later writings were perfectly consistent with his early ones on this score. No one has suggested that he abandoned or at least played down the doctrine of divine illumination in his scientific works. William Wallace's remarks about Grosseteste in *Causality and Scientific Explanation,* vol. I, do, however, begin to suggest that there is something wrong with the traditional view. Although Wallace does not talk about the problem of divine light, he shows how seriously Grosseteste took the formal, logical aspect of the problem of certitude at the time of his scientific investigations and how much he was attracted to the model of knowledge provided by the account of science in Aristotle's works.

[72] *Comm. Post. an.,* I, 17 (pp. 240-41, ll. 38-47).

of the nature of opinion. Here, Grosseteste actually called the spiritual light the first visible:

And I say again that there is a mental sight (*visus mentalis*) that can apprehend intelligibles and there are things visible to that sight that we call intelligibles and knowables and there is a light that floods over the sight and over the visible object and brings about actual vision, just as the light of the sun does in external sight. And although that spiritual light (*lumen spirituale*) is most truly in itself the first visible, just as is the light of the sun to the bodily eye, nevertheless, in the same way that we say that a colored body, because it is the first thing receptive of the light of the sun, is in itself the first visible, so we say that in the case of interior sight (*visus interior*) that which first and in itself receives the spiritual light is in itself the first visible.[73]

From evidence of this sort it would at first seem safe to say that when Grosseteste wrote the *Commentary* he was still thinking of God or God's Truth as the light whereby men knew simple truth. His claim that a spiritual light must shine on intelligible objects to produce knowledge in the mind's eye immediately suggests the way in *De veritate* he showed how the fallen minds of men on earth could know created truth only in the reflected light of the Truth of God. The closeness of the analogy along with the insistence that the spiritual light was the most intelligible of all things makes it hard not to conclude that the same notion of divine illumination was at work.[74] Yet

[73] *Comm. Post. an.,* I, 19 (pp. 279–80, ll. 29–37). The text in Rossi's edition, ll. 36–37, must be repunctuated to read: "... spirituale, esse per se et primum visibile; et...."

[74] There is one more suggestion that Grosseteste still saw God as the normal light of the mind when he wrote his *Commentary*. At the very beginning of the work, when speaking about the way men learn, Grosseteste said that externals like a master or the written word were not teachers in the truest sense, since they merely moved the intellect and made it ready for learning. The real teacher lay inside the mind, where it revealed the truth in a way that commanded assent (*Comm. Post. an.,* I, 1 (p. 94, ll. 33–36). He added that it did this by illuminating the intellect. It sounds as if Grosseteste was here borrowing from the tradition nurtured by the writings of Augustine, according to whom God was within each person

despite the initial plausibility of such an interpretation, the passages in the *Commentary* where Grosseteste used the image of light are not without ambiguity. There is ample evidence he held that the mind itself had a power that could be described as a light and that acted to make intelligible objects visible to it. Such a light could well have been at least partly, if not wholly, what Grosseteste had in mind when he spoke of the spiritual light involved in cognition, and this is a way that would have outdone, or even superseded, the light of God.

In the first passage, for example, Grosseteste himself made the point that the mind had a power capable of shining on things and presumably making them actually intelligible. Whether or not this was the only light he was thinking of there, he must have intended it to play a significant role in the full business of intellectual illumination. In fact, in that very passage he described the function of the spiritual light as one of making knowledge certain. Shortly afterward, when he again spoke of certitude, this time the certitude of universal demonstration, he made it almost imperative to conclude that the spiritual light at the bottom of certain knowledge was the intellect itself. As he said: "The universal is closer to the intellect and farther from the senses. The particular, on the other hand, is closer to the senses. Therefore, universal demonstration makes known that which is less mixed with material images and closer to the spiritual light through which is attained certain intellectual vision."[75] Indeed, there can be no doubt that Grosseteste thought the intellect was, properly speaking, a kind of intelligible or spiritual light. At the end of the *Commentary*, in an effort to clear up a troublesome spot in the original text, he tried to explain what Aristotle could have

---

the teacher of the heart and the mind (see Augustine, *De magistro,* XI, 38, and XII, 40—in the edition by Günther Weigel, CSEL, 77, 1 [Vienna, 1961], pp. 47 and 48-49). If this internal light, necessary to apprehend the truth, was the same as the spiritual light Grosseteste spoke of later, then this would mean that the spiritual light was itself directly from God.

[75] *Comm. Post. an.,* I, 17 (p. 249, ll. 211-14).

meant when he said that the intellect (*intellectus*) was the principle of science and the principle of principles (*scientie principium, et principium principiis*).[76] One explanation he proposed depended on the notion of a spiritual light: "Perhaps he [i.e., Aristotle] wanted to show by those words that the same nature that is the intellectual power is that by which something is accepted as a first principle, without a cause. For, as has been said above, the spiritual light that is in itself visible to the sight of the mind is a nature of this kind."[77] Clearly, he was saying that the light by which the intellect came to understand principles, and thus also to perceive the first objects of simple cognition, was identical with the intellect itself.[78] In other words, the intellect was its own illuminator. What is more, Grosseteste seems to have directed this message back to that earlier passage where he spoke about spiritual light and a first visible.[79] The intellect was the spiritual light that was "in itself visible to the sight of the mind." It was, therefore, in the language of the earlier passage, the "first visible" itself. Here is a way to read the image of intelligible light without making any reference to God at all, and it appears to have the explicit approval of the author himself.

The ultimate impression left by the passages in the *Commentary* that refer to a spiritual light is, therefore, somewhat confusing. From one perspective it seems as if Grosseteste meant to speak of the light of God's Truth, while from another it

[76] Aristotle, *Posterior Analytics*, II, 19 (100b15-16). For the Latin text used by Grosseteste, see Aristoteles Latinus, IV, 1-4, ed. Minio-Paluello and Dod, p. 107.

[77] *Comm. Post. an.,* II, 6 (pp. 407-8, ll. 103-7).

[78] Crombie read the passage to mean that the intellect was illuminated by God (see *Robert Grosseteste,* p. 57). Apparently he took the word *natura,* the first time it appears in the passage, to be in the ablative case, so that "something by nature the same as the intellectual power" was what accounted for knowledge of principles, and this something similar to but different from the intellect was the spiritual light. This reading is grammatically awkward—it is difficult to see why "something the same" (*eadem*) should be in the feminine or why "by nature" (*natura*) should be followed by a relative clause—and it seems unlikely that it is correct.

[79] See above, n. 73.

would seem he was talking about a light solely from the human mind. Alone, the passages themselves provide no way of deciding whether Grosseteste really intended one interpretation or the other, or both. Yet there is another group of passages in the same work where he spoke in greater detail of the procedure by which men came to know simple truth, and in these cases he totally ignored divine illumination. What makes this silence about a role for God even more impressive is that these were the passages that focused most explicitly on analyzing the mechanism itself by which the mind came to know simple truth. In this way they differ from the passages dependent on the image of light, all of which were primarily concerned with establishing the degree of certitude that attached to various objects as they were known. The image of light, with all its ambiguity, seems to have been perfectly satisfactory for that purpose, but not for closely analyzing the intellectual process itself. With this new goal in mind Grosseteste turned to a less imagistic, more complicated model, one that was free of ambiguity. Instead of describing simple cognition as occurring in some sort of intelligible light, all the passages of the second group offer a more pedestrian but definitely more precise account in terms of powers of the soul and processes of formal reason. Here Grosseteste left no place for God but rather concentrated on the notion, inspired by Aristotle, of the primacy of sensible particulars in human cognition. Thus, these passages mark a continuation along the intellectual path Grosseteste had taken with his more mature views on the nature of truth and the referential conditions of simple knowledge, and this alone explains their significance for the historian of medieval thought. If this new, more Aristotelian description of the cognitive process had not yet totally displaced the old idea of divine illumination, it had clearly come to center stage, not only pushing the older view aside but actually undermining its purpose, even its legitimacy, as a foundation for the reliability of the procedure by which the mind came to know simple truth.

The problem that concerned Grosseteste in this second set of passages had to do with the formation of simple universals. He wanted to explain how it was possible for the mind to come to knowledge as he had described it in his theory of the reference of universal terms. This meant, in effect, accounting for the discovery of the universal concepts, the basis for all science, and Grosseteste recognized, perhaps even more than Aristotle, the importance as well as the difficulty of the task. As Grosseteste had said, the formal expression of the knowledge of what a thing was, its essence (*quod quid est*), was the definition.[80] Consequently, the art by which men acquired true knowledge of simple things could be called the art of definition or of discovering definitions, and it consisted in establishing the proper definition for each definable thing.[81] The difficulty was that although the definition lay at the heart of all demonstration—for Grosseteste's science, like that of Aristotle, was ultimately a matter of essential characteristics—it could not be found or even substantiated by means of demonstration itself.[82] There had to be some other way to ascertain simple knowledge.

Most of the second book of the *Posterior Analytics* was occupied with the formal procedures of the art of definition, and in his *Commentary* Grosseteste went into great detail on how he thought Aristotle's method should be interpreted. For the purposes of this study, however, it is not necessary to follow Grosseteste through his enumeration of the specific steps for arriving at a definition. What is important is to examine what he thought were the psychological and logical foundations for the process. They were the aspects of his epistemology that tied his formal logic and his notion of science to his theory of simple truth. The most important and the most extensive single passage where Grosseteste dealt with this problem came at the end of the fourteenth chapter of his commentary on the first book. In his discussion of a rather brief text from Aristotle, Grosseteste undertook to explain why humans had scientific knowledge only of those things they knew through the senses, and what Aristotle meant by induction. He did this by giving a

---

[80] See above, this chapter, nn. 7 and 11.

[81] *Comm. Post. an.,* II, 1 (pp. 287-88, ll. 11-24).

[82] *Comm. Post. an.,* II, 2 (pp. 308-10, ll. 113-20 and 131-39). On the importance of definition, see below, Chapter VII, n. 98.

complete account of the process by which the intellect formed simple concepts.[83]

After some preliminary considerations about the kind of knowledge available to God and the higher intelligences, intended primarily to guarantee God's omniscience and to serve as a contrast to what he would have to say about human understanding, Grosseteste turned to the problem that concerned him: the workings of men's minds. Here, at the very outset, he took care to eliminate any direct illumination from a higher light in normal human cognition. As he explained things, the higher part of the human soul, the intellective power or intellect, had been by nature designed to operate without the aid of any bodily organ but instead to receive an irradiation from some superior light from which it would derive all its scientific knowledge, beginning with that of simple universals. This irradiation or illumination would have been direct, the sole intelligible object being the source of light from which the mind would receive immediately the exemplary images that caused its knowledge. There would have been no need to look on lower created beings. Since Grosseteste did not specify what source of light he had in mind, he presumably meant to include both God and the celestial intelligences. In short, he was referring to that sort of knowledge he had previously described in his first two levels of universal cognition. If, however, this sort of divine or celestial illumination had once been natural to the human mind, it could not account for human understanding in his life. Immediately after describing the process by which the mind could know something through a superior light, Grosseteste insisted that in fact this way to knowledge would be available to the fallen soul only after it had left the body, with the possible exception of a few unusually pure souls who had cut themselves off completely from bodily affections.[84] Direct illumination from the divinity or an intelligence

[83] *Comm. Post. an.,* I, 14 (pp. 212–14, ll. 216–52). The discussion that follows will refer back to this passage unless otherwise noted.

[84] See also above, this chapter, n. 34.

was not part of human understanding in the world, but it was reserved for an occasional mystic and for the blessed after the Resurrection.

Grosseteste traced the plight of the intellect on earth to its peculiar relation with the body. At one point he said that the sight of the mind (*mentis aspectus*) or reason had been clouded over because of bodily contagion, and he often spoke in such antimaterialist terms as if any contact with the body would have sufficed to destroy the original intellectual powers of the soul.[85] When he took care to be more precise, however, he admitted that it was not the body in itself that accounted for the deterioration of the workings of the mind but rather the condition of the body as well as the mind after the Fall. In this he followed the example of many medieval thinkers in Christianizing the Neoplatonic view of the history of the soul and the nature of its union with the body. William of Auvergne had taken the same position. Simply put, then, Grosseteste held that the original purity of the mind's eye had been clouded and weighed down by the corrupted body. In this state the natural powers of reason were so overwhelmed with the corporeal mass to which they were attached that they could not act, at least not as they were intended to do. They were, in a manner of speaking, asleep (*quodammodo sopite*).

For all this sober language, however, Grosseteste shared very little in the skepticism of some Neoplatonists. The sleepy minds of men in the world might be cut off from the direct illumination of those higher lights that were supposed to give them knowledge, but they were not thereby prevented from obtaining scientific understanding. Grosseteste was, in fact, more sanguine about the everyday possibilities of reason than was William of Auvergne. He had inherited Aristotle's enthusiasm for knowledge in the world; the problem was how to account for this knowledge. If, as Grosseteste held, the mind could no longer turn directly to the divine light for knowledge, then there had to be some way to compensate for the

---

[85] See *Comm. Post. an.,* II, 6 (p. 406, ll. 69–72).

loss. It has already been shown how he intended the theory of illumination he sketched out in *De veritate* to be a way to get around the impossibility of any direct vision into God in this life. What is striking about the group of passages in the *Commentary on the Posterior Analytics* where he explicitly analyzed the mechanics of simple intellection is that in them there is not even a trace of such a view. Indeed, the precise terms in which he explained the procedure did not rely at all on the image of an intelligible light. Instead, he devoted all his attention to Aristotle's theory that the mind works entirely from sensation, using the tools of division and induction.

On this point he was insistent. All human knowledge in this life depended on or arose from sensation. As adequate proof of this he noted that anyone lacking one of the senses also lacked intellectual knowledge of the objects of that sense.[86] Consequently, it was clear that even knowledge of universals, whether simple or complex, found its source in sensory perception.[87] Yet the senses apprehended singulars and not the universal.[88] There had to be some special process by which the intellect could work from sensory data to the proper cognition of universal concepts. According to Grosseteste, and according to Aristotle, the way was through induction.[89] Grosseteste later revealed that the inductive method he and Aristotle meant in this case was not the same as enumerative induction (*inductio per singularia*), which was properly limited to proving a fact (*quoniam est*).[90] In enumerative induction one listed all singular examples, making clear that there was no instance contrary to the general rule. Proof of this sort was inappropriate, even

---

[86] See *Comm. Post. an.,* I, 14 (p. 212, ll. 203-15).
[87] See above, n. 85, and also below, Chapter VII, n. 137.
[88] See *Comm. Post. an.,* I, 18 (p. 265, ll. 134-40).
[89] ". . . ipsum universale non est acceptum nisi per inductionem." *Comm. Post. an.,* I, 14 (p. 212, ll. 210-11). Grosseteste was commenting on Aristotle, *Posterior Analytics,* I, 18 (Aristoteles Latinus, IV, 1-4, ed. Minio-Paluello and Dod, p. 40). See also *Comm. Post. an.,* II, 6 (p. 406, ll. 67-69).
[90] *Comm. Post. an.,* II, 2 (p. 322, ll. 394-400). See Aristotle, *Posterior Analytics,* II, 7 (92a34-b3).

impossible to attain, when it came to identifying the genus or the species of objects in the world. Instead, the sort of induction involved in discovering universals was something less logically formal, although still a cognitive inference drawn from the examples at hand. It was, somehow, closely associated with division, at least highly dependent upon it. Grosseteste plainly stated that the art of definition consisted in division, the analysis of a complex notion into its simple parts, and indeed it was the method of division that occupied nearly the whole of his commentary on the second book of the *Posterior Analytics.*[91]

The way he accommodated both division and induction without contradiction was to see them as two stages in a continual process. The process began with sensation, although Grosseteste pointed out, much like William of Auvergne, that sensation was not the cause of scientific knowledge but only the occasion for it.[92] He held that after a certain amount of activity on the part of the senses, in which they took note of various sensible objects, the mind (*ratio*) of fallen man was roused to action, or more precisely, having been asleep it woke up (*expergiscitur*). Yet the senses not only awakened the mind; they carried it to the sensible objects as in a boat ([*ratio*] *in sensibus quasi in navi delata ad sensibilia*). This image served to explain how the mind, an intelligible power, was able to gain cognizance of sensible, singular things otherwise below its range of perception. As at the same place in William of Auvergne's epistemology, the whole idea apparently depended on a notion of the soul derived from Augustine, who stressed the unity of the soul and its powers. The mind could follow the senses to their objects because it was essentially identical with whatever lower faculty took cognizance of sensation, or at the very least it was, in Grosseteste's exact words, mixed with the senses (*ipsis sensibus admixta*)—by which he presumably meant

---

[91] On definition and division, see, for instance, *Comm. Post. an.,* II, 2 (pp. 312–13, ll. 186–217).
[92] *Comm. Post. an.,* I, 18 (p. 265, ll. 133–34).

that it was open to, or aware of, sensible impressions. Thus, it saw singular objects literally through the eyes of the body.

If up to this point, where the intellect first came into contact with external, individual objects, Grosseteste's description of cognition ran very much like that of William of Auvergne, from here on he gave an account that has no parallel in the writings of his Parisian contemporary. William simply skipped over the process by which the mind came to apprehend the essence of singular objects; Grosseteste examined it in some detail. According to him, the first part of the intellectual process was division. It is true that he had said that the reason was awakened only after the senses had confronted sensible objects many times (*per multiplicem obviationem sensus cum sensibilibus*), and if he meant that the same sense had to react to many objects of the same class many times before the reason was aroused, then perhaps there was here a sort of preliminary induction before the mind began to act on its own. Once reason had been awakened, however, and confronted by the senses with a singular, sensible object, its first act was to divide (*dividere*) or, as Grosseteste explained it, to consider separately those qualities that had been lumped together (*confusa*) in sensation. To give an idea of what he meant, he noted how the sense of vision confused color, size, shape, and body and took them in its judgment to be all one thing. Reason, on the other hand, was able to differentiate the various accidental qualities and to distinguish them from the body that supported them, finally coming to an apprehension of the substance that lay beneath them all. In like manner, reason could distinguish in any object its essential characteristics, which logically ordered would produce a definition. By a kind of shorthand he said the process was at once division and abstraction—that is, it resulted in a properly divided concept of definition that was at the same time sufficiently removed from particulars to be ready to serve in universal predication.

Of course, by speaking of division and abstraction in the same phrase Grosseteste somewhat obscured the distinction between the two, as in fact he often failed to draw a sharp line between logical processes and the more purely psychological or noetic functions of the mind. But he did, on one occasion, give a clearer indication of how he thought abstraction, by itself, came about.[93] He claimed, just as Aristotle had, that there was already a sort of preliminary abstraction in sensation and that sensory knowledge therefore possessed in a primitive form the conceptual foundations for the eventual intellectual cognition of essential characteristics themselves. Sensation was, to be sure, properly of individual things, but the first impression any sense had of a singular object was in a way universal—that is, it was an impression of the singular object under a universal aspect (*intentione universali*). It was this universal impression that formed the basis for the later concepts in the mind.

By way of example, Grosseteste followed Aristotle in describing the sensible apprehension of the man Callias. Whoever saw Callias approaching from a distance would at first see only an animal. Then, as the object came closer he would recognize that it was a man, and finally that it was Callias himself. Consequently, in sensory perception alone there would already be three different ways of viewing the same singular object: as an animal, as a man, and as the particular man Callias. Here was a sort of abstraction before any act on the part of the intellect. Furthermore, the results of this sensory abstraction were arranged according to a definite priority, furnishing already some basis for the more logical procedure of division itself. All that was needed was for the mind, by reasoning over the work of the senses, to raise a crude perception to the rank of true understanding.[94]

To return to the passage in Book I, Chapter 14, once the

---

[93] *Comm. Post. an.,* II, 6 (pp. 405-6, ll. 56-72).

[94] Grosseteste's interpretation of the process differed somewhat from the way Aristotle had described it. Aristotle had held that the senses perceived the different aspects of their objects in an order just the reverse of what Grosseteste said—that is to say, for Aristotle the senses went from man to animal, from less to more abstract. Likewise, it seems that for Aristotle the mind cooperated with the senses at each stage in the procedure, so that their mutual working toward the general concept involved some sort of induction. For Grosseteste a sense worked through the whole series of its impressions in a single, continuous act, and only then submitted its raw data to the intellect for consideration. See Aristotle, *Posterior Analytics,* II, 19 (100a14-b5).

mind had finished the process of division it possessed a concept or definition that could serve as the basis for a universal—that is, it had a general idea of an object like man or animal. But it did not yet know the idea as universal. For that, another step was needed. The initial concepts of the mind provided abstract knowledge only of individual essence. Universal knowledge demanded that the mind come to know that the same concept that referred to one or the other external object of the same class could be used to refer to them all. In other words, it had to realize that its concept or definition was capable of being used as a universal term, one thing in many. Here was where induction came in. As Grosseteste explained it: "Nevertheless, the mind does not know that this [abstracted concept] is in fact universal until, after it has made this abstraction from many singulars, it occurs to it that one and the same thing, according to its judgment, has been found in many singulars."[95] He could not have stated more clearly the rational nature of the universal as opposed to the abstracted idea, and his belief that it could be arrived at only after repeated exposure to the same general type. It was after having seen the same nature several times in several different objects that the mind concluded, or rather was induced to believe, that this nature was in fact characteristic of a class and should therefore be recognized as universal. This was the intuitive act Crombie spoke of when discussing Grosseteste's principles of science.[96] Yet rather than coming after induction, it lay at the heart of the inductive process itself. It was what allowed the mind to cut short the intellective process and establish the universal without enumerating every possible individual.

With induction the mind capped a procedure that had begun with the senses and ended with certain intellectual knowledge of universal terms. Using language much like that

[95] *Comm. Post. an.,* I, 14 (p. 214, ll. 247–50).
[96] Crombie, *Robert Grosseteste,* p. 71. Crombie's notion of this intuitive act actually conflates two *habitus* that were separate in Grosseteste, *intellectus* and *sollertia.* See below, Chapter VII, n. 166. Only *intellectus* was involved here.

of William of Auvergne, Grosseteste said that it was this way that the mind "hunted out the simple universal among singulars." The role of the senses was crucial, but the mind transformed their perceptions with its own methods of division and induction. The whole procedure was one of a gradual heightening of awareness and intelligibility: "First comes sensible knowledge of singular things, and from these knowledge ascends until it comes to simple universals."[97]

Clearly Grosseteste had developed an alternative to explaining the process of understanding simple truth by means of the image of a spiritual light. And although the account at the end of Chapter 14, Book I, provided the epitome of this alternative way, there are other places where he elaborated a similar notion as well. At the end of the *Commentary*, for example, he described the process from the point of view of psychology alone, making essentially a summary of Aristotle's ideas from the end of the *Posterior Analytics* and the beginning of the *Metaphysics*.[98] As before, he emphasized the role of sensation. The universal came to be known as a result of a prolonged procedure of comparison and abstraction performed by a hierarchy of the soul's powers, all open to receive knowledge from below. Another relevant passage comes in the middle of the second book.[99] Here, Grosseteste dealt with the purely logical aspects of the problem. His discussion is long and complicated, and it represents one of his most important attempts to come to grips with the logical implications of an epistemology that left the mind dependent on information it could draw from the sensible world. In each of these two cases the stress lay on the primacy of the existing material object for human knowledge. In neither was there reference to any sort of divine intervention. Indeed, it is difficult to see how there could have been a place for the divinity, given the concrete and worldly nature of the procedures and the objects involved.

---

[97] See above, n. 93.
[98] *Comm. Post. an.,* II, 6 (p. 404, ll. 24–40). For the Aristotelian texts, see *Posterior Analytics,* II, 19, and *Metaphysics,* I, 1.
[99] *Comm. Post. an.,* iI, 2 (pp. 322–40).

In the end, then, one must recognize not only the new direction taken in the passages in the *Commentary* where Grosseteste carefully examined the mechanism of coming to know simple truth but also the importance they hold for a final appreciation of his thought. In contrast to those other places in the very same work that only peripherally concern the cognitive process while focusing more directly on the question of certitude, these passages avoid using the image of light. Where the others suggest or at least make room for a role for God, these seem to exclude the divinity outright. But perhaps most important, where the one group of passages is vague or ambiguous, these are straightforward and clear. They represent the areas of his thought that he had worked out most carefully and, presumably, that he had come most recently to embrace. The degree of articulation they attain surely marks them as the fruit of his most deliberate consideration of the problem of human intellection.

It is evident, therefore, where the new departures in Grosseteste's thought led—toward the notion of a concrete mechanism of intellection tied to an appreciation of the logical steps involved, and away from the language of illumination. It was his formal analyses of the cognitive procedure, inspired by Aristotle, and not his ambiguous references to a guiding light that represented the significant growth in his thought. Here lay the foundation for an epistemology to complement the notion of reference he had worked out before. Together, the two provided theoretical support for a new definition of simple truth and for confidence in a program of scientific investigation in the world. In short, it would seem that Grosseteste had turned away from the explanation of simple cognition he had given in *De veritate*. He had simply changed his mind about the process of knowing simple truth.

This did not, however, force Grosseteste to forsake all use of the old language, as his discussion of the certitude associated with various intelligible objects makes clear. In fact, insofar as the image of divine light carried theological implications he would not forgo, even in a scientific treatise like the *Commen-*

tary on the Posterior Analytics, he could reintroduce it with very much the force it had held for him before. The notion of divine illumination provided a basic link between man and God; it suggested an intimacy that was otherwise hard to imagine. Like William of Auvergne, Grosseteste found a way to preserve this link.[100] If, as the *Commentary* generally implied, illumination was reserved for the final state of glory, it was tied to this life by an intellectual progress that led the mind from sensible impressions in this world to divine light in the next.

At the very end of his discussion of human intellection in Chapter 14 of Book I, Grosseteste tackled the problem of explaining how it was that the corrupted body had been able to contaminate the workings of a spiritual substance like the mind. In giving his answer, he was led to speculate on the path the soul took toward its final and most exalted operations.

The reason that the soul's vision is clouded by the mass of the corrupted body is that the feeling (*affectus*) and the sight of the soul are not divided and so its sight cannot attain to [any object] to which its feeling and love do not attain. Therefore, when the soul's love and feeling are turned toward the body and toward bodily enticements, they necessarily carry with them the [soul's] sight and deflect it from its light, which is to it as the sun is to the eyes of the body. Now when the sight of the mind has been deflected from its light it is necessarily turned toward darkness and idleness until it comes forth in some way through the bodily senses and finds in some way in external sensible light a trace (*vestigium*) of that light originally intended for it. And when it comes upon this [trace of its light], it is, so to speak, excited by it and begins to seek out its own light, and the more the [soul's] love is diverted from corruptible bodily things, the more its sight is turned to its light and the more it recovers it.[101]

Up to a point, Grosseteste was describing here the very process he had outlined in his account of human knowledge earlier in the same passage. The mind's own proper light (*suum lumen*

---

[100] For William's views, see above, Chapter IV.
[101] *Comm. Post. an.,* I, 14 (pp. 215–16, ll. 279–91).

or *proprium lumen*) was clearly the higher illumination, either from God or from a celestial intelligence, that Grosseteste had spoken of before. Because of original sin, human souls had lost contact with this light, and consequently every mind began its career in idleness or, as Grosseteste had previously said, in sleep. It was the business of the senses to arouse the intellect and call it back to activity. They not only did this, however, but they also mediated between the intellect and the objects of knowledge in the external world. For this reason the knowing mind did not turn back immediately to its proper intelligible light but instead came to depend on sensible light as the agent of its cognitive illumination. Knowledge in the world was a matter of interpreting sensible images, not reading messages sent down from above.

It was only in the last two sentences that Grosseteste went beyond the terms of his newly espoused theory of universal cognition. He began by saying that in coming to know objects in the world—that is, by means of material images received through the senses—the aroused intellect found, in a manner of speaking, a trace of its originally intended light. Yet by reintroducing in this way the higher light of Truth he did not intend to forsake his new epistemology or to imply that the mind in the world actually made contact with the higher light in itself. The intellect that had found the trace was still engaged in the worldly process of extracting simple universals from sensory data by means of division and induction, and this process had provided merely the evidence for, not the experience of, a higher intelligible reality. Instead, the mention of a vestige of a higher world apparent in the processes of human intellection here below signaled a change in the train of Grosseteste's thought. With this, he turned away from the matters of pure noetics and epistemology that had concerned him up till then and focused his attention on the soul's struggle for moral perfection. Suddenly his account was swept up in a dynamic that led directly into the next world and that had more to do with ends than with stages along the way.

As he explained it, once the mind had come to recognize the

traces of a higher intelligible reality, it remembered what had been lost through corruption and began to search for the illumination that had originally been its due. The immediate results of this shift in purpose were not intellectual but moral. The soul withdrew its love increasingly from worldly things and presumably fixed it on more secure objects above. The more the soul attached its love to higher objects, the more the intellect found its proper intelligible light, which was in the end God Himself. Of course, according to what had been said before, the ultimate confrontation with God and the real return of the soul to its intended light occurred only in the state of beatitude, so that the words of the last sentence of the passage actually referred to the long-term journey of the soul from this world to the next.[102] Grosseteste resorted to this literary acceleration simply to bring into greater relief the goal toward which the whole process tended and to cast back the shadow of the end on everything that came before. He was not constrained, nor was he concerned, to delineate every step along the road through life, death, and the final Resurrection. He did not even care to determine whether or not the mind actually found any more than a trace of God's light in this life. All he wanted to show was that however long it took and however many stages were required, the mind searching for truth was on its way to the blessed end in God.

Just like William of Auvergne, therefore, Grosseteste found a way to revitalize the notion of divine illumination by inserting it into a dynamic view of intellectual and ethical development. He thereby elevated the soul's efforts to find the worldly truth he had defined in the *Commentary* not by claiming they somehow involved seeing God, or the light of His Truth, but

---

[102] In a later work, his commentary on the Pseudo-Dionysian *De divinis nominibus,* Grosseteste reiterated his insistence on the distinction between the mental vision in his life, which had to be by forms and figures, and that in beatitude, where the soul could participate directly in the divine light. See the text from Chapter 1 of the commentary in Francis Ruello, "La *divinorum nominum reseratio* selon Robert Grossetête et Albert le Grand," *Archives d'Histoire Doctrinale et Littéraire du Moyen Age* 34 (1959), 153-55.

by asserting that they were a necesary stage in moral regeneration. In this way he armed himself with a strong defense against those who might have attacked his speculative efforts as unworthy of a serious Christian. But he also affirmed his faith that the most worldly operations of the human mind, if performed with an awareness of the end to which they tended, were capable of leading men to God. This was, indeed, what the image of an intelligible light, as Augustine had used it, was primarily intended to do. This was the theological argument Grosseteste had wanted to preserve.

VII

The Truth of Complex
Knowledge

===

IF GROSSETESTE'S examination of truth as it pertained to simple cognition constituted a signal achievement for his time, his
theory of the truth of complex knowledge made an even more
substantial contribution to the thirteenth-century discussion of
human understanding. Here again his innovative ideas appeared toward the end of his activity in the natural sciences.
Yet this time it appears that his mature views on the subject
did not so much replace or modify earlier ones, as had been the
case with simple truth, as fill what had been until then a lacuna
in his thought. It is not hard to understand why this should
have been so. Theological speculation of the sort involved in
Grosseteste's early treatises depended very little on a coherent
and critical notion of complex truth. In those works he was interested in truth as it provided evidence for God's presence in
the world, and for that purpose he did not have to go beyond
its simplest form. This did not prevent him from mentioning
complex truth, but it meant he did not have to examine it very
deeply. In those few places in *De veritate* where he turned to
the subject, he gave only cursory attention to the question of
the nature of such truth, totally ignoring the critical issue of
reference, and he made no comment at all on the way the mind
came to knowledge of it. When, on the other hand, it came to
establishing a system of scientific thought, the problem of
complex truth became a central concern and one that had to be

examined in some detail. Science was constructed from statements about reality, and they had to be ones that could be held
with certainty and identified as true. A theory of complex truth
that would fix the standards to be followed lay therefore at the
very heart of a scientific program.

Grosseteste devoted himself to scientific investigations beginning in the early 1220s, and his work on the problem of
identifying complex truth and describing how to attain it was
essentially a product of his interests in those years. It is likely
that his research in science prodded him on various occasions
to seek answers to different sides of the question and that he
only gradually brought all of them together into a coherent
doctrine. The culmination of the process appeared with his
Commentary on the Posterior Analytics. It is only with this work
that one can speak of an articulate theory of complex truth in
his thought, and this text must serve practically alone as the
basis for an examination of his ideas on the issue. In the *Commentary,* Grosseteste revealed his debt to Aristotle as well as the
independent force of his own intellect, able to proceed from
the inspiration it found in Aristotle's logic to the articulation
of a complicated theory that could appeal to contemporaries.
As might be expected, this theory shared fully in the character
of Grosseteste's intellectual outlook at the time. It is imbued
with the same preoccupation with the worldly foundations of
knowledge that had marked his later thought on the question
of simple truth.

I. THE NATURE OF COMPLEX TRUTH

Grosseteste, like William of Auvergne, viewed the truth that
pertained to complex knowledge as something quite different
from that of simple cognition. One had to explain it in completely new terms. Whereas simple truth was something that
attached to the object of knowledge, complex truth was,
loosely speaking, a quality of knowledge itself. Therefore, although one spoke of the knowledge of simple truth in the
same way one referred to the knowledge of horses or whiteness,

it was proper to talk about the truth of complex knowledge and, of course, its falsehood as well.

The distinction was so fundamental to Grosseteste's thought that it was apparent even in his early work, *De veritate*. In fact, it was in this work, where there is otherwise so little attention to complex truth, that he gave his only explicit formulation of the definition of complex truth. As he saw it, when men spoke of "truth," it was the truth that applied to complex cognition they most often had in mind—that is, the word "truth" commonly signified the truth of a statement or proposition (*oratio enuntiativa*).[1] He thought that this sort of truth was best described as a relation between two things. Unlike William of Auvergne, he did not expressly use the word "relation" on this occasion, but he did cite the traditional definition upon which such a view of truth was founded.[2] He claimed that he agreed with those who held that truth was an accommodation between language and reality (*adaequatio sermonis et rei*) or an adequation of the object to the intellect (*adaequatio rei ad intellectum*).[3] The way William of Auvergne interpreted this definition, the accommodation could be read either way, so that truth could be predicated of both the extremes, language and objective reality; and Grosseteste, too, made use of this double direction at other places for other kinds of truth.[4] When it came to complex knowledge, however, he apparently did not see the relation as symmetrical. Statements accommodated to things were true, but the truth of referents did not depend on any corresponding accommodation to statements. He added that the relation was firmest when it linked reality to the con-

---

[1] See above, Chapter V, n. 2.

[2] See below, n. 52, for an occasion where Grosseteste did use the term "relation" to describe a condition of truth.

[3] *De veritate* (*Phil. Werke,* p. 134). See also *De veritate propositionis* (*Phil. Werke,* p. 144). On the possible origin of this definition, see above, Chapter III, n. 11.

[4] For instance, see Grosseteste's discussion of the simple truth of things, *De veritate* (*Phil. Werke,* pp. 134–35), where he relied on the definition as an accommodation, this time between created things and the word of God.

ceptual language of the mind. Such a view rested on the assumption he held in common with many medieval thinkers that mental concepts referred immediately to their object, while spoken or written words pointed to external reality only indirectly, through their foundation in the intellect.[5] Consequently, complex truth in its purest state related mental propositions to external things.[6] For all practical purposes, however, any statement, whether existing in the mind or outside it, could be considered to have a relation with external reality and, depending on the nature of the bond, called true or false.

Of course, the Latin term in Grosseteste's definition, *adaequatio,* suggested as much some sort of equivalence as it did an accommodation. Grosseteste, like most thinkers at all influenced by Aristotle, recognized that it was impossible for there to be an exact equivalence between two things of such different natures as languages or concepts and objective reality, and so the truth relation had to be worked out in a way that made clear it was something less than identity. Like William of Auvergne, Grosseteste relied on the link between language and objects already established by his theory of semantics. If his readers understand how language referred to reality, then they could make the requisite transformation between the way things existed in themselves and the way they were implied in propositions. The accommodating nature of truth could then be described quite easily. The relation called truth was, as Aristotle had maintained, simply the condition that prevailed whenever the objective reality a statement referred to was exactly as that statement held it to be.[7]

[5] The idea can be traced back to Aristotle, *De interpretatione,* I, 1. Again, William differed with Grosseteste on this score, and he seems to have been unusual in his apparent reluctance to assign a priority in reference to either words or concepts. See above, Chapter II, n. 13 and Chapter III, n. 14.
[6] See *De veritate* (*Phil. Werke,* p. 134).
[7] "Et haec veritas, sicut dicit philosophus, non est aliud, quam ita esse in re signata, sicut dicit sermo." Ibid. See also *De veritate propositionis* (*Phil. Werke,* p. 144): "Haec autem adaequatio nihil aliud est, quam ita esse in re, sicut sermo vel opinio dicit...." In referring to Aristotle, Grosseteste seems to have had in mind *Metaphysics,* IV, 7. See above, Chapter III, n. 18.

Yet Grosseteste had another way of talking about this relation that expressed even more immediately the connection to
semantics. According to the principles of his thought, simple
concepts expressed the essence of their object without indicating whether or not their referent actually existed, while complex cognition revealed the state of existence. It described the
actual fact of the matter, either the simple being of a substance
or a complex set of circumstances. Consequently, complex cognition could be said to be true when it correctly indicated existence as it was in the real world. Put in more formal logical
terms, this meant that a proposition was true when it predicated being of that which actually existed and nonbeing of that
which did not.[8] Since this involved an accommodation of language to objective reality, it did not depart in principle from
the other definition. It did, however, allow Grosseteste to
speak of truth in another way: as the proper signification of
being.

2. REFERENCE IN COMPLEX KNOWLEDGE

When Grosseteste came to write his *Commentary on the Posterior
Analytics,* he could simply rely on the definitions of complex
truth he had given earlier in *De veritate*—those defining it
either as a relation of accommodation or as a signifier of being.
These notions had been borrowed in large part either directly
or indirectly from Aristotle and were therefore admirably
suited to the sort of speculation in which he was engaged in
the 1220s. Yet now he had to work out the particulars concerning the nature of such truth, and this in light of the problems posed by his interest in science. Here, there were matters
that could not have been treated in brief formal descriptions.

One aspect of the nature of complex truth he had not dealt
with adequately in his definitions was the matter of reference.

---

[8] "Veritas autem propositionis, a qua est propositio vera, nihil aliud
est, quam significatio esse de eo, quod est, vel non esse de eo, quod non
est." *De veritate* (*Phil. Werke*, p. 143). Grosseteste drew this language almost verbatim from Anselm, *De veritate*, 2 (Schmitt, ed., *Opera omnia*, I,
178).

While the problem of how words referred to objects under the conditions of complex truth overlapped with the corresponding problem in the case of simple cognition, the two were not precisely the same. The simple words and concepts making up propositions still referred to simple substances and qualities, yet there were additional aspects of reference introduced just by the fact that the words were combined into sentences. Complex knowledge referred as much to states of being and to context as it did to essence alone. A theory of reference adequate to complex truth had to explain under what conditions a true statement could be said to hold as well as what actual objects it should be taken to signify. The problem was complicated even further by the question of immutable or eternal truth. Grosseteste had in fact raised the issue early on in a passage in *De veritate,* where he asked about the eternal foundations of certain special propositions.[9] On that occasion he implied that some true statements had to refer and thereby relate to something divine in order for their truth to have the supertemporal characteristics it required. By the time of the *Commentary* his answer had become more explicit and more complicated and, of course, had taken on a somewhat different philosophical cast.

A. The Types of Complex Truth

In order to deal with the problem of reference as it pertained to complex truth, Grosseteste had to make a careful distinction among the levels of complex knowledge the mind could attain. Just as in the case of simple cognition, where he differentiated among the ways the mind could know universals, so here his classification depended on both the nature of the object and the way the intellect seized it. According to the *Commentary on the Posterior Analytics,* there were three mental dispositions or states of understanding that had to do with complex truth. They were *intellectus, scientia,* and *opinio.*[10]

---

[9] *De veritate* (*Phil. Werke,* pp. 139–41).

[10] *Comm. Post. an.,* I, 19 (p. 282, ll. 95–96). The idea that there were three basic states of mind that concerned complex truth came from Aristotle himself, and Grosseteste lifted the three names by which he identified them directly from the Latin translation of the *Posterior Analytics,* I,

Opinion was the weakest of the ways the mind could grasp the truth. There were, however, three different ways to use the word "opinion."[11] Broadly speaking (*dicta communiter*), opinion was just knowledge with assent—that is, it was the state of holding that something was true. Grosseteste explained that another term for this first sort of opinion was *"fides,"* and it was in fact a category so general that it included all forms of complex knowledge, whether held with certainty or not. Properly speaking (*proprie dicta*), opinion involved accepting something as true, presumably with some evidence, but without being absolutely certain about it. If one held an opinion of this second sort, one could not be free of some doubt (*timor, suspicio*) that the contrary was in fact the case. All kinds of truths could be known in this way, both those that were necesary and those that were not, although knowing a necessary truth with the force of opinion proper meant that one did not know it as necessary.[12] In its strictest sense (*magis proprie dicta*), opinion was assent to the evident truth of a contingent fact. Opinion of this third sort could not be held of a necessary truth, for it involved recognizing the contingency of the fact that was known.[13] This was the narrowest and the weakest of the three

---

33 (see the translation by James of Venice in Aristoteles Latinus, IV, 1-4, ed. Minio-Paluello and Dod, p. 65).

Grosseteste normally used the word *habitus* as Aristotle did to mean simply a mental disposition or state of understanding (see, for instance, n. 15 below), and this is how it is translated here and generally throughout this work. Occasionally, however, he spoke as if the different *habitus* were powers of the mind. For the most part this involved nothing more than transferring the name of a cognitive configuration to the intellectual potential that underlay it, as when Grosseteste referred to *intellectus* as a power of mind that was somehow responsible for the knowledge of principles (see below, n. 20). Sometimes, however, Grosseteste was willing to stretch the meaning of the term even further, as when he called quick wit (*sollertia*) a *habitus*. Here, there was no question of associating a potential with a definite configuration; quick wit was the power to perform a process and not the psychological counterpart to a cognitive state. This ambiguity in the use of the word is the same as that found in William of Auvergne.

[11] *Comm. Post. an.,* I, 19 (pp. 278-79, ll. 16-29).

[12] See *Comm. Post. an.,* I, 19 (p. 282, ll. 99-101). On opinion properly speaking, see also above in Chapter VI, 2.

[13] See *Comm. Post. an.,* I, 19 (p. 282, ll. 97-99).

categories of opinion, for it excluded any kind of knowledge of a necessary truth. It was, however, the most precise; it made clear that the level of assent attained was the best that could be expected given the nature of the subject known.

The *opinio* Grosseteste had specifically in mind when he listed the three ways to know the truth, and indeed the meaning he thought Aristotle had intended when he used the word in his *Posterior Analytics,* included both the second and the third ways of speaking about it: properly and more properly. As was clear from common parlance, the hallmark of this sort of knowledge was that it was not certain (*non certa*).[14] Whether this uncertainty arose from the object or from the way the mind apprehended it, it always came down to the same epistemological failing. The logical quality of opinion—that it did not seize truth with the firmness of higher sorts of knowledge—derived from the fact that the mind had apprehended its object through material conditions. In contrast, when the mind had certain knowledge of complex truth, it saw things in the purity of their essence.[15]

Opinion was therefore to be regarded as a source of intellectual error. The problem was clearest in the case of opinion properly so called. There the mind might judge a condition that was in itself necessary according to the contingent material accidents by which it had come to be perceived. Under such circumstances it was highly likely that reason would make a mistake.[16] As Grosseteste said, the intellect that could arrive at no more than this kind of knowledge about some proposition was like an infected eye that could not clearly see what it was looking at.[17] Yet either sort of opinion, properly or more properly so called, exhibited the same fundamental weakness. Opinions were *habitus* that the mind developed virtually indiscriminately about complex ideas. Unlike higher states of intellection, they provided no reliable criteria by which to distinguish between

---

[14] *Comm. Post. an.,* I, 19 (p. 282, ll. 101–6).
[15] *Comm. Post. an.,* II, 6 (pp. 406–7, ll. 80–88). See also *Comm. Post. an.,* I, 19 (p. 280, ll. 65–67).
[16] See *Comm. Post. an.,* I, 19 (p. 280, ll. 47–65).
[17] Ibid.

truth and falsehood.[18] They were consequently of no value for science, and they contributed nothing positive to Grosseteste's critical theory of complex truth. Indeed, he took little interest in opinion or the problem of how it was formed.

In order to be able to discriminate with certainty between truth and falsehood, one had to turn to the higher states of understanding, *intellectus* and *scientia.* These two *habitus* directed the mind to the essential nature of things and could be formed only about necessary truth.[19] Here, Grosseteste had in mind precisely those two states of mind as they had been described by Aristotle. He explained it was by *intellectus* that the mind grasped a complex truth without having recourse to any middle term, while in the case of *scientia* it achieved true knowledge only after reasoning through a middle.[20] This meant that even though both involved certain knowledge, *intellectus* was unique in being immediate, arrived at without the use of the discursive powers of the mind. What is more, the object of *intellectus* was of a kind that necessitated this immediate procedure. It was something in itself visible to the intellect, first among the objects of understanding (*primum et per se visibile interius*).[21] In short, *intellectus* was, as Aristotle would have said, evident apprehension of the principles of science. It was a higher form of cognition than any other normal act of the human mind. More immediate than *scientia,* it was also more certain.[22] Since all other knowledge of complex truth was derived from it, it could itself be called the principle or basis of scientific cognition (*principium scientie et principium principiis*).[23]

Scientia, or reasoned knowledge of complex truths, was a more complicated matter to explain. One problem was that in

[18] *Comm. Post. an.,* I, 19 (p. 282, ll. 96–97). See also above, n. 15.
[19] See above, n. 15.
[20] *Comm. Post. an.,* II, 6 (p. 406, ll. 76–79).
[21] *Comm. Post. an.,* I, 19 (p. 279, ll. 37–38). I have suggested that the punctuation of this text be amended from Rossi's reading. See above, Chapter VI, n. 73.
[22] *Comm. Post. an.,* II, 6 (pp. 406–7, ll. 79–98). See also *Comm. Post. an.,* I, 2 (p. 103, ll. 91–93), and I, 19 (p. 278, ll. 3–7). In fact, knowledge of principles was the most certain form of cognition. See *Comm. Post. an.,* II, 6 (p. 403, ll. 10–13).
[23] *Comm. Post. an.,* I, 19 (p. 281, ll. 89–91), and II, 6 (p. 407, ll. 98–99).

its broadest sense, the word "to know" (*scire*) included any apprehension of the truth. In order to show what was special about science according to a stricter usage of the term, one had to introduce distinctions. Grosseteste identified four ways to use the word.

It should be no secret to us that one can use [the words] "to know" (*scire*) in a general way and properly and more [properly] and most properly. For knowledge (*scientia*) generally speaking is the comprehension of truth, and irregular contingent events (*contingentia erratica*) are known in this way. And knowledge properly speaking is the comprehension of the truth of those things that always or quite frequently (*frequentius*) happen in one way, and natural [events]—that is, natural but contingent [events] (*naturalia, scilicet contingentia nata*)—are known in this manner. Of [the truth of] these events there can be demonstration, in a general sense of the word. Now, knowledge more properly speaking is the comprehension of the truth of those things that always happen in one way, and in this manner are known not only the conclusions but also the principles of mathematics. Yet since truth is that which is (*illud quod est*) and the comprehension of the truth is the comprehension of that which is, and furthermore since the being of something that depends on something else cannot be understood except through the being of that thing on which it depends, it is clear that knowledge (*scire*) most properly speaking is the comprehension of something immutable through the comprehension of that thing from which it gets its immutable being, and this is through the comprehension of that cause which is immutable in being and in causing. Therefore, to know (*scire*) simply and most properly speaking is to understand (*cognoscere*) the immutable cause of a thing in itself—immutable, that is, in causing. And with respect to this sort of knowledge, Aristotle calls all other ways of knowing sophistical and [knowledge] only in a manner of speaking. And this kind of knowledge is the most specific goal of this science [of the *Posterior Analytics*], and it is acquired through demonstration in the strictest sense of the word.[24]

---

[24] *Comm. Post. an.*, I, 2 (pp. 99-100, ll. 9-27). Crombie has translated this same passage in *Robert Grosseteste*, pp. 58-59. His version is essentially the same as the one given here, except that he mistakenly interprets "this

Grosseteste had arranged his four categories of knowledge in order of increasing specificity. The first and broadest consisted in complex knowledge pure and simple, limited only by the stipulation that it be true. This set knowledge in general against opinion properly speaking, which could be of things both true and false. In other words, knowledge in the broadest sense involved the first and most basic degree of certainty. One could not "know" a complex something unless one knew for certain it was true. Intellection at this lowest and broadest level of complex comprehension extended to the knowledge of contingent events of single and chance occurrence—this is what it meant to say it could be about erratic contingents—and so it included the category of opinion defined most strictly. Because of this, this first category of knowledge went beyond science in any proper sense of the word. According to the laws of Aristotle's logic that Grosseteste was following, demonstration was the sole basis for scientific understanding, and he recognized that there could be no demonstration of any chance event.[25]

Above the lowest level, one could begin to speak of science in some proper sense of the word, and the degree of propriety varied according to the strictness of the criteria for certitude. The second category, scientific thought properly speaking, was knowledge of facts or events that were either always the same or quite frequently so. This meant that the truth of proposi-

---

science" in the last sentence to be metaphysics. From the beginning statements of the chapter in which this passage occurs, it is clear that Grosseteste was trying to elucidate the end or goal of the science treated in the work he was commenting on, and this was the logical science of analytics. He explicitly referred to "the science Aristotle intends to teach in this book," and he said that it was proper for Aristotle to begin his discussion of that science with its definition. Since the definition most suitable for Aristotle's purposes was the definition drawn from the end of the thing, it was appropriate for him to identify this end, which in this case was knowledge (*scientia*) itself. What Grosseteste meant when he called his fourth level of knowledge "the most specific end of this science" was that it was the final goal toward which the science of analytics was directed—that is, fully certain and demonstrative cognition.

[25] On demonstration and science, see *Comm. Post. an.,* I, 1 (pp. 93-94, ll. 2-25), and I, 2 (p. 100, ll. 29-40). On the nondemonstrability of chance events, see *Comm. Post. an.,* I, 18 (pp. 264-65, ll. 115-32).

tions about them was more or less invariable. Because this kind of understanding included knowledge of propositions that were true only in most instances, not always, it could not be science in a strict sense. Grosseteste allowed that such propositions could be proved true by demonstration, but demonstration only in a manner of speaking, and therefore not strictly scientific. He called the complex objects that could be known in this way natural contingent events.

The third level narrowed the focus to knowledge of events that invariably held the same way. This was, then, the area of strictly immutable, and necessary, truth. Grosseteste had to stretch the definition of science for his third category, since in it he included knowledge of the principles as well as the conclusions of scientific thought. Knowledge of principles was not science strictly defined as reasoned or demonstrated knowledge of the truth but rather *intellectus,* immediate comprehension of those truths that could not be proved in any way. Yet Grosseteste was willing to admit that one could be said to "know" (*scire*) principles if the word "know" were taken in a broad way (*communiter*).[26] It made sense to do so here, for principles made up a significant number of the truths that accounted for science and they fit quite well into the pyramid of levels of intellectual assent Grosseteste had in mind.

The fourth level constituted science according to its strictest Aristotelian definition. This was knowledge of a necessary and immutable conclusion by means of knowledge of its immutable cause. In other words, it was reasoned knowledge, properly demonstrated through a middle term referring to something that invariably, or immutably, caused the object or condition described by the conclusion to be the way it was. As Grosseteste said, it was the primary purpose of the *Posterior Analytics* to show how to attain this kind of knowledge, science strictly and most properly speaking.

Thus, among the kinds of complex cognition discussed in this description of the four levels of *scientia,* there were actually

---

[26] *Comm. Post. an.,* I, 3 (p. 106, ll. 24–30).

only two that were not more properly denominated by some other technical term, such as *opinio* or *intellectus.* They were knowledge of natural contingent events and demonstrated knowledge of immutable truths, the peculiar ingredients of the second and fourth levels. These were, in fact, the only two that constituted science strictly speaking, as Aristotle had originally conceived it, and they were what Grosseteste had in mind whenever he used the word *scientia* in a technical sense. In order to understand them fully and to see how they differed it is necessary to look more closely at both the objects to which they could apply and the kind of demonstration appropriate to each.[27]

It is easier to begin with the mode of demonstration. Grosseteste's highest category, his fourth level of science, fit Aristotle's model of demonstrative science best.[28] According to the strict principles of Aristotelian logic, demonstration consisted in syllogizing from necessary premises to necessary conclusions.[29] This meant syllogizing with premises and conclusions referring to conditions or natures that could not be other than they were—that were in themselves immutable—for this is what it was to be necessary.[30] Now demonstration in its simplest and most perfect form depended on finding a middle term from which to construct the premises proving the conclusion, and Grosseteste held that the proper middle for scientific demonstration was the cause expressed by the object's defini-

---

[27] Grosseteste held that these were the two sources for the differences in certitude among the sciences: the form of demonstration and the nature of the cognitive object. See *Comm. Post. an.,* II, 6 (p. 408, ll. 112-14).

[28] This is not only the explicit conclusion of the passage given above, n. 24, but also what Grosseteste said in interpreting Aristotle in *Comm. Post. an.,* I, 4 (p. 110, ll. 24-26): ". . . 'what is according to demonstrative science' (that is, that to which demonstrative science applies) 'is necessarily knowable (*scibile*)' (that is, knowable simply and most properly)."

[29] See *Comm. Post. an.,* I, 4 (pp. 109-10), and I, 6 (pp. 129-31). On Aristotle's full criteria for demonstrative science, see Jonathan Barnes, "Aristotle's Theory of Demonstration," *Articles on Aristotle,* I: Science, eds. Jonathan Barnes, Malcolm Schofield, and Richard Sorabji (London, 1975), pp. 65-87.

[30] See, for instance, *Comm. Post. an.,* I, 4 (p. 109, ll. 15-16).

tion—that is, the formal cause.[31] If the object were immutable, or perhaps just understood as universal, then its formal cause would be immutable too, necessarily and unchangeably associated with it as cause to effect. For Grosseteste, therefore, the paradigm of scientific demonstration was to prove a conclusion through a middle term that expressed the formal nature of the object to be understood. And these were precisely the stipulations he set down for the fourth and highest level of scientific thought. His words had been that science most strictly construed was knowledge of something immutable through the understanding of the immutable cause of its being. By "immutable cause" he did not mean some higher substance but rather the universal principle that defined the object and made it, immutably, what it was. To know something through such a cause was to know a necessary proposition concerning some immutable essence or condition through premises that expressed its formal or essential nature.[32]

Naturally, science of this sort entailed knowing a conclusion through its proximate cause. And this was, as Grosseteste explained, technically called knowledge of the reasoned fact (*propter quid*).

Therefore science acquired by demonstration either is acquired through the proximate cause of the thing known or it is acquired through a cause of the thing known that is not proximate. Now that science which is acquired through the proximate cause is called science of the reasoned fact (*propter quid*), and this is science most strongly and most properly so called. Moreover, the demonstration by which such science is acquired is demonstration most strictly speaking.[33]

[31] *Comm. Post. an.,* I, 13 (p. 201, ll. 44–60).

[32] Neither Crombie nor Palma have interpreted Grosseteste's remarks about knowledge through the immutable cause and demonstration in the strictest sense in this way. Yet considering all else Grosseteste said about the methods of logical argument, it seems there is no other way to read him consistently. Grosseteste himself stated that demonstration properly so called was demonstration of incorruptible propositions, in contrast to the weaker demonstration of predictable contingencies. See *Comm. Post. an.,* I, 18 (p. 265, ll. 126–29).

[33] *Comm. Post. an.,* I, 12 (p. 189, ll. 23–27).

In purely formal terms, knowledge of the reasoned fact usually depended on the first mode of the first figure of Aristotle's syllogistic logic.[34] One could, in sum, have science in the highest degree only when one had demonstrated the scientific conclusion from premises drawn from the proximate, formal cause and when the demonstrative syllogism followed Aristotle's first figure.

If it was a relatively simple matter to explain the most proper kind of science, given the standards of demonstrative logic, the same was not the case when it came to science that applied to natural contingent events. The difficulty here was that the rules of demonstration would seem to have prohibited any scientific knowledge whatsoever of contingent truths. Grosseteste himself had said that there were just two classes of complex truth, contingent and necessary, and that it was from necessary truth alone that one could construct a demonstration.[35] He was able to escape this dilemma and make a place for a science of contingent truths only by allowing for demonstration in a weakened form.

This weaker demonstration depended on a necessity lower, or lesser, than that involved in demonstration of the strictest sort. As he explained, there was a degree of necessity in some types of continguent event—those with a kind of predictability greater than chance. This was called natural necessity (*necessitas naturalis*), and it stood opposed to the simple necessity (*necessitas simpliciter*) of conditions or events that were immutable, always holding in one way.[36] The conditions or events possessing natural necessity were all natural occurrences (*res naturales, contingentia nata*) that followed the sort of regularity often found in the world of nature, less rigid than the absolute invariability of events subject to necessary truth in the strictest sense. Such occurrences were, of course, still contingent, but they could be expected to turn out according to an established pattern unless prevented by some accidental impediment. In

[34] *Comm. Post. an.,* I, 13 (pp. 199–200, ll. 20–21 and 38–39).
[35] *Comm. Post. an.,* I, 4 (p. 110, ll. 31–34).
[36] *Comm. Post. an.,* I, 18 (pp. 264–65, ll. 119–24).

scholastic parlance, they were said to happen frequently (*frequenter*).

Upon natural necessity Grosseteste established his weaker form of demonstration, and out of this he built the notion of a science of natural, nonimmutable phenomena.[37] There were, in fact, two ways he did this, and for both of them he drew upon suggestions in the text of Aristotle. On the one hand, he worked out a variant to strict demonstration of the reasoned fact, dependent not on the necessity that the conclusion refer to a condition or event that always held but rather on the possibility of specifying the conditions under which the conclusion would be invariably true.[38] On the other hand, he explained that even in those cases where it was not possible to give such *propter quid* demonstration, one could sometimes provide demonstration through a middle that was not the proximate cause. This constituted, in contrast to a science of the reasoned fact, science of the fact (*scientia quia*), and it worked *per posterius* by using as a middle, instead of the formal cause, the result or another cause that was more remote.[39] It thereby established the truth of a fact without explaining why it was so. For all their weaknesses both forms of demonstration permitted science in many fields of thought where the unaided human mind could not attain to the height of scientific certitude in its strictest sense.

Yet Grosseteste's division among the sciences did not rest solely on the kind of demonstration attained in each, for this variation itself was connected with distinctions among the real objects to which the demonstrations were applied. Here the theory of two basic levels of science linked up with an old and

[37] See *Comm. Post. an.,* I, 18 (p. 265, ll. 126–30).

[38] See below, nn. 62 and 64.

[39] *Comm. Post. an.,* I, 12 (pp. 188–90). Grosseteste's description of *scientia quia* was taken straight from the text of Aristotle upon which he was commenting—*Posterior Analytics,* I, 13. It is interesting to note that later, in a sermon that Servus Gieben dates around the year 1240, Grosseteste called this kind of knowledge of events that happen frequently not science but art. See Gieben, "Robert Grosseteste on Preaching," *Collectanea Franciscana* 37 (1967), 139.

established tradition of the schools. He maintained that the sciences available without revelation could be divided into two sorts: *rationales* and *doctrinales*. The doctrinal sciences were more certain than the rational ones, and the reason was that in them alone there could be demonstration in the strictest sense. In the others, one could demonstrate a conclusion only in a certain way of speaking, reasoning rationally (*rationaliter*) and according to less than absolutely demonstrative argument (*probabiliter*) rather than scientifically (*scientifice*).[40] In other words, these were essentially the same two categories discussed so far. Now, however, one can see exactly what kinds of things could be known in each, and here there were some inclusions for which the reader might be unprepared. The specific sciences Grosseteste had in mind were, for doctrinal science, mathematics alone, by which he most likely meant to include the whole medieval quadrivium; and for rational sciences not only natural science but also logic insofar as it was a true science and not an art, metaphysics, and ethics.[41] The division is, in general outline, precisely the same as that found in William of Auvergne, and it had been known in the West since the days of Boethius.[42] Grosseteste differed only slightly in his terminology, in part because he stuck rather closely to the text of Aristotle, which suggested a distinction between *doctrinae* and *rationes*.[43]

The reason Grosseteste had seen fit to expand the rational sciences—those with weaker than perfect demonstration—beyond the natural sciences alone had to do with the imperfect way the mind came to know things in this world. For here below, several kinds of objects in themselves far above materiality were received by the mind only through the senses and had, therefore, to be treated in demonstrative argument essen-

[40] *Comm. Post. an.,* I, 11 (pp. 178–79, ll. 109–42).
[41] Same as above, n. 40, and also *Comm. Post. an.,* I, 12 (p. 188, ll. 12–16).
[42] See above, Chapter III, n. 56.
[43] See *Posterior Analytics,* I, 12 (77b27–33) (Aristoteles Latinus, IV, 1–4, ed. Minio-Paluello and Dod, p. 28).

tially the same as the material objects of natural philosophy. Metaphysics, for example, fell among the lower sciences in this classification, although Grosseteste clearly did not think this was its proper place in the absolute scheme of things. For him metaphysics, which he also called divine science, was about subjects just as immutable as those of mathematics and just as capable of being ordered into a science in the strictest sense of the word.[44] In fact, were man able to regain the original brilliance of his intellect, he would know divine things the most immediately of all objects of his reason, and metaphysics would thereby become the most certain science of all. It was the Fall that had clouded man's reason and made it such that under normal circumstances it was mathematics, which properly depended on the corporeal imagination, that was the most immediate and most certain subject of speculation.[45] Logic, too, deserved a higher place than mathematics, due to the more abstracted nature of its subject, and again only the fallen state of the mind accounted for its relative obscurity in this life. Among all the rational sciences, natural science alone was lower than mathematics because of the nature of its subject, which was fully material and not amenable to any more certain understanding than it normally received.[46] It was, therefore, the science that provided the paradigm for demonstration of the weaker sort.

B. Grosseteste's Theory of Reference

Although Grosseteste had sketched out a complicated array of states of knowledge, from the weakest (opinion) to the highest (doctrinal science), only three basic levels were pertinent to the problem of reference in complex knowledge of the truth: the apprehension of simple contingents, and the two classes of properly scientific knowledge—rational science and demonstrative science pure and simple. Opinion was too low to be included, while *intellectus,* the remaining major category, simply duplicated the referential conditions of the demon-

---

[44] *Comm. Post. an.,* I, 18 (p. 264, ll. 119–22).
[45] See *Comm. Post. an.,* I, 17 (pp. 256–57, ll. 344–65).
[46] See *Comm. Post. an.,* I, 11 (p. 179, ll. 130–37).

strated propositions constituting science of the strictest sort. Both related the mind to a complex object that was immutably and necessarily true.

Grosseteste's task was to show where to locate the complex referent of a true proposition in time and space.[47] The first case, that of simple contingents of chance occurrence or what he called *contingentia erratica,* never actually received his explicit attention. Propositions about such contingent events could be verified by the evidence of sense perception, and this made them more reliable than mere opinions. Yet such propositions could never be known with the certainty of scientific understanding, for the condition they referred to was not necessary in any sense of the word nor could its truth be confirmed by even the weakest sort of demonstration. What is more, statements of simple contingent fact were, by their nature, not universal; all their terms had to be singular. It is not surprising, therefore, that a thinker with Grosseteste's scientific predilections should have taken little interest in them.

Despite his silence on the issue, however, it is not hard to imagine how he would have decided the questions of time and space for the reference of such propositions had he chosen to do so. Although he leaned toward a theory of the indirect cognition of singular objects, in the present case it actually made no difference whether the mind related to individuals directly or indirectly.[48] What a singular concept referred to did not depend ultimately on the means by which the mind arrived at such knowledge but rather on the final object it attained, and Grosseteste never wavered in his insistence that the real object of a singular concept was an individual substance in the world of creation. Since propositions about contingent events of chance occurrence were made up exclusively of terms representing such concepts, their reference had to be a complex con-

[47] This was essentially the same problem as had faced Grosseteste when he considered the reference of simple concepts. For universals, of course, the complex referent had to be shown to exist somehow always and everywhere.

[48] For Grosseteste's views on how the mind seized particular objects, see above, Chapter VI, n. 22.

figuration of substantial beings in external reality. Furthermore, the propositions themselves, since they each referred to a single event, necessarily specified time and place, if not explicitly then indirectly through the circumstances of their use. The specificity and particularity of simple contingents therefore predetermined their referential limits. A proposition on this first level of knowledge was true when and if it expressed the relation that held among a group of real, individual objects at a definite time and in a particular place.

Above the level of simple contingency the problem of reference in true knowledge became more complicated. Both kinds of complex knowledge that made up science proper were universal. In part this meant nothing more than that the propositions of science had to be composed of universal simple terms, and to this extent the conditions of reference in scientific knowledge were adequately accounted for by Grosseteste's theory of the reference of universals in simple cognition. The terms going into propositions known to be scientifically true each distributed over a general class of real individuals, all existing at some time in the created world. The referents of scientific knowledge were therefore located in reality just as the individual referents of contingent propositions, with the difference that the range of time and space was much wider. Yet this simple explanation in fact obscures a real difficulty that invariably arose in explaining the temporal foundation for universality. Universals had to exist in a way that simple individuals did not. As Grosseteste showed in his theory of simple universals, one had to find a way of making clear how they could be said "always" to be. In the case of complex truths the task was doubly hard because one was dealing not only with discrete units of reality, the essences, but also with the complex conditions in which they were involved.

According to Grosseteste, for scientific truths to be universal they had to be purely and simply perpetual (*simpliciter perpetua*), which is to say that their truth had to be incorruptible.[49]

---

[49] See *Comm. Post. an.,* I, 7 (p. 139, ll. 88-95).

Such language suggests the problem of eternal truth in much the way it had been traditionally approached in the Middle Ages and as it initially appeared in William of Auvergne's handling of the truth of scientific propositions. Yet as was the case with Grosseteste's stand on the incorruptibility of simple universals, his notion of the perpetuity of necessary truth was different from anything imagined in such a traditional view.

The key to Grosseteste's ideas on this subject can be found in one of his early theological treatises, *De scientia Dei*. In that work he explained that there were two kinds of perpetuity, or as he said, two ways something could be said to exist incessantly (*incessanter esse*). One of these was for the thing to exist throughout all eternity (*in simplicitate aeternitatis esse*); the other, for it to exist throughout all time (*in omni tempore esse*). Another way of making the same distinction was to say that perpetual being could be measured either by the standard of infinite eternity (*mensuratio aeternitatis infinitae*) or that of the totality of time (*mensuratio a temporis totalitate*).[50] The division rested on a commonly accepted differentiation between the all-encompassing present of God's eternity, above time and incapable of being determined by it, and the sequential sweep of all time, where there was truly a before and after and where some things could be said to endure longer than others, some even forever.

These two different sorts of perpetuity were attached to two distinct forms of necessity or necessary truth. First there was the necessity that inhered in the very being and nature of a thing. Grosseteste called this "antecedent necessity" (*necessitas antecedens*), since it predetermined the way a thing or condition would be. It was the sort of necessity that one found in the laws of nature, and as an example Grosseteste cited the inevitability of solar and lunar motion that brought about an eclipse. Another example he could have given was the essential truth that man was a rational animal. If something were true by this sort of necessity, then it would have to be true for all time, be-

---

[50] *De scientia Dei* (*Phil. Werke*, p. 146).

cause its truth would be embedded in the very nature of reality. The second kind of necessity was the sort that followed the existence of a thing—what Grosseteste called "consequent necessity" (*necessitas consequens*). It was this kind of necessity that existed for all events of past occurrence once they had in fact occurred. This type, however, in contrast to antecedent necessity, could not be said to put any fetters on the being or nature of a thing, for any thing or condition would have been what it was or would come to be what it would come to be without any reference to this sort of necessity after the fact.[51] All things necessary by the first kind of necessity were also necessary in this way, but this second category included in addition a whole new class of subjects that could never be said to involve any natural necessity in the real world. In particular Grosseteste mentioned God's knowledge of future contingents, which was necessarily true but which did nothing to prejudice the theoretical possibility that the events to which it referred would never occur. He noted that truths dependent on this sort of necessity, although they were not invariably true over all time, possessed nevertheless their own sort of perpetuity. They could be said to be perpetually true in the simplicity of God's eternity.

Grosseteste's theory, by providing him with two ways to talk about the perpetuity of truth—eternal or over all time—allowed him to resolve the problem of the incorruptibility of universal truths without having to call upon the notion of eternity or of knowledge in God. All truths, of any sort, insofar as they were known by God, were true in the simplicity of God's eternity. Yet this was not a statement about the nature of things or the character of true knowledge in general but rather an explanation of what it was for God to know something. On the other hand, only those special truths having to do with the laws of nature, or even more those concerning the

---

[51] Ibid. Grosseteste's ideas about antecedent and consequent necessity are practically identical with those of Anselm in *Cur deus homo*, II, 17 (Schmitt, ed., *Opera omnia*, II [Rome, 1940], p. 125). One source for the distinction may be Boethius, *Philosophiae consolatio*, V, pros. 6 (Bieler, ed., pp. 103-4).

laws of logic and mathematics, held over all time. Thus these truths were special not because of the nature of the knowing subject but because of the kind of objective condition to which they referred. They were the truths that made up science. Now in *De veritate,* Grosseteste had spoken of eternal, complex truths, and he had traced their eternity back to the eternity of ideas in the mind of God.[52] But in doing this he had provided no explanation for the special temporal qualities of scientific truth, which had to be true not just in God but also in the world, for all time. For perpetuity of this sort Grosseteste needed another explanation, and it was only in the *Commentary on the Posterior Analytics* that he provided it.

At the very top of the structure of science came scientific thought most strictly speaking, consisting of propositions that were true without exception or variation. Given the circumstances of normal human cognition on earth, this category was comprised exclusively of the doctrinal or mathematical sciences, which included truths like the arithmetical verity that seven plus three equals ten and the conclusion of geometry that the sum of all the angles of a triangle is equal to two right angles.[53] Metaphysics would have been a part of most proper science had Adam not fallen, and it apparently would return to its place of pre-eminence after the Resurrection, when men regained their intended intellectual powers. In the present, however, its truths could not be held with the certainty required

[52] *De veritate* (*Phil. Werke,* pp. 139-41). It is interesting to note that in this discussion of complex eternal truth Grosseteste employed an explanatory device also found in the work of William of Auvergne. In order to show how the relation that constituted eternal truth did not demand the eternal existence of the objective correlative—the referent of God's knowledge—he pointed to the fact that not all relations required the simultaneous existence of all the related terms. Certain *"passiones"*—corresponding to what William would call "passive predications" (see above, Chapter III, n. 28)—held true even when there was no subject to receive the quality by which they were designated. Thus, Caesar could be praised eternally, even though he lived only the span of a normal human life.

[53] Both these examples are propositions that Grosseteste mentioned at one time or another. See *De veritate* (*Phil. Werke,* p. 140), and above, Chapter VI, n. 50.

for this highest degree. For the purposes of a theory of reference, the principles of science had also to be included in this
general category of the most certain complex objects of human
thought. Although they were not scientific at all in the true
sense of the word, they were held with as much certainty as the
most carefully demonstrated formulas of mathematics, and
they exhibited an equally rigid necessity. Grosseteste himself
had lumped such truths together with fully demonstrated
propositions in his third category of knowledge, science more
properly speaking. Included among the principles of science
were all immediate propositions about the natures of things,
such as statements drawn from unshakable definitions, and
most of the fundamental truths of demonstrative logic.

When it came to explaining how the highest truths of science and first principles reflected objective conditions that were
somehow perpetual or incorruptible, Grosseteste could merely
turn to his theory of perpetuity among the universal objects of
simple cognition. This was because the propositions expressing
these highest truths all referred to the essential nature of their
subjects, and so the invariability of their truth was a direct
function of the invariability of essential reasons. It will be remembered that Grosseteste had explained the incorruptibility
of simple universals in two ways.[54] The universal nature always
remained the same either because, as a logical entity, it was un-
affected by the normal corruptions of time or because, as a real
entity, it was constantly being replenished by the succession of
individuals within a species. Clearly, the perpetuity Grosseteste
was aiming at did not extend beyond the limits of time. And if
one thinks carefully about his distinction between perpetuity
in eternity and perpetuity in all time, it is easy to see how this
says nothing about the question of the eternity of the world.
No matter how long or how briefly the world existed, the species that populated it would be perpetual so long as they maintained a continuous succession throughout its complete existence. Truths referring to the essential characteristics of such
species would likewise be perpetual. The whole question was

[54] See above, Chapter VI, 3.

independent of whether the world and such true relations were never-ending or limited by a definite beginning and end.

After the highest and most rigorous kind of complex knowledge came the truths of rational science, Grosseteste's second and lower category of *scientia*. Although metaphysics, logic as a science, and ethics fell under this rubric for the duration of man's journey through the world of sin, it was natural science that constituted its pre-eminent type. The truths of natural science were by their very nature suited to the less conclusive kind of demonstration that characterized this weaker form of scientific thought.

Just as in the case of the higher sciences, propositions at this level of complex thought were composed of universal terms referring directly to real things in the world. In contrast, however, they did not typically reveal the nature of simple essences but instead reported or explained more complicated conditions, usually events occurring regularly enough (*frequenter*) to be scientifically predictable and thus reducible to laws of nature. In general, these laws were of two kinds. On the one hand were the laws of nature that worked continuously unless impeded by some accidental object, like the rules that the natural motion of earth was downward toward its proper sphere while that of fire was upward beyond the sphere of air. On the other hand were laws that described what would happen whenever the circumstances were right, such as the fact that an eclipse would occur whenever the moon, earth, and sun were correctly positioned. In either case the referent of the proposition stating the law could not be reduced merely to the several simple universal objects that were the referents of its separate terms. The propositional referent had also to include the configuration or event that related the simple objects.

Strictly speaking, these configurations or events were contingent, despite the fact that they followed the laws of nature. Sometimes the real objects would not be arranged in the required configuration or behave in the way prescribed. Earth could be prevented from falling, and eclipses were not always occurring. Yet at such times there would be no real particular referent—that is, no complete one. Given Grosseteste's theory of the immanence of universals, this meant that at these times there would not be any complete universal referent either.[55] Clearly, propositions that referred to such impermanent complex objects were significantly different from higher scientific truths, whose reference was to unchanging essential natures, and it would seem that the incorruptibility of their truth could not be accounted for in precisely the same terms, merely by referring back to the perpetuity of universals. Yet in order to qualify as scientific these propositions still had to be true perpetually. The problem was to find some way to identify a referential base, even at times when there actually was no specific referent, so that the inviolability of such truths could be preserved.

Grosseteste said that Aristotle offered a solution to this dilemma in his *Posterior Analytics,* although he admitted that it was not easy to understand what Aristotle's brief remarks on the subject actually meant.[56] He suggested that there were two ways Aristotle's confidence in the feasibility of this lower science, and especially the science of nature, could be defended. Following Aristotle, he took as an example the natural law concerning an eclipse of the moon. One way to provide a perpetual referent for the truth of this law was to say that an eclipse of the moon existed forever in its causal reasons. "There is not an eclipse at every moment, unless we are to say that an eclipse always (*semper*) exists because it always exists in its causal reasons (*rationes causales*). For an eclipse pure and simple (*simpliciter*) always exists in its causal reasons, although no particular eclipse always exists in its causal reason."[57] But itself this passage is difficult to interpret, primarily because Grosseteste did not say precisely what he meant by the causal reasons.[58] To get some idea of what he had in mind, it is

---

[55] See *Comm. Post. an.,* I, 7 (pp. 143–44, ll. 189–94).
[56] The reference was to *Posterior Analytics,* I, 8.
[57] *Comm. Post. an.,* I, 7 (p. 144, ll. 197–200).
[58] Father Wallace has suggested that in this passage Grosseteste was drawing on the work of Sacrobosco and other Neoplatonists in order to claim that a scientific, and therefore perpetual, universal for the lunar

necessary to turn to another passage where he used similar language—that is, to his description of the five referential levels of simple universals.[59] There he differentiated among the foundations for universals according to a hierarchical scheme of existence. He said that the bases for universals in the divinity were the reasons of things to be created (*rationes rerum creandarum*) or the formal exemplary causes (*cause formales exemplares*), in intelligences they were the exemplary forms (*forme exemplares*) or the created causal reasons of things to be made (*rationes causales create rerum fiendarum*), in the stars and planets they were the causal reasons (*rationes causales*), and on earth they were the formal causes (*cause formales*). Any of these causes or reasons might have been the causal reasons Grosseteste referred to when speaking of the perpetuity of an eclipse. The problem is to decide which ones.

Grosseteste gave an indication of which ones he meant by stipulating that it was the eclipse pure and simple (*simpliciter*), as opposed to any particular eclipse, that could be said to exist always in the causal reasons.[60] This idea is itself difficult to interpret, but Grosseteste's theory of the definition offers a clue. According to what he said in the second book of his *Commentary,* the definition pure and simple (*simpliciter*) was the formal definition: that notion of a thing which was taken from its form but which could be used cognitively to represent the whole substance, form and matter together.[61] Since the language Grosseteste used on this occasion follows so closely the language he used to describe his fourth level of simple universal cognition, it seems clear that what he meant by knowledge

---

eclipse could be obtained in the eternal causal reasons of a higher world (see Wallace, *Causality,* p. 33). Although there is no reason to doubt that Grosseteste had such sources in mind, it seems most likely that he did not interpret causal reasons in precisely the same way the Neoplatonists did, especially not as eternal causes on a higher plane of existence. As the present study indicates, Grosseteste's "causal reasons" were probably the essential forms of things in the world.

[59] See above, Chapter VI, n. 24.
[60] See above, n. 57.
[61] See *Comm. Post. an.,* II, 2 (p. 337, ll. 704-11).

of the definition pure and simple was this fourth level itself, the kind of universal knowledge commonly available to the scientific mind. There seems to be every reason, therefore, to assume that when Grosseteste spoke of the eclipse pure and simple he meant to refer to the eclipse as it was known in its formal causes, the forms of the fourth type of universal knowledge. Consequently, when he claimed that universal statements about an eclipse had a perpetual referential base in the causal reasons of eclipse pure and simple, he meant that whatever perpetuity such statements possessed lay in the perpetuity of the formal causes of an eclipse. The formal causes of an eclipse were, quite simply, the real forms of the sun, the moon, and the earth, the constituent elements of an eclipse. It seems therefore that the perpetuity of these simple forms was enough to ensure a perpetual referent for any universal statement about eclipses.

If this is what Grosseteste had in mind, then his first solution to the problem of how universal statements of natural science could have some perpetual referent was after all not much different from the way he solved the problem for simple universals, or for statements of truth in science of the highest, most properly demonstrative sort, in spite of the additional complications involved in locating the complex object to which the truths of natural science referred. This solution merely argued that it was irrelevant that the intended configuration of the referents did not exist at all times; it was enough that each of the formal constituents could be identified and their perpetuity explained in the same way as all other essential natures of real things. In the case of an eclipse, which involved celestial substances, the perpetuity of the formal causes came down to the fact that the forms of the sun, moon, and earth existed unchanged for all time. In the case of many other truths of natural science the substances referred to were objects in the sublunary world, and their universal forms could be said to exist forever as they were constantly renewed by regeneration. In either case perpetuity was in some way ensured.

There was, however, a second way Grosseteste thought Aristotle could be interpreted. In his own words:

Perhaps one should say that Aristotle did not intend to say that an eclipse always (*semper*) exists but rather he intended to say that the conclusion in which [the cause of] an eclipse is demonstrated is a proposition that is true at any moment, whether there [actually] is an eclipse [at that moment] or not.[62]

Here, for the first time, Grosseteste turned away from the problem of finding an incorruptible referent and asked if there were not some other way to account for the perpetuity of scientific truth. His response was to shift some of the philosophical burden away from matters of ontology and toward the logic of demonstration itself. According to this second explanation, perpetual truth was dependent on the enduring ability to construct a logical argument. A proposition was true perpetually if a demonstration could be made of its truth at any time. In order to free this rational process from the limits of the existence of an object at any particular moment, one had only to cast both premises and conclusions as conditional statements and not as assertions of actual circumstances in the real world.[63]

And this is what Aristotle intended to say, that is, that when it comes to demonstrating those things that occur with natural regularity (*frequenter fiunt*), the conditions [must be stipulated] which [would make] such things true at any time.[64]

In the case of an eclipse what was perpetually true was that if and whenever the sun, moon, and earth lined up in the proper manner, the moon went into eclipse.

It was a major step for Grosseteste to come to this conclusion, or rather to discover in Aristotle a doctrine that had until then been unfamiliar in the West. By setting the arguments of

---

[62] *Comm. Post. an.*, I, 7 (p. 144, ll. 200–204). Grosseteste followed this with an example of the kind of demonstration he meant.

[63] This is essentially the conclusion Father Wallace arrives at concerning the same passage, although the fact that he reads the word *propositio* (see above, n. 62) as *proximo* means that he does not realize that Grosseteste's theory allowed him to explain how the conclusions of science were actually true at all moments, even at times when the conditions that made them true did not actually hold. See Wallace, *Causality*, pp. 32–33.

[64] *Comm. Post. an.*, I, 7 (p. 144–45, ll. 211–14).

natural science in terms of conditionality he made it possible to divorce the search for universal truth from either idealism or realism of an extreme sort. This was perhaps the most radical moment in his effort to free the idea of the logical invariability of scientific truth from the notion of a strictly unchanging or eternal existence. Even though he never went further than applying this theory to one small area of science, he had uncovered a doctrine of extraordinary intellectual power, capable eventually of being extended to the whole structure of human thought.

It might be noted that Grosseteste believed that both of his explanations for the incorruptibility of complex, natural universals contradicted the principle that universality could be preserved only if the real referential base continued undiminished throughout all time.[65] The succession of individuals, by which he had accounted for the preservation of simple universals, would clearly not apply to the case of an eclipse, which occurred only on occasion. Here, rather than follow up the insights of his new appreciation of conditional argument, he turned back to examining the referent to find a way out. Just like William of Auvergne, when on a slightly different occasion he had wanted to speak of truth where there was no existing referent in the world, Grosseteste relied on the notion of a privation (*privatio*).[66] Yet where William had compared the whole relation of truth to a state of privation, Grosseteste applied the term to the objective correlative alone, in this case an eclipse. He said that an eclipse was not a real nature but rather the absence of one.[67] For this reason it made no sense to talk as if the nature of eclipse could be increased or diminished, and so this was one place where the general rule about universals simply did not apply.

Despite this momentary retreat, however, it is unquestionable that Grosseteste's analysis of the nature of truth in complex human knowledge constituted a formidable achievement

[65] On this principle, see *Comm. Post. an.*, I, 7 (pp. 141-42, ll. 154-57).
[66] See above, Chapter III, n. 30.
[67] *Comm. Post. an.*, I, 7 (p. 145, ll. 214-19).

for his day. By following the logical solutions to problems as far as he did, he began to sketch a coherent vision of truth independent of the older ways of approaching the issue. He had found a means of explaining complex truth and solving the problem of its real reference without making a formal appeal to any divine or superintellectual intervention. This was a significant step in the history of medieval thought, and it opened the way for the refinements in the theory of method that appeared later in the thirteenth century.[68]

3. THE WAY TO KNOWLEDGE OF THE CONCLUSIONS OF SCIENCE

Although Grosseteste did give some slight attention to the problem of the nature of complex truth in his early treatise, *De veritate,* he reserved all his thoughts on the way men arrived at such truth for the *Commentary on the Posterior Analytics.* What is more, his treatment of the issue in that work is extensive, covering the matter far more completely than the scattered ob-

---

[68] In particular, Grosseteste's reasoning about conditional arguments in the natural sciences seems to have laid the foundations for the fuller understanding of *ex suppositione* demonstration in Albert the Great and others later in the Middle Ages. See William A. Wallace, "Aquinas on the Temporal Relation between Cause and Effect," *The Review of Metaphysics* 27 (1974), 569–84; "Albertus Magnus on Suppositional Necessity in the Natural Sciences," in *Albertus Magnus and the Sciences,* ed. James A. Weisheipl (Toronto, 1980), 103–28; "The Scientific Methodology of St. Albert the Great," in *Albertus Magnus Doctor Universalis 1280/1980,* eds. Gerbert Meyer and Albert Zimmerman (Mainz, 1980), 391–93; and "Aristotle and Galileo: The Uses of Ὑπόθεσις (*Suppositio*) in Scientific Reasoning," in *Studies in Aristotle,* ed. Dominic J. O'Meara, (Washington, D.C., 1981).

In his commentary on Book II, Chapters 8 and 9 of the *Physics,* where Aristotle had expounded his ideas on the matter in much greater detail than in the *Posterior Analytics,* Grosseteste did pick up the term *ex suppositione,* and noted that such argument depended on recognizing the final cause (*propter finem*), although he did not explain himself any more completely. See *Commentarius in VIII libros Physicorum Aristotelis,* ed. Dales, p. 47. Grosseteste's comments on *Posterior Analytics,* II 12, another place where Aristotle touched on the same issue, also foreshadow Albert's ideas, but here the term *ex suppositione* does not appear (see *Comm. Post. an.,* II, 3 [pp. 358–61, ll. 274–326]).

servations on the same subject to be found in the contemporaneous writings of William of Auvergne. To be sure, Grosseteste did not organize all the elements of his theory systematically, nor did he exhaustively follow every aspect of the problem to its final solution. This kind of thoroughness came only with the more highly refined philosophy of the later thirteenth century, when thinkers could build on the foundations laboriously established by men like Grosseteste during the preceding fifty years. Yet the comments dispersed throughout the *Commentary* come together to give at least the outline of a coherent response to the whole question and constitute one of the earliest attempts in the medieval West at a comprehensive examination of the ontological and epistemological problems of evidence in complex human understanding of the real world.

Grosseteste never dealt explicitly with the question of how men came to know the truth of statements of particular fact, the *contingentia erratica.* Presumably he would have answered the question in just the way that has been suggested for William of Auvergne.[69] It was only when it came to universal propositions, those that could be held with certainty, that he took an interest in the problem of the evidence leading to knowledge of complex truth. Here, there were two basic categories: knowledge of conclusions, which was demonstrated knowledge, and knowledge of principles, which was undemonstrated. It is convenient to consider first his discussion of the conclusions of demonstration, that knowledge which was truly scientific in the proper sense of the word.

To his mind it was a difficult problem to determine when one knew something scientifically—that is, when one knew with certainty that a universal statement had been proven to be true—and when not.[70] This was increasingly to become an issue for thirteenth-century scholastics, who, encouraged by the example of such thinkers as Grosseteste and William of Auvergne, set out to identify the whole body of certain knowl-

---

[69] See above, the beginning of Chapter III, 3.
[70] *Comm. Post. an.,* I, 8 (p. 153, ll. 158–70).

edge. Grosseteste claimed that Aristotle's *Posterior Analytics* held the key to this problem, for it was written to reveal the absolute criteria for scientific thought.[71] It was undoubtedly his confidence that Aristotle had found the answer that encouraged him to publish his long commentary on the work, hoping thereby to make available to his fellow scholars the ideas somewhat obscured by the brevity and opaqueness of the Latin text. Subsequent generations of medieval thinkers shared Grosseteste's enthusiasm and apparently trusted him as a faithful interpreter of the original, for the *Commentary on the Posterior Analytics* continued to be read and quoted frequently long after his death.[72] Ironically, this work of textual explication served as one of the primary conduits of Grosseteste's thought to the minds of the rest of the Middle Ages.

He maintained that it was an essential characteristic of scientific knowledge that when the mind first grasped the meaning of a scientific proposition, it could not be sure whether that proposition was true. Indeed, it might suspect it was false.[73] Another way of putting this was to say that the mind could always raise initial objections (*instantia*) to the truth of a statement of science. Even though such objections were invariably revealed to be invalid in the final analysis—for it was of the nature of scientific propositions that they be necessarily true— their weakness was never immediately apparent, and some additional reasons had to be introduced in every case before the objections could be put aside.[74] It was this requirement that distinguished scientific cognition from the knowledge of principles, true statements that aroused no doubt and therefore did not need to be proved. Now the way to allay the doubt and come to recognize the truth of the conclusions of science was through finding a middle or cause that could establish their validity.[75] In short, scientific truths came to be known mediately through propositions that served as premises for a proof. The

[71] See *Comm. Post. an.,* II, 5 (pp. 401–02, ll. 236–50).
[72] See above, the introductory remarks to Part Two, n. 17.
[73] See *Comm. Post. an.,* I, 1 (p. 94, ll. 26–31).
[74] See *Comm. Post. an.,* I, 8 (p. 158, ll. 273–77).
[75] See above, this chapter, n. 20.

only way to the certain knowledge of science was by means of the demonstrative syllogism.

Like William of Auvergne, Grosseteste had no intention of detailing all the rules of syllogistic reasoning. He did mention that demonstration did not involve such processes as induction or division, for true to the principles of Aristotle, he insisted that science properly speaking consisted solely of knowledge arranged deductively.[76] Beyond this general statement, however, he had little to say about the formal rules of demonstrative logic, and even those few places where he commented on Aristotle's analysis of the material conditions of demonstration need not be considered here.

Yet although he eschewed the role of logician, he did feel called upon to justify man's grasp of the syllogism and his consent to it as a compelling mode of argumentation, and in this way he differed somewhat from his fellow theorist William of Auvergne, who made no attempt to underwrite a process he apparently took to be patently reliable. By Grosseteste's account, reason (*ratio*) was the human faculty responsible for coming to know something that was previously unknown. It did this by finding something already known from which it could infer the intended conclusion. When the unknown thing to be learned was a complex truth—that is, when it was a proposition of science—then reason came to know it or hold it with certainty by discursively passing over (*discurrere*) a syllogism that proved it and that could therefore be called, in a secondary sense of the word, the reason (*ratio*) for that particular truth.[77] The question was, why did the process of syllogism prove anything?

According to Grosseteste, it was the principle of identity that lay at the heart of all scientific reasoning and provided the true foundation for the syllogism: "For this rule constitutes the [compelling] force of all syllogistic necessity: that whatever things are identical to one and the same thing, they are them-

---

[76] *Comm. Post. an.,* II, 2 (p. 312, ll. 195-96).
[77] *Comm. Post. an.,* II, 2 (pp. 343-44, ll. 837-44).

selves identical."[78] He said that a syllogism simple enough to make manifest to the penetrating intellect the identity of its three terms—the two extremes and the middle—was called a perfect syllogism.[79] Because such a syllogism laid bare the foundation upon which all logical argument rested, it needed nothing more than to be exposed to reason or the sight of the mind (*aspectus mentis*) in order to convince the mind of the truth of its conclusion. It was, as William of Auvergne had held of simple syllogism, compelling in itself (*per se*). Later in the *Commentary,* Grosseteste noted that syllogisms of this type, immediate and accepted only through themselves, had to be in the first mode of the first figure of Aristotle's syllogistic logic. Since these were the only kind of syllogisms that in effect argued for themselves, they constituted the building blocks of all demonstrative science, so that all other demonstrations, no matter how complex, could ultimately be broken down into components that were themselves perfect syllogisms and from which the more complex arguments derived their logical force.[80]

Beyond this essentially logical or formal explanation of the power of syllogism, Grosseteste also offered an account that delved more deeply into the epistemological side of the discursive process. He maintained that the conclusion of a demonstrative argument was already known in a universal way (*in universali*) in its premises before the full argument had been made. Drawing the conclusion, which is to say completing the syllogistic demonstration, merely allowed the mind to know fully (*simpliciter*) and in itself (*in seipso*) a statement that it had previously understood in only this vague and incomplete manner.[81] He explained that he was not referring to the sort of universality that attached to the natures of things. Instead, he

---

[78] *Comm. Post. an.,* I, 13 (p. 202, ll. 67–69).
[79] *Comm. Post. an.,* I, 8 (p. 158, ll. 266–73).
[80] *Comm. Post. an.,* I, 13 (p. 202, ll. 74–80). Grosseteste was here expanding on ideas found in the Aristotelian text upon which he was commenting, *Posterior Analytics,* I, 14.
[81] *Comm. Post. an.,* I, 1 (pp. 96–97, ll. 77–94).

meant that the premises were more universal in the sense that they were more inclusive and less specifically defined than the conclusion. In short, the syllogism was a process of increasing specification or manifestation that worked within an identity. This idea was related to the theory in which he described syllogism logically as a manifestation of the identity of terms. Now, however, the identity was not between simple concepts but rather between propositions. The premises contained in a generalized way the very same truth as the conclusion, although each premise contained more specific truths than any single conclusion could express. What the mind required was a rational or demonstrative argument to reveal this identity and, in a word, to transform the universal knowledge of the premises into the specific instance of the conclusion.

Yet Grosseteste would go even further and, much like William of Auvergne, base the epistemology of demonstrative syllogism directly in the ontology of cause and effect. He suggested that certain knowledge (*scientia*) of true premises was the efficient cause and origin of certain knowledge (*scientia*) of true conclusions. By this he meant not only that knowledge of premises was the instrumental agent by which conclusions came to be known as true but also that it in effect provided the cognitive material out of which such knowledge could be generated.[82] Furthermore, just like William of Auvergne, he associated this primarily epistemological phenomenon with an even more fundamental reality in the external world. The causal bond between knowledge of premise and knowledge of conclusion constituted the cognitive counterpart to the link between premise and conclusion themselves, or more precisely, between the actual facts to which they referred. The premises were truly the cause of the conclusion, not only of knowledge of it but of its very being.[83] In the end, Grosseteste could defend the procedures of logic with a realism that held that they simply reflected the way things were in the objective world. It remained only to add that the existential connection between premises and conclusion acquired the epistemological force

[82] *Comm. Post. an.,* I, 2 (pp. 100–101, ll. 40–52).
[83] *Comm. Post. an.,* I, 16 (p. 235, ll. 139–42).

necessary to induce in the mind certain knowledge of the conclusion through the process of joining the propositions themselves together in proper syllogistic form or, as he put it, through the process of ordering premises cognitively to conclusions.[84] Interestingly enough, it was *intellectus*—in this case as much a faculty of the mind as the *habitus* responsible for the knowledge of principles—that achieved this ordering. Perhaps it was a sign of Grosseteste's stress on the real foundation of the rational process in the external world that he felt he could extend the powers of this essentially receptive *habitus* to include the dynamic operation of discursive reason.

4. THE WAY TO KNOWLEDGE OF THE PRINCIPLES
OF SCIENCE

Mention of *intellectus* reintroduces the problem of the undemonstrated principles of science. Explaining how to recognize their truth was a more difficult and complicated task than explaining how to know the truth of scientific conclusions, and it revealed more about Grosseteste's thoughts on the foundation of certain knowledge. It is here that one must give the greatest attention to what he had to say about the way the mind attained complex truth.

Grosseteste emphatically supported Aristotle's view of the importance of principles for scientific understanding. In his words, the discovery of principles opened the way for the work of demonstration.[85] *Intellectus*, the *habitus* of mind by which principles were known, was itself the principle or foundation of science, and without this primary perception of complex truth no certain understanding would ever have been possible.[86] Furthermore, knowledge of principles was the clearest form of cognition available to man.[87] It provided the ideal of plain truth, which the mind could only approximate by any other

---

[84] *Comm. Post. an.,* II, 6 (p. 407, ll. 99–103).
[85] *Comm. Post. an.,* II, 1 (p. 289, l. 54).
[86] *Comm. Post. an.,* I, 3 (p. 106, ll. 30–34); I, 19 (pp. 281–82, ll. 89–95); and II, 6 (p. 407, ll. 94–99).
[87] *Comm. Post. an.,* I, 2 (p. 103, ll. 91–93); I, 15 (p. 226, ll. 190–92).

means of complex cognition. Before going on to examine Grosseteste's account of the mechanism for attaining these principles, however, it is necessary to see just what kinds of principles he thought there were and to try to find some examples of each.

A. The Kinds of Principal Cognition

According to Aristotle there were three fundamental elements—*principia,* in a broad sense of the word—that went into science, three things to be known through immediate cognition before one could construct a demonstration. These three were, first, the subject of the science (*genus subiectum*); second, the first principles or axioms of demonstration (*dignitates*); and third, the immediate properties of the subject (*per se passiones*).[88] Grosseteste once called them the *precognita,* those things that had to be known before science could proceed, and he referred to them simply as *subiectum, dignitates,* and *passiones.*[89] At times he expanded the middle category to include complex principles other than just the axioms of all science, so that he could speak of *subiectum, principia* (this time in its more proper sense), and *passiones.*[90]

Now of these three, *principia* clearly constituted a kind of complex principal cognition; they were, by their very name, principles of science. But the subject, too, provided the basis for a kind of complex principal cognition. To understand how, it is necessary to go back to one of the analytical foundations of Aristotle's thought.

At the beginning of the second book of the *Posterior Analytics,* Aristotle stated that there were four general questions all knowledge was designed to answer. They were the question of

[88] Aristotle, *Posterior Analytics,* 1, 7 and 10 (75a39–b2, 76b11–16). See the translation by James of Venice in Aristoteles Latinus, IV, 1–4, ed. Minio-Paluello and Dod, pp. 19 and 24.

[89] See *Comm. Post. an.,* I, 1 (p. 96, ll. 77–81); I, 7 (pp. 136–37, ll. 39–44); and I, 8 (pp. 153–54, ll. 171–77, and p. 155, ll. 195–97). Rossi has punctuated incorrectly on p. 96, ll. 79–81. The text should read: ". . . sunt tria: principia ex quibus est syllogismus, et esse et quid est quod dicitur de subiecto, et quid est. . . ."

[90] See *Comm. Post. an.,* I, 1 (p. 95, ll. 46–49, and p. 96, ll. 77–81).

fact (*quia est*), the question of reason (*propter quid est*), the question of existence (*si est*), and the question of nature or essence (*quid est*).[91] As Grosseteste explained in his *Commentary,* two of these, and third and the fourth, were asked with reference to a simple object, inquiring whether something was and then what it was, while the other two, the first and the second, had to do with complex conditions, asking whether something was true of something and, if so, for what reason.[92] When one turned from the nature of the object to the kind of knowledge their answers provided, however, one came up with a different division between simple and complex. Here, the first three questions had to do with complex cognition, for answers to them were properly expressed as statements or propositions. Only the last concerned simple knowledge and had to be answered with a nonstatement, a phrase. It was this distinction Grosseteste had in mind when he said that it was at least theoretically possible to respond to the first three questions with a syllogistic argument or demonstration, but not to the last.[93] What a thing was (*quid est*) came to be known only through the definition, which did not predicate something of something else but merely expressed a concept of the simple essence.[94] Therefore, it did not have to do with propositional knowledge and could not be verified or supported by syllogism. Grosseteste took pains to explain that even the question concerning the existence of a simple essence (*si est*), although it did not refer to a complex object in the world, was a question of fact and had to be answered with a complex truth—one that predicated existence of a subject.[95]

It should be clear that among the four questions, only *propter quid* could have nothing to do with Grosseteste's, and Aristo-

---

[91] Aristotle, *Posterior Analytics,* II, 1 (89b23–25). See the Latin text in Aristoteles Latinus, IV, 1–4, ed. Minio-Paluello and Dod, p. 69.

[92] *Comm. Post. an.,* II, 1 (p. 290, ll. 64–69). It must be noted that Grosseteste used *si est* and *an est* interchangeably.

[93] *Comm. Post. an.,* II, 1 (p. 287, ll. 5–11).

[94] See above, Chapter VI, nn. 11 and 12. It was because Aristotle established the notion of essence on the basis of this question, *quid est,* that he called the essence by the name scholastics translated as *quod quid est.*

[95] *Comm. Post. an.,* II, 1 (p. 297, ll. 210–14).

tle's, three fundamentals. Knowledge of the fundamentals or *precognita* was immediate, which was to say that it had to be accepted as true without any reason other than itself. The question *propter quid,* on the other hand, specifically asked for a cause or reason. Indeed, the sort of knowledge with which it was associated, knowledge of the reasoned fact—likewise called *propter quid*—could be said to be the hallmark of demonstrative science.[96] The remaining questions could and did apply to fundamental or immediate knowledge, for it was possible to answer each of them without having recourse to a cause or middle from which a true conclusion was inferred. Two of them, *quia est* and *si est,* could, to be sure, occasionally be answered with a demonstration, but there was nothing about the nature of such questions that prevented their answers from being verified at other times simply on the evidence of immediate perception. The answer to the question *quid est* was, quite simply, technically incapable of being demonstrated under any circumstances.

With these three questions, then, Grosseteste was able to explain exactly what was known about each of the three fundamentals. In doing so he followed closely in the footsteps of Aristotle.[97] When it came to the principles proper (*principia*), both the axioms and other immediate propositions of complex truth, one knew without any demonstration simply the fact of a complex existence (*quia est*). For the subject, simple essences, one knew immediately both the definition (*quid est*) and the fact of existence, in this case simple (*si est*)—that is to say, one could define each specific member of the general subject and at the same time, without demonstration, affirm that it existed.

---

[96] *Comm. Post. an.,* I, 6 (p. 132, ll. 67-72). Although, as noted above, knowledge *quia est* and *si est* could also be given in some sort of demonstration, Grosseteste held that all demonstrative knowledge could be called *propter quid* in a general way insofar as it provided the reason or cause for knowing something. In a strict sense, however, knowledge *propter quid* was limited to demonstrative knowledge that revealed the immediate prior cause.

[97] See *Comm. Post. an.,* I, 1 (pp. 95-96), and I, 8 (pp. 153-55). Aristotle's comments on the matter appear in *Posterior Analytics,* I 1 and 10.

So far as the undemonstrated knowledge of the properties was concerned, one knew on the primary level nothing more than the definition (*quid est*).[98] Here, the simple fact of existence had to be proved by demonstration through a cause.[99]

Of these three fundamental forms of knowledge, only immediate knowledge of the properties did not involve any complex cognition and therefore did not belong among the complex principles of thought.[100] Such knowledge generated many of the definitions necessary for scientific investigation, but it was not attached to any certain knowledge of reality, knowledge that could be expressed in the form of a proposition. Examples of such properties were, in geometry, the substantive "triangle" and the adjectives "right," "rational," "reflex," and "curved"; and in arithmetic, the notion of uneven numbers, squares, and

[98] At one point Grosseteste expressed the view, taken from Aristotle, that all the questions of science could ultimately be reduced to a search for a definition. In some way, therefore, definition could be said to be the sole basis for all that Grosseteste and Aristotle held to be scientific knowledge (see *Comm. Post. an.*, II, 1 [p. 288, ll. 32–35]). This was true, however, only if "definition" were taken in a broad sense, where it could be identified sometimes with the nature of a simple thing, sometimes with the description of a complex state of existence, and sometimes with the cause of a fact (compare n. 96, above). Only the first of these cases constituted definition in the strict sense of the word—that which expressed *quod quid est*. Strictly speaking, therefore, science was founded on immediate knowledge of more than just definitions. The truth of Grosseteste's contention that science was reducible to definition lay in the fact that Aristotle's science emphasized explaining things by their formal nature, which was what the definition was intended to express.

[99] See *Comm. Post. an.*, I, 8 (pp. 153–54, ll. 173–81, and pp. 155–56, ll. 211–17).

[100] Once in his *Commentary*, Grosseteste divided all the fundamentals into two groups, simple and composite principles. Composite principles consisted of the immediate propositions of science, whereas simple principles were the subjects of the sciences and immediate properties (see *Comm. Post. an.*, I, 18 [p. 277, ll. 377–82]). This did not mean, however, that Grosseteste thought immediate knowledge of the subjects was limited to simple cognition. In making this special division he was calling knowledge both of the subject and of the properties simple because the real objects in either case were simple essences, not because the knowledge they both provided could not be expressed in the terms of a proposition—the trademark of complex cognition. This latter limitation was true only of properties.

cubes.[101] The two remaining kinds of cognition could serve, according to Grosseteste's philosophy, as the immediate complex bases for science. Together they constituted, in a broad sense, the principles of demonstrative thought, and they were, on the one hand, complex principles proper and, on the other, statements affirming the definition and the existence of the members of the subject of each science.[102] It is to these two groups that one must turn in order to understand Grosseteste's views on the way to certain knowledge of undemonstrated complex truths.

B. Knowledge of the Subjects of Science

The first group of principles to consider consists of those drawn from the subject. Grosseteste maintained that the subject of a science was composed of the fundamental objects with which that science had to deal, thus interpreting the term broadly enough to allow for more than one specific member in the general subject of any single science. For arithmetic he gave the example of unity; for geometry he listed magnitude and points and lines.[103] There were innumerable specific subjects in the natural sciences, perhaps as many as there were substantial species in the world.[104]

As has been shown, it was necessary to have immediate knowledge both of the definition (*quid est*) of the elements in the subject of a science and of the fact of their existence (*si est*).

---

[101] *Comm. Post. an.*, I, 8 (p. 154, l. 178, and p. 155, ll. 211–14).

[102] This distinction is basically the same as that introduced above to analyze the thought of William of Auvergne. Compex principles proper can be identified with the first and the third of the categories used in the section on William; statements about the subject are identical with the second category.

[103] *Comm. Post. an.*, I, 1 (p. 95, ll. 57–58) and I, 8 (p. 154, ll. 177–81, and p. 155, ll. 207–11).

[104] Grosseteste did not explain exactly what he meant by a subject in the natural sciences, but he did give some indication. Once he said that the definition of man was the sort of thing one knew in knowing a subject of natural science. This implies that each of the universal substances with which the natural sciences had to deal was a subject. See *Comm. Post. an.*, II, 2 (p. 313, ll. 201–7).

Knowing the definition was a matter of simple cognition, for, as Grosseteste made clear, the definition taken as a definition did not predicate anything of anything else but just revealed an essence.[105] For example, one definition of man was "a two-legged walking animal." Knowledge of this sort was immediate in the way all simple cognition was immediate cognition. In order for this understanding to become a principle of science, however, it had to be converted into a statement that could serve as a premise in a demonstration—that is, it had to become the basis for a complex truth. This meant that some assertion had to be made about the existence of a subject of which the definition pure and simple could be predicated. As Grosseteste explained for the case of the definition of man, one could use this definition as a proposition (*enuntiative*) if one did not intend just to explicate the subject but rather to state the fact that man is man (*dicere quod homo est homo*).[106] The complex principle was, therefore, "man is a two-legged walking animal."

To pass from evident simple cognition to a complex principle about the nature of a subject, one had to rely on what Grosseteste, following Aristotle, called hypothesis (*suppositio*). If one knew the definition, one merely hypothesized the existence of a subject, thereby making it possible to predicate one of the other.[107] Grosseteste specifically defined hypothesis as

---

[105] See above, Chapter VI, n. 14. Grosseteste was here just reporting the sense of the Aristotelian text upon which he was commenting. See *Posterior Analytics*, II, 3 (90b33–38).

[106] *Comm. Post. an.*, II, 2 (pp. 306–7, ll. 71–82). *Quod est* was here the declarative equivalent of the interrogative *si est*. Thus, he was referring here to Aristotle's cognitive category of knowing the fact of the existence of a simple thing, one of the forms of complex cognition.

[107] See *Comm. Post. an.*, I, 8 (p. 155, ll. 207–11), and II, 2 (pp. 337–38, ll. 716–24). Grosseteste was drawing on Aristotle's discussion of hypothesizing the existence of the subject in *Posterior Analytics*, I 10, and II, 9. See also *Posterior Analytics*, I, 2 (72a18–21).

Grosseteste maintained that one hypothesized principles from the formal definition alone. Material definitions had to be proved by demonstration. See *Comm. Post. an.*, II, 2 (pp. 337–38), and I, 7 (pp. 142–43). For an indication of how Grosseteste thought hypothesis might be justi-

the formal assumption of an indemonstrable truth that was not immediately apparent to all minds.[108] At other times he said that one simply accepted (*accipit*) this kind of principle or, to be more precise, accepted it without any necessary inference (*absque consecutione necessaria*).[109] Yet a third way of saying the same thing was that one postulated (*petit*) the principle, although according to the Latin terminology Grosseteste employed, the term *petitio* was more properly restricted to mean the unproved assumption of a truth that was in theory demonstrable in contrast to the hypothesizing of absolutely indemonstrable statements such as those drawn from the subject.[110] Whatever the term used to describe this process, however, Grosseteste insisted that it invariably led to knowledge of the truth, even though this knowledge was not supported by demonstration. Because the truth of hypotheses was not always immediately manifest to everyone—for not everyone was familiar with the subjects of all the sciences—in some cases it might be necessary to turn to some less-than-demonstrative explanation (*aliqua levis dialectica explanatio*) in order to induce assent.[111] Yet this could not gainsay the fact that hypothesis was a legitimate way to complex truth and one that did not ultimately rest on any discursive process.

Grosseteste never bothered to explain hypothesis any more than this or to justify it, but it is possible to see how he could have done so. Given his attitude toward reference and truth, hypothesis concerning the subject was just a legitimate and indeed logical extension of the evidence of simple cognition. Early in his *Commentary*, when he was examining the nature of complex principles, he offered an analysis of evident truth that

---

fied on one occasion, look at the passage quoted in Crombie, *Robert Grosseteste*, p. 58, n. 3.

[108] *Comm. Post. an.*, I, 8 (pp. 158–59, ll. 283–85).

[109] *Comm. Post. an.*, II, 2 (p. 313, ll. 201–7).

[110] Ibid. On *petitio* proper, see *Comm. Post. an.*, I, 8 (p. 159, ll. 285–93). Grosseteste's notion of *suppositio* and *petitio* was drawn from Aristotle, although it did not exactly coincide with his usage. See *Posterior Analytics*, I, 10 (76b27–31).

[111] *Comm. Post. an.*, II, 2 (pp. 337–38, ll. 716–23).

focused on the nature of the relation among a proposition's terms: "The truth of a proposition is known when one sees the substantial identity (*identitas in substantia*) of predicate and subject."[112] Another way of making the same point was to say that a true proposition consisted of several reasons or forms— at least two, one predicated of the other—that in fact coincided in the same subject.[113] In short, a true proposition expressed an identity, wherein the predicate represented just another way of describing the object already named in the subject. Propositions where this identity was not immediately evident could, presumably, be analyzed or broken down into propositions where it was. This was, after all, the business of demonstrative science.

In the case of statements of principal cognition drawn from the subject, the relation of identity between subject and predicate was immediately apparent. All valid hypotheses predicated a definition of some real subject existing in the world. Yet the proper subjects of science were all natures that had been fully revealed to the mind through the processes of simple cognition, including of course the division necessary for most definition. Consequently it was evident, at least to a teacher who could explain matters to his students, both what these subjects were and that they existed. To translate such knowledge into a hypothesis suitable to serve as a complex principle, one had merely to formulate the appropriate proposition. Its truth would be immediately apparent without any additional inference. Certitude here on the level of complex knowledge was the immediate outgrowth of evidence already obtained on the level of simple perception.

C. Knowledge of the Complex Principles Proper

It was not such an easy matter to explain the way to knowledge of the truth of complex principles proper. At the very least, one had to introduce a number of categories and subdivi-

---

[112] *Comm. Post. an.,* I, 8 (p. 158, ll. 268–69). This idea is, of course, intimately related to the belief that the fundamental purpose of the syllogism was to reveal the identity of terms.
[113] *Comm. Post. an.,* I, 8 (p. 160, ll. 321–28).

sions that made any attempt at explanation more complicated. Grosseteste divided complex principles into two sorts: first principles and those that were not first. Only first principles were true principles, known through that disposition of immediate cognition called *intellectus.* The principles that were not first actually constituted a kind of scientific or discursive knowledge, since they were in fact proved to be true by means of the first principles.[114] They were called principles only because they were sometimes introduced without proof among the premises of scientific demonstration. In such cases they were literally *suppositiones,* this time not in the absolutely proper sense of hypothesized statements drawn from the subject, or *petitiones;* they were complex truths that were assumed without proof for the purposes of demonstration but that could in fact be demonstrated in a higher science.[115] Since certain knowledge of the truth of these propositions had to be explained in the final analysis according to the laws of demonstration, it was not truly a case of immediate knowledge and need not be considered any further.

What Grosseteste had to explain was certain knowledge of the first principles of science. Again, further subdivision is in order. There were two classes of first principles: proper and common—that is, those exclusive to any one science and those common to all.[116] The common principles were the axioms (*dignitates*), the basic laws of science, which, however, had to be fitted or appropriated to the subject of a particular science before they could be used as premises in a demonstration.[117] For example, one common principle was the law stating that if equals are subtracted from equals, the resulting differences are equal. When employed in geometry, this law had to be ex-

---

[114] *Comm. Post. an.,* I, 2 (p. 102, ll. 80–82, and p. 103, ll. 91–94).

[115] *Comm. Post. an.,* I, 8 (pp. 158–59, ll. 281–93). Contrast this definition with the one given for *suppositio simpliciter,* n. 108, above. For a short discussion of how truths in one science were proved in a higher science, see Weisheipl, "Classification of the Sciences," pp. 73–75.

[116] *Comm. Post. an.,* I, 8 (p. 154, ll. 184–85).

[117] *Comm. Post. an.,* I, 8 (p. 154, ll. 185–91).

pressed or at least understood in terms of magnitude, but the arithmetician understood it in terms of number.[118] This process of appropriation in effect transformed common principles into proper ones, a logical metamorphosis that Grosseteste thought was absolutely necessary, since, like Aristotle, he held that demonstration arose only from premises properly suited to the conclusion.[119] He divided common principles into two subcategories. On the one hand were the rules of exposition (*dispositiones enunciationis*), on the other those of quantification (*dispositiones quantitatis*). The former were applicable to all sciences, once they had been duly fitted to the various general subjects, while the latter were used only in the mathematical sciences as well as the natural sciences and metaphysics.[120] As an example of a rule of exposition Grosseteste cited the law of excluded middle; among rules of quantification he mentioned the principle about subtracting equals from equals and also the law that things equal to one and the same thing were equal to each other.[121] The most common of all common principles were the two rules of exposition, the law of excluded middle and the principle of noncontradiction. They were so basic to rational thought that even the most obstinate opponent could not deny them.[122]

Among proper principles there also seem to have been several sorts. One class consisted of the first principles peculiar to each science. These were propositions that predicated the first essential (*per se*) property or accident of the general subject of the science, and for this reason there was generally only one for each science. Even in those sciences where there was more than one essential property, the number of such principles was very

---

[118] *Comm. Post. an.*, I, 8 (p. 155, ll. 204-7). For another example, see *Comm. Post. an.*, I, 7 (p. 137, ll. 51-55).

[119] *Comm. Post. an.*, I, 8 (p. 154, ll. 191-94).

[120] *Comm. Post. an.*, I, 10 (pp. 170-71, ll. 14-26). The mathematical sciences were those Grosseteste also called doctrinal sciences, and in them alone could men on earth achieve certitude in the strictest sense of the word. See above, Chapter VII, 2, A.

[121] See above, n. 120, and also *Comm. Post. an.*, I, 7 (p. 137, ll. 51-55).

[122] *Comm. Post. an.*, I, 9 (p. 162, ll. 7-14).

small.[123] As examples, Grosseteste cited two laws of arithmetic: that number is a collection of units and that number is expandable into infinity. It is probable that he also intended to include among this type of proper principle two laws he mentioned earlier in his *Commentary:* that a line is a one-dimensional figure (*longitudo sine latitudine*) whose extremities consist of two points and that a straight line is an extension from one point to another.[124] A second class of principles Grosseteste designated as proper contained those principles already discussed above, statements drawn from the subject alone.[125] Although they were not strictly speaking first principles, they constituted one of the major categories of the proper principles of science, and Grosseteste himself often listed them alongside such true first principles as the ones given above. In fact, he was frequently ambiguous about the difference between principles taken from the definition of the subject and those predicating the first essential accident. Some of the examples of the latter sound more like definitions pure and simple than statements predicating a property of its natural subject. Finally, there was the class of principles that had to do with the regular but still contingent laws of nature.[126] Despite the fact that Grosseteste never explicitly spoke of these as proper principles, it is clear that they were and that they fell under neither of the previous two categories. As will be shown below, they were simply explanations of the facts of nature, arrived at through induction. An example Grosseteste gave of this type of principle was the law that every male, when he reached the age of

---

[123] *Comm. Post. an.,* I, 18 (p. 276, ll. 352-58).

[124] *Comm. Post. an.,* I, 8 (p. 155, ll. 202-4). There is some difficulty in seeing the second proposition as an example of a first proper principle, since the subject has already been modified by the adjective "straight." Nevertheless, Grosseteste insisted it was a proper principle and not a statement drawn from the definition of a subject or even of a predicated property of the science. Perhaps it is best not to hold Grosseteste strictly to his own rules on this point.

[125] *Comm. Post. an.,* I, 8 (p. 155, ll. 207-12). See also *Comm. Post. an.,* I, 18 (p. 277, ll. 380-82).

[126] Grosseteste clearly held that there were principles in the natural sciences. See *Comm. Post. an.,* I, 18 (p. 274, ll. 316-18).

maturity, was able to fulfill his generative function. It was true in every case, provided there was no extraordinary obstacle.[127]

With these various classes in mind it is possible to examine how Grosseteste explained the acquisition of knowledge of first principles, those propositions the understanding of which Aristotle characterized by the state of mind or *habitus* called *intellectus*.[128] Since such understanding arose immediately from an act of perception, without reference to any middle term or reason why, without any intervening act of deduction, the evidence for the truth of first principles had to be provided totally in the fundamental, nondiscursive processes of mind. For Grosseteste, therefore, the problem was to identify the conditions under which the evidence was produced and to locate the driving force, the efficient cause, that accounted for the eventual formulation of the principle proposition itself.

Just as was seen to be the case in his account of the way men arrived at simple truth, Grosseteste's explanation of the process by which the mind obtained knowledge of the truth of complex first principles followed two different lines, ones that do not initially seem to have been completely compatible. On the one hand, he turned to the metaphorical language of light, reinforced by a direct analogy to sensory vision. The single account he gave in these terms shares much with traditional descriptions of divine illumination, although it does not mention God and need not necessarily be interpreted along these lines. On the other hand, Grosseteste devoted several passages to a more straightforward and analytical examination of the way men knew first principles, and on these occasions he adhered closely to Aristotle's this-worldly line. Besides being more precise than the description by metaphor and analogy, this analytical approach seems to have constituted for Grosseteste a more congenial line of thought, for he turned to it several times and took care to elaborate it with a considerable degree of explicitness and detail.

[127] *Comm. Post. an.,* II, 3 (p. 363, ll. 371-77).
[128] See *Comm. Post. an.,* I, 19 (p. 279, ll. 35-40). On changing the punctuation of this text, see above, Chapter VI, n. 73.

Grosseteste's metaphorical explanation of the knowledge of first principles depended on a model of cognition that attributed activity to the object and saw the mind primarily as a passive receiver. The model was an extension of the logical characterization of principles as truths known immediately or in themselves (*per se*).[129] Although in strictly logical terms this meant merely that the mind knew they were true without having to demonstrate the fact through a middle term, it was possible to argue that the words *per se* involved the additional implication that the principles somehow revealed themselves. Grosseteste chose to interpret them this way, but he added the important qualification that the driving force behind such revelation was not ultimately the principles, or whatever real referent might stand behind them, but rather a spiritual or intelligible light that shone upon them.

According to his explanation, it was the intelligible light involved in all cognition, and not any particular cognitive object, that was, properly speaking, in itself visible (*per se visibile*) to the mind and known first of all things.[130] One could, however, transfer these qualities to some other objects of cognition if they were not, in turn, revealed to the mind through the medium of anything else but this primary light. From the vantage point of the unreflecting intellect these objects would in fact seem to be revealing themselves without the aid of any other agent, for the mind saw them and not the light that carried their image to it. Grosseteste tried to make his point clearer by drawing an analogy with the circumstances of sensory vision. Everyone would agree that it was the sun that was in itself visible and that its light accounted for sight. Nevertheless, since in most cases it was not the sun itself that men saw but rather colored bodies illuminated by its radiation, it was common practice to call these colored bodies the first objects of sight and to claim that they were in themselves visible. It was at heart a matter of what one was first conscious of perceiving. Grosse-

---

[129] See *Comm. Post. an.,* I, 15 (p. 226, ll. 192–93).
[130] See above, the passage cited in Chapter VI, n. 73.

teste added that the intelligible objects corresponding on the intellectual level to colored bodies in sensation were things known by immediate perception or *intellectus*. If they were complex and therefore the basis for complex truths, then they could be called the principles of demonstration.[131]

There can be no doubt that in this instance Grosseteste attributed efficacy—that is, efficient causation—in the process leading to *intellectus* to a spiritual light. The problem is that it is not clear exactly what that light was. Did Grosseteste mean the light of God, or did he have in mind something else, a radiation from the human intellect itself, this time considered from the point of view of its active, not receptive, function? As has already been shown in the chapter on simple truth, it may not be possible to answer this question conclusively. One can say, however, that Grosseteste believed the intellectual power did possess a light of its own and that in fact this light was involved in the process by which it came to accept first principles as true.[132] Whether the light of God was involved in addition, he did not explicitly say.

It is perhaps significant that there were no other occasions in the *Commentary* where Grosseteste used the image of an intelligible light to explain the way to knowledge of first principles. At all other times he turned to a more analytical model, the foundations for which lay in Aristotle's thought. Here, he took great care to be precise about the driving force or efficient cause of *intellectus*. This was the mind itself, considered now as an active power and the real mover behind the first and most certain complex cognition. It is this concrete, worldly model that dominates Grosseteste's discussion of knowledge of first principles. And in it there is not even the hint of a notion of divine intervention.

The most general statement of Grosseteste's more analytical view of the process leading to *intellectus* came in the last chapter of his *Commentary*. Like Aristotle, Grosseteste firmly re-

---

[131] *Comm. Post. an.,* I, 19 (p. 279, ll. 37-40). This follows immediately after the passage cited in Chapter VI, n. 73.

[132] See above, Chapter VI, n. 77.

jected the theory that the knowledge of principles was innate. Those who adhered to this doctrine, including Plato, held that such knowledge was hidden to the mind until something triggered the memory, which then recalled the principle in fact already known. Grosseteste thought this was manifestly absurd.[133] Yet if the knowledge of first principles was not innate, then it had somehow to be acquired. Grosseteste agreed with Aristotle that the mind could not learn first principles the way it learned the conclusions of science, inferring or demonstrating them from premises, for principles were immediate and therefore not derived from any other intellectual knowledge.[134] The problem was that it was just as wrong to hold that the mind simply came to knowledge of the principles without any preparation or previous cognitive foundation. Grosseteste believed that Aristotle had satisfactorily shown that everything acquired in intellection had to be derived from some pre-existing knowledge.[135] The way Grosseteste solved this problem was to follow Aristotle's cue and maintain that knowledge of principles was neither innate nor truly acquired *de novo*. Instead, it was realized from a potential that preceded it in the soul.[136]

He argued that this potential was not itself any sort of principle or primary knowledge; in fact, it was not intellectual knowledge at all. The potential for knowledge of first principles was sensory cognition.[137] Nothing could illustrate more clearly the worldly, almost material character of Grosseteste's theory of the acquisition of first principles. Here, at the very foundation of his doctrine of *intellectus,* he placed a kind of cognition that was fully of this world and not in any way dependent on an intelligible light, whether of the mind or from some higher source. What is more, he insisted that the way the

---

[133] See *Comm. Post. an.,* II, 6 (pp. 403-4).
[134] See *Comm. Post. an.,* II, 6 (p. 403, ll. 13-16).
[135] *Comm. Post. an.,* II, 6 (p. 403, ll. 16-17).
[136] *Comm. Post. an.,* II, 6 (p. 403, ll. 17-20).
[137] *Comm. Post. an.,* II, 6 (p. 404, ll. 23-24). The idea is clearly stated in Aristotle, *Posterior Analytics,* II, 19 (100a10-11).

mind moved from potential knowledge of principles in sensory data to actual understanding of them on an intelligible level was through induction.[138] Again, this turned him away from a notion of knowledge dependent on some form of illumination. It was not an external spiritual light that accounted for what the mind knew of principles but rather the internal power of intellect itself.

The way Grosseteste described the inductive process by which knowledge of first principles was drawn from sensation was taken largely from Aristotle, showing how the universal was gradually abstracted as knowledge passed from the power of sense through the imaginative power, estimative power, and memory to the highest of all, the reason or intellect.[139] At each stage knowledge of the object became more rarefied and less material, until one arrived at a concept that could serve for scientific cognition. The literal significance of this passage is, therefore, relatively clear. What is not so easy to understand is how it can be applied to the problem at hand. Grosseteste explicitly said that he had in mind the induction of complex as well as simple universals—that is, all the fundamentals of scientific knowledge, including first principles.[140] Yet his analysis did not go beyond simple cognition.

It is perhaps significant that in the very chapter Grosseteste was commenting on, Aristotle himself did the same thing: he stated his intention to explain the acquisition of complex principles but then went on merely to describe the formation of simple universals.[141] Yet even though Aristotle may not have realized the incompleteness of his solution, it would seem that Grosseteste did. Describing the formation of universal concepts went only halfway to solving the problem. It made the point that the kind of knowledge he was talking about was

---

[138] *Comm. Post. an.,* II, 6 (p. 406, ll. 67–69).
[139] *Comm. Post. an.,* II, 6 (p. 404, ll. 24–40). This is the same passage referred to above, Chapter VI, n. 98.
[140] *Comm. Post. an.,* II, 6 (p. 406, ll. 67–69).
[141] See, for instance, Jonathan Barnes in Aristotle's *Posterior Analytics,* p. 249.

drawn immediately from the evidence of sensation. But it did not explain exactly what it was that allowed the mind to go beyond simple intellection and judge that some propositions in which these simple concepts served as terms were true, without any discursive reason to show why this was so. To explain this judgment, some additional analysis was required. As if to provide it, Grosseteste referred his reader back to his commentary on the first book.[142]

In fact, the first book contains two accounts of the way to knowledge of the truth of first principles, each one tailored to a different category of principle, the axioms and the laws of nature. To explain how the mind perceived the truth of common principles, the axioms (*dignitates*) of scientific thought, Grosseteste turned to the rules of logic. He began by saying that Aristotle had shown that axioms had to do with conditions that were necessary in themselves (*per se*), and by this he meant that there was no middle or separate cause upon which their existence depended as well as no external reason or syllogism that served to reveal them to the discerning mind. To illustrate what he meant, he drew an analogy between knowledge of axioms and vision in sensory light. A bright visible object did not stand in need of anything else—that is, any additional light—in order to be seen by the eyes, so long as they were directing their vision toward it. In the same way, an axiom needed only the attention of the reason (*aspectus mentis*) in order to be made known; it depended on no other agent, logical or otherwise, to manifest its truth.[143]

The reason for this had to do with the way such primary ob-

---

[142] *Comm. Post. an.,* II, 6 (p. 406, ll. 69–72).

[143] *Comm. Post. an.,* I, 8 (pp. 157–58, ll. 255–73). At l. 262, Rossi's text must be repunctuated to read: ". . . nisi ratione que sita est in anima sicut visus in oculo; et sicut. . . ."
This might be seen as another use of the notion of an all-pervasive intelligible light to explain knowledge of first principles. But strictly speaking, Grosseteste was drawing an analogy with sight not to introduce the idea of an intelligible light but rather to make clear that the principles, or whatever objects they stood for, provided themselves the evidence for their own truth.

jects fit with the logic by which the mind knew truth. According to Grosseteste, the immediate (*per se*) intelligibility of axioms depended on the evident identity of their terms. Here he appealed to the rule that the mind knew the truth of a proposition when it saw the substantial identity of subject and predicate. If the mind could perceive that identity without having to infer it from a middle term or conclude it on the basis of some external, formal reason—that is, if the identity was in itself manifest to human reason—then the proposition whose truth was known in this way could be called an axiom of scientific thought.[144] Grosseteste went on to say that one practical consequence of this fact was that no one could raise even a tentative objection to an axiom.[145] All other knowledge, including the most certain truths of science, could be doubted until proven true. Only axioms could never be doubted at all.

For Grosseteste, therefore, the only true noetic process involved in knowing the truth of axioms was the process by which the mind formed the simple concepts of which they were composed. The judgment of the truth of the way the concepts related followed as an immediate and noninferential outgrowth of simple cognition. One could almost say that knowing the truth of an axiom was equivalent to seeing that a complex statement was not complex at all, from the point of view of reference, but instead a complicated way of describing a single nature. This means, of course, that Grosseteste's description of the way to knowledge of the truth of axioms was very much like the way he would explain knowledge of the truth of those other fundamentals of science, principles drawn immediately from the definitions of the members of the subject. The formal configuration of the two types of proposition was not precisely the same, for axioms did not necessarily take the simple pattern of a subject followed by a definition. Yet the underlying logical and referential circumstances for each sort of

---

[144] *Comm. Post. an.,* I, 8 (p. 158, ll. 268–73).
[145] *Comm. Post. an.,* I, 8 (p. 158, ll. 273–79).

principle seem to have been identical. Perhaps the similarity extends even to knowledge of the first proper principles, ones that joined the subject of a science with its first inherent property.[146] Grosseteste never explained how one acquired such principles, but it must be imagined that there, too, an immediately apparent referential identity was at the bottom of knowledge of truth.

To a certain extent, the formal correspondence among these three types of immediate cognition must be accepted as a fundamental aspect of Grosseteste's thought and indeed the result of a conscious parallelism in his explanations of the epistemological foundations for science. He occasionally maintained that all scientific thought could ultimately be reduced to a matter of definition, and although he could not have intended this statement to be taken literally without some reservations, it did reflect one of his basic attitudes about the workings of the mind.[147] Moreover, this was an attitude that would have tended to reduce all forms of principal cognition to one basic type. Yet Grosseteste did distinguish among the kinds of principles. He clearly held that knowldege of axioms should not be confused with other sorts of immediate complex cognition, such as true statements drawn from the subject. If in his descriptions of how the mind attained such types of knowledge he did not make it clear how they were different, this should not be taken to mean that the distinction was one he could not have explained in detail had he thought that it was important.

In fact, if one reads the *Commentary* carefully one can find a few hints as to how he might have handled the issue. It seems that what distinguished axioms from other kinds of principles was the elevated nature of the simple concepts from which they were formed. This idea would not have been unfamiliar to other scholastics of Grosseteste's day. William of Auvergne, for

---

[146] See above, n. 123.

[147] See above, n. 98. Even in the case of natural science Grosseteste sometimes spoke as if discovering principles was no more than a matter of finding the proper definition. See, for example, his *Commentary on the Physics,* I (*Commentarius in VIII libros Physicorum,* ed. Dales, p. 1).

example, explicitly noted that axioms could be set apart from all other kinds of knowledge since they alone were made up of terms referring to the first intelligibles.[148] Now at one point in the passage where Grosseteste explained the knowledge of principles by drawing upon the notion of an intelligible light, he made the observation that not all the complex conditions that were in themselves (*per se*) visible to the mind—and therefore foundations for principal cognition—were constituted from simple natures that were also per se visible.[149] The implication would seem to be that there were some principles, but not all, for which not only the complex truth of the whole proposition but also the nature of the simple referents of the terms were per se visible. In the face of Grosseteste's silence on the matter, one can only speculate about the difference between the terms of principles that were visible per se and those that were not, but it would be reasonable to suppose that the former consisted of concepts that were immediately and without exception known to all rational minds. They would have been simple concepts so basic to the process of thinking that no one could have failed to perceive what they were, very much like William's first intelligibles. Furthermore, the propositions in which they were found would necessarily have been the most fundamental of all rational thought—in short, truly the very first principles of science.

It is, therefore, hard not to conclude that Grosseteste was referring to a notion of the nature of axioms parallel to that found in the work of William of Auvergne.[150] There may even be an indication in Grosseteste's *Commentary* of how he thought this idea was related to Aristotle's view of the hierarchy of the sciences. The axioms were, it must be remembered, the common principles of science, and at one point Grosseteste commented that such common principles were explained, al-

---

[148] See above, Chapter III, n. 72.

[149] *Comm. Post. an.,* I, 19 (p. 279, ll. 40–42).

[150] This is not to imply that Grosseteste agreed with William's theory that the mind received its knowledge of such concepts through illumination.

most verified, in a common philosophy, some overarching field like metaphysics or the topics.[151] He was evidently referring to the weak, dialectical explanation that he had said was the closest thing to a proof one could expect for immediate propositions drawn from the subject of a science.[152] Yet this implies that axioms were nothing more than hypotheses based on the definitions of the subjects of the very highest sciences. In this case they would indeed be like the other hypothesized principles, except that their subject terms would be so basic and so abstract that they would be implied in every type of scientific thought and handled explicitly only in the most general of all.

Whether or not this accurately represents Grosseteste's real views on the matter, the fact remains that his explanation of the way to knowledge of axioms or common principles, like his explanation of statements drawn from the subject, depended almost exclusively on his general notion of the relation between propositional truth and an identity of terms. The same idea could not, however, have been so successfully applied to the category of proper principles consisting of regular although ultimately contingent laws, most notably the laws of natural science. Here, something more than the simple vision of the referents of terms was required. Indeed, it took an elaborate procedure for the mind to come to know the truth of such principles, although the whole process was still formally less than a true demonstration. Grosseteste's account of this procedure came in the same place where he examined the induction of simple concepts.[153] Immediately after sketching the way the mind worked its way to simple universals, he turned to analyze the induction of complex truths. As he made clear, he was not on this occasion interested in all complex truths, only those that expressed fundamental natural laws, what he called experimental complex universals (*universalia complexa experimentalia*).

---

[151] *Comm. Post. an.*, I, 8 (p. 152 ll. 136–39).
[152] See above, n. 111.
[153] *Comm. Post. an.*, I, 14 (pp. 214–15, ll. 252–71). The passage in Grosseteste's *Commentary* immediately preceding this, pertaining to simple cognition, has been discussed above. See Chapter VI, n. 83.

Grosseteste recognized that just as in the case of the knowledge of any other complex truth, the induction of the complex principles of natural science followed upon the prior induction of simple universal terms. In other words, experimental induction was only the second part in a two-stage process. The first stage consisted in the procedure whereby the mind divided and induced its way to simple universals. The second stage began where the first left off, and it operated wholly within the realm of complex thought. This second stage was, however, itself divisible into two further substages. According to Grosseteste, induction on the complex level brought the mind only to the point of formulating a proposition whose universal truth it wanted to test. The testing itself came through what he called experiment (*experientia*), which is why he referred to the principles obtained by this whole procedure as experimental universals. What is more, he meant the word "experiment" in very much the sense in which it is used today, a controlled procedure intended to verify a scientific hypothesis. Such a notion of experimentation is not to be found in Aristotle, and Grosseteste probably came upon the idea in the works of Arabic science. Indeed, he may have lifted his experimental theory in toto from Avicenna, perhaps as transmitted through the works of al-Ghazali, for the example he used to illustrate experiment is precisely the one first employed by Avicenna in his *Logic*.[154] When these two processes, induction and experimentation, were put together, they provided the mind with a single, continuous procedure permitting it to identify natural principles and to know that they were true.

[154] The example had to do with scammony and the purging of red bile (see below, n. 155). Crombie suggested that Grosseteste may have taken his example from Avicenna's *Canon medicinae* (see Crombie, *Robert Grosseteste,* p. 81). Julius Weinberg has, however, succeeded in locating the exact source of Grosseteste's example in Avicenna's *Logic.* He notes that the *Logic* was only partly translated into Latin but that Grosseteste could well have found the example repeated in al-Ghazali's *Logic,* which was the first part of his *Tendencies of the Philosophers.* According to Weinberg, this same example was used after Grosseteste by Albert the Great and Duns Scotus, and it probably was the basis for William of Ockham's remarks on induction. See Julius R. Weinberg, *Abstraction, Relation, and Induction* (Madison, Wisc., 1965), pp. 133–35.

Grosseteste began his description of the procedure by re-
marking that here, as in the case of the acquisition of simple
concepts, the human intellect in its weakened condition after
the Fall was reduced to seeking knowledge through the instrument of the bodily senses (*sensus ministerio*). He followed with
a straightforward account of induction and experimentation.

Now when the senses several times apprehend two sensible objects, of which one is the cause of the other or in some other way
related to it, and they do not apprehend the mediating relation itself, as, for example, when someone many times sees the eating of
scammony accompanied by the discharge of red bile and he does
not see that scammony attracts and draws out red bile, then from
the frequent perception of these two visible things [the power of
sense] begins to form a notion (*estimare*) of the third, invisible
element, that is, [in this case,] that scammony is the cause that
draws out red bile. And on account of this notion (*intentio estimata*), formed many times and stored in the memory, and on account of the sensory perceptions (*intentiones sensate*) from which
this notion (*intentio estimata*) is derived, the reason wakes up.
Now the awakened reason begins to wonder and to consider
whether things really are as the notion in the memory (*estimatio
memorata*) says, and these two lead the reason to an experiment
(*experientia*), that is, that it give scammony [to someone] to eat
after all other causes purging red bile have been isolated and removed. Then when it has many times administered scammony
with the definite (*certa*) isolation and removal of other causes that
draw out red bile, there is formed in the reason this universal: that
all scammony of its nature (*secundum se*) draws out red bile. And
this is the way by which one proceeds from sensation to an experimental universal principle.[155]

By this account the whole first half of the process, the business of complex induction, took place on a sensible level,
below the intelligibility of reason. After the external senses had
many times perceived two objects that were in fact related as

---

[155] *Comm. Post. an.,* I, 14 (pp. 214-15, ll. 254-71). Some elements of
the translation given here have been borrowed from Crombie's translation of the same passage (*Robert Grosseteste*, pp. 73-74), but there are also
significant differences.

cause and effect, some internal power below reason made the guess, or more precisely the inductive inference, that there was a third, unperceived cognitive element that had to be taken into consideration, namely the relation between the two objects as cause and effect. It is clear by the fact that Grosseteste referred to the process of making the inductive inference as *estimare* and called knowledge of the relation an *intentio estimata* that he had in mind the cognitive power known commonly in medieval texts as the estimative.[156] This mental faculty on the border between sense and intellect was what came up with the first, tentative form of the proposition that would eventually be made a principle of science. In accordance with Grosseteste's understanding of psychology, the knowledge of the relation uniting the two objects was stored in the memory, while the fundamental sensible knowledge of each of the two objects alone was perceived in the imaginative power.[157]

Once the senses had seen the two objects together many times and the estimative had often been led to infer the existence of a relation between them, the reason was finally aroused to activity. Grosseteste seems to have been implying that here, too, some sort of induction came into play, because otherwise there would have been no need to say that the preliminary sensory process had to occur many times; but he offered no more formal explanation than to suggest metaphorically that the senses had to nudge the intellect several times before it woke up. The data that lay before the reason when at last it began to function were the sensible images of the separate objects preserved in the imaginative power and the notion of a causal relation between them (*intentio estimata*) that had been stored in the memory. It was the job of the reason to decide whether

---

[156] Grosseteste also made reference to this power in the passage noted above, Chapter VI, n. 98. On the history of the notion of an estimative power, see Pierre Michaud-Quantin, *Etudes sur le vocabulaire philosophique du moyen âge* (Rome, 1970), pp. 9-24.

[157] In the same passage referred to in Chapter VI, n. 98, Grosseteste explained that the function of the imaginative power was to retain sensory forms and that of the memory to retain *intentiones estimatas*.

this notion, or more exactly, the proposition in which knowledge of this relation was expressed, was true. Grosseteste made this clear by using the precise terms of his formal definition of complex truth: the reason had to judge if the knowledge suggested by the estimative power stated things as they actually were in reality. The way the reason went about making this judgment was to find an experiment by means of which it could test the veracity of the proposition relating the two simple objects. When it had performed the experiment many times, taking care that it had done so under carefully controlled circumstances, and when the result had come out as the hypothetical proposition would have predicted, then the reason felt satisfied of the proposition's truth and accepted it as a universal statement of fact. Verified by experiment, the proposition could stand as a principle of science.[158]

This brief description of a complicated mental process constituted a truly significant moment in medieval thought. It represented the first attempt in the medieval West to formulate a theory of the induction of complex scientific laws and to suggest an experimental method for verifying them. Even William of Auvergne, himself an innovative thinker, had never thought to explain the process by which the mind arrived at these sorts of natural principles as a form of induction, and he offered no way, other than pure intuition, to judge their truth. By combining Arab ideas on induction and experimentation with a vision of science otherwise largely inspired by Aristotle, Grosseteste had gone further than anyone in his time to provide the epistemological foundation for a new attitude toward the mind's search for truth, cutting it off from the traditionally supposed dependence on intuition or on a higher light and replacing that dependence with a novel reliance on a critical, definable procedure. What is more, the effects of such a speculative innovation were independent of whether or not men were im-

---

[158] It is important to remember that Grosseteste held that the principles of science were verified by experiment, but not the conclusions. Scientific reasoning per se was deductive, concerned with the formal, logical inference of conclusions from certain principles.

mediately capable of putting the new theory into practice. Grosseteste himself was, after all, no great experimenter. What his ideas did was rather to change the way men of science explained the processes of their thought, the way they defended what they held to be true, and the way they taught such truths to others. In the end, Grosseteste's views on complex induction encouraged scholastics in their attempt to establish a systematic organization of all knowledge in this life and convinced them that they could find in the world discernible criteria by which to do so.

For all its importance, however, as an indicator of a new attitude toward the way the human mind attained and verified its knowledge of the external world, Grosseteste's vision of the process of complex induction and experimentation had its limitations. First of all it did not actually apply in its fullness to all contingent or natural principles, not even to all those of the natural sciences. There were natural conditions involving a principle of regularity that were not fully observable and thus, to Grosseteste's mind, not subject to induction, yet this did not prevent one from formulating valid laws to describe or explain them and from knowing that the laws were true. A case in point was the frequently cited example of an eclipse of the moon. Although the senses could not actually perceive the earth, the moon, and the sun in their relative positions in space, the mind was nevertheless able to come to know the principle that an eclipse would follow whenever the three lined up so that the earth cast its shadow on the moon. In such instances there would have to be some other procedure besides induction and experimentation by which the intellect arrived at complex knowledge and recognized its truth. Yet the problem went beyond the question of observability, for Grosseteste admitted that even if one could by some special dispensation observe a lunar eclipse from a vantage point where it was possible to see earth, sun, and moon all at once, one would not on that account alone be justified in formulating a proposition that could stand as a principle of astronomy. One would, to be sure, have seen the singular constituents of an eclipse and have witnessed the configuration of light and shadow that was its cause in that particular instance, but there would seem to be nothing in this from which the mind could logically infer a universal principle to explain an eclipse in every case.[159]

The difficulty was essentially the same as that mentioned before in discussing the universality of simple concepts. Even if the mind knew all the existing examples of a specific nature, it would not by that fact alone be able to form a universal to represent that nature. Some other, universalizing procedure was necessary. Similarly, when it came to complex cognition, even if one was permitted to observe the cause of a regular phenomenon at any single moment, one could not be sure that the knowledge one had could be expressed in terms of a principle or a statement of universal fact. That is to say, one could not say with certainty that the cause one had observed revealed the true nature of the complex phenomenon and did not merely represent a set of accidental circumstances that accounted for its occurrence in that particular case. In the earlier example concerning scammony and the discharge of red bile, it was the process of complex induction, carried out on the level of the estimative power, followed by a series of controlled experiments that provided the mind with the requisite certainty that its knowledge was universal. And Grosseteste actually referred to this account of experimental knowledge when he raised the problem of finding the universal cause of an eclipse, saying that if one were to observe an eclipse many times from some point in space, one would be able to work one's way to knowledge of the principle in the way he had described before.[160] Yet such fantasy did not offer a real solution to the dilemma. One could not fully observe the facts or perform experiments in the case of natural laws about phenomena like an eclipse.

To resolve the issue Grosseteste offered a corollary to his longer explanation of the way the mind arrived at knowledge of the complex truths of the natural world. He said that al-

[159] *Comm. Post. an.*, I, 18 (pp. 267–68, ll. 174–80). Grosseteste took this directly from Aristotle, *Posterior Analytics*, I, 31 (87b39–25).
[160] *Comm. Post. an.*, I, 18 (p. 268, ll. 180–83).

though knowledge of the complex principles of science was dependent on sensation, as he had explained in his account of induction and experimentation, the senses were not in any proper sense the cause of such knowledge. They provided only the occasion. This was clear even in those instances, such as the imaginary one where someone was elevated to the moon to view an eclipse, where the senses directly perceived both the separate elements involved in the phenomenon and the causal relationship that bound them together. For all the suggestive value of such observations, in themselves they amounted to no more than apprehending the singular cause of a particular event. And that was not the same thing as scientific knowledge of a universal principle, nor did one kind of knowledge follow inevitably from the other. The fact that in the human mind universal, complex knowledge did sometimes follow immediately (*statim*) upon complete sensory perception of a single incident was not, therefore, because there was a strictly logical or necessary connection between the two but rather because there was something special about the intellect that permitted such an inference to be made.[161] Grosseteste repeated an example he found in Aristotle, that most men did not know the cause why light could pass through glass simply because they could not see the pores in glass that allowed light to go through. If, however, they could once see those pores, they would immediately know the scientific, universal cause, even though the vision of the pores itself did not constitute scientific knowledge but only the occasion for it.[162]

---

[161] *Comm. Post. an.,* I, 18 (pp. 268–69, ll. 189–207). See also *Comm. Post. an.,* II, 1 (pp. 301–2, ll. 298–315).

[162] *Comm. Post. an.,* I, 18 (pp. 269–70, ll. 207–27). The example came in *Posterior Analytics,* I, 31 (88a14–17). Grosseteste—like Aristotle elsewhere in his own works—did not accept the theory that glass was transparent because it contained pores, and he was evidently perplexed by the fact that Aristotle cited that theory to illustrate his point. His response offers an interesting example of how he dealt with an authoritative text in a case where he clearly disagreed with its literal meaning. Rather than accuse Aristotle of error, he suggested that he may have been speaking of the pores as a metaphor for the real cause of transparency, which Grosseteste understood to be the lack of earth in glass. Grosseteste defended

What permitted the mind to move sometimes straight from sensation to scientific knowledge of a causal principle was *sollertia,* or quick wit.[163] As Grosseteste explained, quick wit was a *habitus* of the mind, the power (*vis*) of discovering the middle term of a demonstration or the cause of a thing when this was not in itself immediately intellectually perceptible.[164] It could, moreover, go from knowledge of the cause to knowledge of the effect as well as the other way around.[165] What characterized quick wit was that it made this passage instantaneously (*cito, velociter*) and that it did so without having recourse to the discursive power of reason but only to its own intuition. There was, for Grosseteste, nothing magical in all this, for it fully conformed to his realist metaphysics. Causal connections in the world were real, and although they might not be available to the mind the way a simple nature was through *intellectus,* it was conceivable that there existed a mental process capable of following them through on some other level. In short, quick wit was just part of the psychological equipment necessary to deal with external reality. Yet if quick wit was not remarkable as a phenomenon of psychology, it did have an extraordinary and somewhat mysterious role when viewed from the perspective of epistemology. For because it was a power that bypassed the enumerative procedure of normal scientific induction, it allowed the mind to infer a general

---

this interpretation by claiming that it was not unusual for Aristotle to speak in such a cryptic way. Perhaps he subscribed to the opinion that the philosophers tried to hide their real meaning from the vulgar curiosity of the unlearned.

[163] *Comm. Post. an.,* I, 19 (p. 278, ll. 3–7; p. 281, ll. 70–83; and p. 286, ll. 181–88). Aristotle explained *sollertia* in *Posterior Analytics,* I, 34. William of Auvergne also used the notion of this power—even more widely than Grosseteste or Aristotle.

[164] Technically speaking, to use the term *habitus* to describe a power of the mind departed from the strict Aristotelian meaning of the word. William of Auvergne had also used *habitus* ambiguously in this way. Yet even Aristotle was sometimes less than clear on the division between powers of the mind and states of knowledge. See above, Chapter III, n. 97.

[165] *Comm. Post. an.,* I, 19 (p. 286, ll. 181–82).

principle and know its truth given only the singular occasion of sensory perception of particular circumstances. It permitted in a single bound an inference that could not be justified on any more complicated logical grounds.[166]

It does, to be sure, seem as if something like quit wit was implied, although not explicitly mentioned, even in the example where the mind worked its way to knowledge of the principle concerning scammony and red bile. In that case quick wit would have been the psychological power permitting the mind to induce a general proposition from repeated observation of the same fact. It would have worked on the level of the estimative power. Yet if quick wit was already incorporated in this limited way in the theory of induction and experimentation, the use to which Grosseteste put the idea when it came to principles such as those explaining eclipses and the passage of light through glass involved much more. Here quick wit substituted for induction altogether. A single instance where the cause was apparent to the senses was enough for the mind to formulate a general statement of fact. What is more important, quick wit also replaced the subsequent procedure of experimentation itself. It revealed to the mind the truth of a complex principle even when there was no chance of verifying it experimentally. There is, furthermore, no indication that Grosseteste thought that principles obtained in this way were any less reliable than those devised and tested through the former, more complicated procedure.

One must be careful, however, of drawing too great a contrast between Grosseteste's explanation of the acquisition of principles by quick wit and his other account dependent on in-

---

[166] This relates to the problem Serene raised with regard to Crombie's discussion of intuition in Grosseteste (see Serene, "Robert Grosseteste," pp. 101-2, and Crombie, *Robert Grosseteste,* pp. 71-72). It would seem that for most of the proper principles of natural science, Grosseteste did believe that an act of intellect other than induction accounted for justified assent. For some natural laws experimental verification was necessary. For others a special power of mind would do. But this special power was not *nous* (that is, in Latin, *intellectus*), as Crombie has asserted, but rather *sollertia.*

duction and experimentation. As has been suggested, quick wit may have had its place in the latter account as well. Likewise, Grosseteste seems to have wanted to make room for something like induction even in the acquisition of those principles more conveniently explained through quick wit, although, as seen in the case of eclipses, he had to resort to fantasy to do this.[167] It would appear he simply borrowed the notion of quick wit from Aristotle and medieval sources but did not examine very carefully how it fit with his other, inductive-experimental approach. On this score it is important to note that the examples he gave to explain how one might come to knowledge of a principle of natural science when there was no possibility of induction and experimental verification were hypothetical; in not a single instance was it possible even to imagine how the mind might make the preliminary observations required. A case in point was the lunar eclipse. Grosseteste said how things would be if one were raised to the heavens and saw the earth come between the moon and the sun, but he never explained how the principle had actually been arrived at—whether he thought there had been some sort of induction from data gained by observing the stars and if he felt some kind of verifying experiment had been possible. In short, the references to quick wit are no more than an indication that he recognized there was a process of discovery or intellectual invention that could not be fully accounted for in terms of the inductive procedure he had learned from Aristotle and Avicenna. They do not explain exactly what he thought the process was.

This brings us to a second limitation of Grosseteste's whole discussion of the way to knowledge of the truth of the laws of nature. All of his theoretical statements about the procedures for obtaining such knowledge—about verification and discovery—seem far from the real business of science in his time and from most of what he did in his own scientific works. Here, the vagueness of his notion of discovery through *sollertia* was just a symptom of a broader divergence between theory and practice.

[167] See above, n. 160.

Of course, Grosseteste pointed out that Aristotle's *Posterior Analytics* was not a guide to invention—that is, the discovery of new or principal truths as well as the formulation of syllogisms—but rather a handbook for judging demonstrations whose principles and whose form had already been devised.[168] No one could have expected his *Commentary* to go far beyond the scope of the original work. Nevertheless, it might appear curious that he never took the occasion in any of his writings to work out his thoughts about invention or experimentation any more clearly than he did. He plainly realized that the discovery of principles, this time referred to specifically as induction from singulars, was of capital importance for the acquisition of science:

And if there is no induction from singulars there will be in the intellect no universal knowledge of the singulars, because the universal itself can only be obtained through induction. And if there is no universal in the intellect, there will be no demonstration, because demonstration is from universals. And if there is no demonstration, there will be no science, because science is acquired by demonstration alone.[169]

It could even be argued that attaining such knowledge was the most critical aspect of the process of knowing complex truth. On several occasions Grosseteste hinted that demonstration was more or less a matter of putting words in the right deductive order once true principles had been arrived at by the preliminary processes of division and induction.[170] If, then, he did not work out the details of invention, it was not because it was irrelevant to his theory of truth and the way truth was found.

The reason lay instead in the nature of what motivated him to work out such a theory. Grosseteste, along with most of his

---

[168] *Comm. Post. an.,* II, 5 (p. 402, ll. 250–55). More recently, Jonathan Barnes has argued that Aristotle, in the *Posterior Analytics,* had no intention of showing how to conduct research but rather wanted to reveal the best way of teaching what was already known. See Barnes, "Aristotle's Theory of Demonstration," p. 85.

[169] *Comm. Post. an.,* I, 14 (p. 212, ll. 209–14).

[170] See, for example, *Comm. Post. an.,* II, 2 (pp. 314–15, ll. 238–50).

contemporaries in the scholarly world, was concerned more to sort out, organize, and evaluate a body of knowledge already familiar or at least available in works newly translated from Arabic and Greek than to extend the boundaries of science into uncharted areas of thought. Because of this a theory of truth was important primarily insofar as it served to establish the validity of the formal principles of organization. These principles were, for the most part, deductive, the rules of logic concerned with drawing out the implications of what was already known and explaining how known truths related to one another. Therefore, only those aspects of a theory of truth having to do with the articulation of demonstrative or deductive logic were of immediate practical significance. They made it possible to understand more clearly what logic was doing and to manipulate it with greater ease. Among the most important of these aspects of a theory of truth were reflections on the nature of truth itself and on the types of universal reference, for they related knowledge and language to the objective world and consequently provided a link between the maneuvers of logic and reality.

When it came, on the other hand, to those elements of a theory of truth that had to do with the ultimate foundations of true knowledge in undemonstrated principles and with the way such principles were derived and verified, there was much less urgency and indeed much less interest. These aspects of the theory—for Grosseteste, those concerning induction, discovery, and experimentation—were symbolically important, since they validated the whole endeavor of deductive science and argued to men that their analytic system made sense. For this reason Grosseteste took care to sketch out a doctrine that at least suggested how such foundations were laid. Yet this side of the theory of truth was not immediately connected with the business of scientific thought, which was deductive, and so it did not have to go very far. Once an outline had been given, enough to suggest how the procedures of science rested on an adequate base and to affirm that the primary truths from which men reasoned were reliable and drawn from the nature of reality, there was no need to go into greater detail or to work out minor inconsistencies. Since thirteenth-century thinkers were not often interested in opening up new avenues for investigation, since they generally did not intend actually to apply the principles of invention and verification that had been worked out, it was not necessary to indicate exactly what such processes would entail.

It is not hard, therefore, to understand how Grosseteste could have been so eloquent and imaginative when it came to suggesting a theory of truth and solving problems of reference while at the same time he devoted so little attention to invention (including the process of induction) and verification, or to see why the latter processes had so little to do with his actual scientific work.[171] Yet in the end it is not such imbalances in Grossesteste's thought but rather the ambitious nature of his many-sided theory that stands out. He laid the foundations for a comprehensive solution to most of the fundamental problems of scientific knowledge. Especially in the area of complex truth, he went beyond his contemporary William of Auvergne and handled questions of reference and evidence with a subtlety remarkable for his time. Here, his readiness to see the logical side of problems long answered exclusively in metaphysical terms and to fashion a language to deal precisely with this logical element marks his thought as something spe-

---

[171] Bruce Eastwood refers to this tendency when he claims that Grosseteste's " 'scientific' methodology" was pure epistemology, not intended to be practically applied. It is perhaps more precise to say that some of Grosseteste's methodology was not intended to be practical—that part which had to do with induction and verification. Grosseteste also had a lot to say about deductive logic, and this applied directly and practically to what he did in specific scientific treatises. Nevertheless, the general point remains true that Grosseteste's discussion of method and a notion of truth was offered more as an apology for a view of knowledge and the way it referred to the world than as a plan of action for scientific discovery. For Eastwood's views, see "Medieval Empiricism," p. 321, and also "Robert Grosseteste's Theory of the Rainbow. A Chapter in the History of Non-experimental Science," *Archives Internationales d'Histoire des Sciences* 77 (1966), 313–32, and "Grosseteste's 'Quantitative' Law of Refraction: A Chapter in the History of Non-experimental Science," *Journal of the History of Ideas* 28 (1967), 403–14.

cial. Just as important was his ability to multiply the categories available to analyze the nature of scientific thought and to accommodate his theory of truth to each category, from the different kinds of science properly speaking to the varieties of complex principles. His work, by its precision and breadth alone, went a long way toward providing an alternative to the old methods of approaching truth. At the very least, by suggesting that a full alternative was possible he offered an incentive to continue looking for it. Grosseteste gave men a glimpse of a philosophical rationale for the analytic system of thought they so eagerly sought. In this way he contributed greatly to the formation of the mental habits of the thirteenth century.

Conclusion

═══

It is now time to step back and consider once more the broader issues of intellectual change with which this study has been concerned. As was noted in the Introduction, the thirteenth-century discussion about the nature of truth was not at bottom a dispute over specific doctrines—at least this is not what it was for the first few generations of thinkers involved—but rather an effort to come to terms with a philosophical issue that had not been considered in the medieval West before. It was an attempt to arrive at a notion of truth that could serve as the basis for a more critical appraisal of what it meant to know. Yet this attempt was itself part of a larger episode in the history of thought. By coming to a new idea of truth, the most ambitious scholars hoped to lend greater strength to a movement transforming the whole tenor of rational discourse in an increasingly self-conscious intellectual world.

The seeds of this revolution can be found already in the twelfth century. It was then that Western scholars developed their passionate attachment to the business of amassing speculative knowledge about the world they lived in, and they began to seek rational ways to organize and make readily available the collected wisdom of the authors of the ancient and Arabic worlds. Most frequently, this amounted to settling on some Neoplatonized world-view that permitted them to organize all knowledge along the lines of a cosmological scheme. By the thirteenth century, however, after over one hundred years of study and translation, many in the new universities had come to see the complexity of the intellectual tradition to which they were heir, and they sensed the danger of becoming lost in a labyrinth of loose ends and contradictions. All the while, their desire for knowledge had continued to grow, encouraging them to contemplate an almost imperialistic expansion into the realm of natural speculation. It was as if they believed that with only a little effort they could reach the limits—to them the dizzy heights—of human reason.

What was needed was some new way to discriminate among ideas, to sort out opinions according to their worth and fashion the certain ones systematically into a speculative edifice in which scholars could have confidence. To most it appeared that this new way should be along the lines of more purely formal principles, capable of generating a scientific structure from within instead of being applied at a stroke from the outside. The practical tool that was coming increasingly to be seen as the proper guide for such a formal assault on learning lay in the new logic developing in the faculty of arts, both at Oxford and at Paris, especially as this logic was incorporated into the theory and program of science beginning to be extracted from the works of Aristotle. To be able to accept and understand this new tool, however, thinkers needed some further explanation or defense of its validity. Even if their arguments were to amount to nothing more than rationalization for a process that was already underway, they needed some theoretical assurance, an intellectual ideal, to make the shift easier and to justify the arduous task of speculative realignment.

It was this that led some among them to see the question of truth in a new way. They realized, perhaps unconsciously, that the intellectual ideal scholars were looking for was actually a theory of truth, one that was precise and critical in a way that earlier notions of truth had not been and that could thereby buttress new principles of organization that were themselves precise and critical. The conventional ways of describing truth primarily in terms of psychological experience and as an instance of God's revelation to man would no longer work. Those descriptions may have suited the earlier attempts to draw together knowledge along the lines of an authoritative world-view, since their reliance on revelation or internal conviction served primarily to lend authority to opinions and structures that were already formed and well-known. They could not, however, explain what scholars were doing when they appealed to carefully reasoned arguments and a fastidious consideration of logical form. This required both a new doctrine of what truth was and a new notion of what the problem of truth was all about. Here lay the origins of the intense speculation about the nature of truth and the criteria by which it could be identified that characterized the thought of the thirteenth century. William of Auvergne and Robert Grosseteste were among the first thinkers to feel the new need and to concern themselves with the theoretical questions that were involved.

Yet the change in attitude toward knowledge and the way it should be evaluated and organized not only accounted for the rise of a new problem of truth, it also determined some of the peculiarities of the theories advanced to solve the problem and the manner in which they were worked out, especially in the early years when scholars were first coming to grips with the nature of the task that lay before them. First of all it meant that thinkers would look primarily for ways of explaining truth and human knowledge of it that placed the evidence for judgment entirely in the created world. After all, the logic upon which the new science depended claimed that its arguments would be persuasive to anyone with an open mind. There was little room here for Augustine's view of truth as a matter of private and interior revelation or for any theory that depended on an intangible divine intervention that could not be pointed to and accepted by all. Second, the broad philosophical context in which the new problem of truth arose helped to generate within the new theories an uneven balance among the elements of which they were composed. Since the new theories of truth were to serve as a kind of rationale for the scientific procedures of the more forward-looking scholars, their structure naturally would have to reflect the logical biases of the procedures themselves. There was no necessity that they be complete or exhaustive, as would have been the case if medieval thinkers had set out with the purely critical intentions of much of modern philosophy. Scientific thought in the thirteenth century was based on deductive logic and a careful scrutiny of the meaning of words and propositions, and so the theories of truth used to support the new endeavors naturally emphasized the questions of the formal nature of truth and the proper conditions of reference. Little attention was given to the problems of induction and verification, or to any of the more general matters having to do with discovering and establishing new truths. Here, William of Auvergne and Robert Grosseteste set a pattern for their successors when they passed over such issues so lightly.

Finally, the very fact that the new theoretical concern for truth developed as a secondary and more or less apologetic offshoot of the broader and more practical interest in finding an appropriate tool to systematize knowledge accounts for the occasionally awkward or tentative arguments to be seen in the early attempts to deal with it. The same is true for the curious juxtaposition of traditional language and arguments about truth alongside the most innovative and forward-looking attempts to set the problem in completely new terms. This is perhaps the one aspect of early thirteenth-century speculation about truth that is hardest for the modern observer to understand. It is, however, singularly important, for unless one comes to terms with what was going on here one cannot fully appreciate the thought of this period, and indeed one risks misinterpreting it altogether.

The linguistic ambiguities as well as the reluctance of both William and Robert to purge their writings of all traces of a more traditional cast of mind—one that sat only uneasily with their newly gained insights about the nature of human knowledge—make sense only if one remembers how the problem of truth had arisen for them. Those thinkers of the early thirteenth century who had thrown in their lot with a new attitude toward knowledge along the lines of Aristotle's theory of science did so before they understood precisely what that entailed or how their new investigative procedures might be worked out. The formulation of a new notion of truth was one way for them to come to grips with what would remain for some time an awkward if exhilarating program of speculation. Consequently, the problem of truth arose with an urgency that at first strained their ability to work out a satisfactory answer or even to grasp fully all that such an answer would involve.

It was, therefore, inevitable that a complete and consistent theory of truth adequate to the scientific ideal would take a long time to work out. There could be no complete solutions at the beginning, only efforts to define the problem and suggest the directions in which a solution might lie. Thinkers could not talk coherently about new philosophical ideals until they had hammered out a new language with its own syntax, in this case a logical and analytic mode of analysis, and its own vocabulary—a host of new definitions for old as well as new words, like "incorruptible," "universal," "supposition," and "signification." Yet a new language could develop only as scholars came to a clearer understanding of their own ideas. In short, progress had to involve a degree of circularity. It had to come in fits and starts, and the perception of the formal configuration of the problem of truth had to develop slowly and simultaneously with the formulation of specific doctrines to fill out the formal skeleton.

It is likely that the same process occurs whenever there is a transformation in the form of thought, whether on the level of philosophy or not. This would account for the remarkable tenacity of more traditional modes of speech even in areas where their theoretical, or explicit, justification has expired. Such language has literally to be driven out as it becomes impossible to tolerate or even to understand it any longer. In the case of the thirteenth-century discussion of truth it was only when the new philosophical language was fully developed and so ingrained that it had completely colored the outlook of the scholarly world that the old could finally be given up. This happened very late in the thirteenth century, when references to illumination practically disappeared from scholastic epistemology altogether. Even then the old held on in writings where scientific attitudes did not apply, most especially in works of devotion and spiritual advice.

But there is no need here to dwell too long on the survival of the traditional. In the end it is the substantial progress that William of Auvergne and Robert Grosseteste were able to make in articulating new ideas and circumscribing the old that stands out. And for this they needed an extraordinary concentration of vision. One can only admire their confidence in the correctness of their philosophical intuition and in the ultimate validity of the direction in which they were going. Even when they could not fully construct a theory to explain all that they did, they remained true to their intellectual ideal. It is this preliminary, unreasoned confidence that may be the most remarkable and inexplicable aspect of the thirteenth century, an age that otherwise laid such stock in the ability to explain actions in absolutely reasonable terms.

Appendixes

===

A. PASSAGE FROM WILLIAM OF AUVERGNE

De anima, VII, 7 (*Mag. div.,* II supp., 213a–b)

Nihilominus tamen ab ipso mundo inferiori, et informationem, et illuminationem, et inscriptionem [*sic* for: informationum, et illuminationum, et inscriptionum] juxta modos quos audis receptibilem esse vim intellectivam nostram manifestum est. Fit autem istud tribus modis. Primum sensu qui substantias sensibiles,et intellectuales corporibus junctas adducit ad intellectum, verumtamen non pingit in eo formas intelligibiles ipsarum, quoniam nec formas hujusmodi ipsarum ipsemet recipit, sed intellectus per semetipsum substantias illas sub esse varietatibus sensibilium accidentium perpendit. Apprehendit igitur sive videt virtus intellectiva sub operimento substantias hujusmodi, ut jam audivisti, sic ipsam animam humanam ex motibus, et gubernatione corporis tanquam sub veste, vel sub operimento seu vestimento videt, et non ad nudum, sive ut ita dicatur, facie ad faciem; alioquin inter Socratem et Platonem qualiter esset altercatio vel disputatio; cum alter alterum intellectu nec cognosceret, nec videret.

Secundus modus est per abstractionem: et jam declaratum est tibi quid sit abstractio seu spoliatio aut denudatio: haec enim non est nisi privatio apprehensionis formarum individuantium sive individualium, et posui tibi exemplum de hoc in imagine Herculis eidem simillima, et intendo quae clare videnti, et e proximo inspicienti non nisi Herculem repraesentare posset. Si autem elongaretur ab illa pro modo elongationis, imminueretur apprehensio formarum hujusmodi; donec veniret ad hoc ut imago illa non repraesentaret ei nisi hominem vagum, non potius unum quam alium; hic est igitur modus abstractionis seu denudationis

293

formarum ad phantasiam sive imaginationem a sensibilibus venientium, ex quibus non est dubitandum quin intellectus occasionaliter inscribatur formis abstractioribus, et naturae suae congruentioribus. . . .

Tertius modus est per connexionem sive per colligationem, et intendo quod quaedam res colligatae sunt quousque ad invicem, ut sicut una sine altera esse non potest, sic neque cognitio alterius sine cognitione reliquae, cujus exemplum est evidens in causa efficienti conjuncta, et in effectu ejusdem, etc.

B. PASSAGE FROM WILLIAM OF AUVERGNE

De anima, VII, 9 (*Mag. div.,* II supp., 215b)

Neque necesse est ut omnis exitus de potentia in actum sit per actionem, et passionem, sicut vides in exitu virtutis motivae in motum suum; alioquin omnem motum praecederent infiniti. Nata igitur est virtus intellectiva una excitatione etiam levi recipere multas designationes, et fieri liber multarum designationum: causa autem in hoc est, quoniam excitatio hujusmodi applicat illam rebus, atque conjungit conjunctione spirituali. Et propter hoc sicut dicitur de animali quod chamaeleon nominatur; sic se habet, et de virtute intellectiva quae omnium rerum, quibus hujusmodi applicatione conjungitur similitudines vel signa in se recipit: et sicut de simia manifestum est quod opera quae videt ab hominibus fieri prout valet effigiat, et se eis operationibus assimilat: sic virtus intellectiva nata est rebus sic applicata se assimilare, similitudinesque vel signa earum assumere; ad hoc enim nata est naturaliter ut efficiatur liber in effectu sibi ipsi rerum quibus sic conjungitur.

Bibliography

====

PRIMARY WORKS CITED

Adelard of Bath. *Die Quaestiones naturales des Adelardus von Bath*. Ed. Martin Müller. Beiträge, XXXI, 2. Münster, 1934.

Anselm. *Cur deus homo*. In *Opera omnia*, II, 37–133. Ed. Francis S. Schmitt. Rome, 1940.

———. *De veritate*. In *Opera omnia*, I, 173–99. Ed. Francis S. Schmitt. Edinburgh, 1946.

———. *Monologion*. In *Opera omnia*, I, 1–87. Ed. Francis S.Schmitt, Edinburgh, 1946.

Aristotle. *Analytica posteriora*. Aristoteles Latinus, IV, 1–4. Ed. Lorenzo Minio-Paluello and Bernard G. Dod. Bruges, 1968.

———. *Categoriae vel praedicamenta*. Aristoteles Latinus, I, 1–5. Ed. Lorenzo Minio-Paluello. Bruges, 1961.

———. *De anima*. Ed. William D. Ross. Oxford, 1956.

———. *De interpretatione*. Aristoteles Latinus, II, 1–2. Ed. Lorenzo Minio-Paluello and Gérard Verbeke. Bruges, 1965.

———. *Ethica Nicomachea*. Aristoteles Latinus, XXVI, 1–3. Ed. René A. Gauthier. Leiden, 1972–74.

———. *Metaphysica*. Aristoteles Latinus, XXV, 1–1a, 2.. Ed. Gudrun Vuillemin-Diem. Brussels, 1970; Leiden, 1976.

———. *Physica*. Ed. William D. Ross. Oxford, 1950.

Augustine. *De Genesi ad litteram*. PL, 34, 245–486.

———. *De libero arbitrio*. Ed. William M. Green. CSEL, 74. Vienna, 1956.

———. *De magistro*. Ed. Günther Weigel. CSEL, 77, 1. Vienna, 1961.

———. *De Trinitate*. 2 vols. Ed. W. J. Mountain and Fr. Glorie. CC, 50–50A. Turnhout, 1968.

————. *De vera religione*. Ed. William M. Green. CSEL, 77. Vienna, 1961.

————. *Soliloquia*. PL, 32, 869–904.

Avicebron. *Fons vitae*. 3 vols. Ed. Clemens Baeumker. Beiträge, I, 2–4. Münster, 1892–95.

Avicenna. *Metaphysica*. In *Opera in lucem redacta*, ff. 70–109 (second numeration). Venice, 1508. (Repr. Frankfurt a. M., 1961.)

Bacon, Roger. *Opus tertium*. In *Opera quaedam hactenus inedita*, I, 3–310. Ed. John S. Brewer. London, 1859.

Boethius. *De Trinitate*. PL, 64, 1247–56.

————. *In Isagogen Porphyrii commenta*. Ed. Samuel Brandt. CSEL, 48. Vienna, 1906.

————. *Philosophiae consolatio*. Ed. Ludwig Bieler. CC, 94, 1. Turnhout, 1957.

————. *Quomodo substantiae* (or *De hebdomadibus*). PL, 64, 1311–14.

Duns Scotus, John. *Quaestiones in primum librum Sententiarum (Ordinatio)*. In *Opera omnia*, VIII (Vivès). Paris, 1893.

Grosseteste, Robert. *Commentarius in VIII libros Physicorum Aristotelis*. Ed. Richard C. Dales. Boulder, Colo., 1963.

————. *Commentarius in Posteriorum analyticorum libros*. Ed. Pietro Rossi. Florence, 1981.

————. "Ex rerum initiatarum." In Servus Gieben, "Robert Grosseteste on Preaching," *Collectanea Franciscana* 37 (1967), 100–41.

————. *Die philosophischen Werke des Robert Grosseteste, Bischofs von Lincoln*. Ed. Ludwig Baur. Beiträge, IX. Münster, 1912.

————. *Quaestiones theologicae*. In "The *Summa theologiae* of Robert Grosseteste," *Studies in Medieval History Presented to Frederick Maurice Powicke*, pp. 180–208. Ed. Daniel A. Callus. Oxford, 1948.

————. *Robert Grosseteste on the Creation (Hexaëmeron)*. Eds. Richard C. Dales and Servus Gieben. Oxford, forthcoming (1982).

Gundisalvi, Dominic. *De anima*. Ed. J. T. Muckle. *Mediaeval Studies* 2 (1940), 23–103.

————. *De immortalitate animae (Des Dominicus Gundissalinus Schrift von der Unsterblichkeit der Seele)*. Ed. Georg Bülow. Beiträge, II, 3. Münster, 1897.

Isaac Israeli. *Liber de definicionibus*. Ed. J. T. Muckle. *Archives d'Histoire Doctrinale et Littéraire du Moyen Age* 12–13 (1937–38), 299–340.

John of Salisbury. *Metalogicon*. Ed. Clement C. J. Webb. Oxford, 1929.

Plato. *Timaeus a Calcidio translatus commentarioque instructus*. Plato Latinus, IV. 2nd ed. Ed. Jan H. Waszink. London, 1975.

Thierry of Chartres. *Commentaries on Boethius by Thierry of Chartres and His School*. Ed. Nikolaus M. Häring. Toronto, 1971.

Thomas Aquinas. *Commentarium in libros Posteriorum analyticorum*. In *Opera omnia* (Leonine ed.), I. Rome, 1882.

———. *Commentary on the Posterior Analytics of Aristotle*. Trans. Fabian R. Larcher. Albany, N.Y., 1970.

William of Auvergne. *De anima*. In *Opera omnia*, II, supp., 65–228. Orleans-Paris, 1674. (Repr. Frankfurt a. M., 1963.)

———. *De bono et malo* (*Tractatus primus*). Ed. J. Reginald O'Donnell. *Mediaeval Studies* 8 (1946), 245–99.

———. *De bono et malo* (*Tractatus secondus*). Ed. J. Reginald O'Donnell. *Mediaeval Studies* 16 (1954), 219–71.

———. *De fide*. In *Opera omnia*, I, 1–18. Orleans-Paris, 1674. (Repr. Frankfurt a. M., 1963.)

———. *De Trinitate*. Ed. Bruno Switalski. Toronto, 1976.

———. *De universo*. In *Opera omnia*, I, 593–1074. Orleans-Paris, 1674. (Repr. Frankfurt a. M., 1963.)

———. *De virtutibus*. In *Opera omnia*, I, 102–91. Orleans-Paris, 1674. (Repr. Frankfurt a. M., 1963.)

William of Ockham. *Expositio super viii libros Physicorum* (Prologue). In *Philosophical Writings*, pp. 2–16. Ed. and trans. Philotheus Boehner. Edinburgh, 1957.

SECONDARY WORKS CITED

Allard, Baudoin C. "Note sur le 'De immortalitate animae' de Guillaume d' Auvergne." *Bulletin de Philosophie Médiévale* 18 (1976), 68–72.

Altmann, Alexander, and Samuel M. Stern. *Isaac Israeli. A Neoplatonic Philosopher of the Early Tenth Century*. Oxford, 1958.

Baeumker, Clemens. *Witelo, ein Philosoph und Naturforscher des XIII. Jahrhunderts*. Beiträge, III, 2. Münster, 1908.

Barnes, Jonathan. *Aristotle's Posterior Analytics*. (Translation and notes.) Oxford, 1975.

———. "Aristotle's Theory of Demonstration." In *Articles on Aristotle*, I: Science, pp. 65–87. Eds. Jonathan Barnes, Malcolm Schofield, and Richard Sorabji. London, 1975.

Baumgartner, Matthias. *Die Erkenntnislehre des Wilhelm von Auvergne.* Beiträge, II, 1. Münster, 1893.

Baur, Ludwig. "Das Licht in der Naturphilosophie des Robert Grosseteste." In *Festgabe zum 70. Geburtstag Georg Freiherrn von Hertling,* pp. 41–55. Freiburg im Br., 1913.

———. *Die Philosophie des Robert Grosseteste, Bischofs von Lincoln.* Beiträge, XVIII, 4–6. Münster, 1917.

Bérubé, Camille, and Servus Gieben. "Guibert de Tournai et Robert Grosseteste." In *S. Bonaventura, 1274–1974,* II, 626–54. Grottaferrata, 1973.

Bettoni, Efrem. "La dottrina bonaventuriana dell'illuminazione intellettuale." *Rivista di Filosofia Neoscolastica* 36 (1944), 139–58.

———. *S. Bonaventura.* Brescia, 1945.

Beumer, Johannes. "Robert Grosseteste von Lincoln der angebliche Begründer der Franziskanerschule." *Franziskanische Studien* 57 (1975), 183–95.

Bonafede, Giulio. *Il pensiero francescano nel secolo XIII.* Palermo, 1952.

Bowman, Leonard J. "The Development of the Doctrine of the Agent Intellect in the Franciscan School of the 13th Century." *The Modern Schoolman* 50 (1972–73), 251–79.

Callus, Daniel A. "The Date of Grosseteste's Translations and Commentaries on Pseudo-Dionysius and the Nicomachean Ethics." *Recherches de Théologie Ancienne et Médiévale* 14 (1947), 186–210.

———. "The Oxford Career of Robert Grosseteste." *Oxoniensia* 10 (1945), 42–72.

———. "Robert Grosseteste as Scholar." In *Robert Grosseteste, Scholar and Bishop,* pp. 1–69. Ed. D. A. Callus. Oxford, 1955.

———. "Robert Grosseteste's Place in the History of Philosophy." In *Actes du XIe Congrès International de Philosophie,* Brussels, 20–26 August 1953, XII, 161–65. Amsterdam, 1953.

———. "The *Summa theologiae* of Robert Grosseteste." In *Studies in Medieval History Presented to Frederick Maurice Powicke,* pp. 180–208. Oxford, 1958.

Chenu, Marie-Dominique. "Notes de lexicographie philosophique médiévale: Disciplina." *Revue des Sciences Philosophiques et Théologiques* 25 (1936), 686–92.

———. *La théologie au douzième siècle.* 2nd ed. Paris, 1966.

——. *La théologie comme science au XIIIe siècle*. 3rd ed. Paris, 1957.

Copleston, Frederick C. *A History of Medieval Philosophy*. London, 1972.

——. *A History of Philosophy*. II: Mediaeval Philosophy (2 pts.). New York, 1962.

Corti, Guglielmo. "Le sette parte del *Magisterium divinale ac sapientiale* di Guglielmo di Auvergne." In *Studi e ricerche di scienze religiose*, pp. 289–307. Rome, 1968.

Crombie, Alistair C. "Grosseteste's Position in the History of Science." In *Robert Grosseteste, Scholar and Bishop*, pp. 98–120. Ed. Daniel A. Callus. Oxford, 1955.

——. *Robert Grosseteste and the Origins of Experimental Science, 1100–1700*. Oxford, 1953.

——. "Robert Grosseteste on the Logic of Science." In *Actes du XIe Congrès International de Philosophie*, XII, 161–73. Brussels, 20–25 August 1953. Amsterdam, 1953.

Dales, Richard C. "Robert Grosseteste's *Commentarius in Octo Libros Physicorum Aristotelis*." *Medievalia et Humanistica* 11 (1957), 10–33.

——. "Robert Grosseteste's Scientific Works." *Isis* 52 (1961), 381–402.

de Rijk, Lambertus Marie. *Logica modernorum*. II (2 pts.). Assen, 1967.

de Vaux, Roland. *Notes et textes sur l'avicennisme latin aux confins des XIIe-XIIIe siècles*. Paris, 1934.

De Wulf, Maurice. "L'augustinisme 'avicennisant.'" *Revue Néo-Scolastique* 33 (1931), 11–39.

——. "Courants doctrinaux dans la philosophie européenne du XIIIe siècle." *Revue Néo-Scolastique* 34 (1932), 5–20.

Dondaine, Hyacinthe-François. "L'objet et le 'medium' de la vision béatifique chez les théologiens du XIIIe siècle." *Recherches de Théologie Ancienne et Médiévale* 19 (1952), 60–130.

Eastwood, Bruce S. "Grosseteste's 'Quantitative' Law of Refraction: A Chapter in the History of Non-experimental Science." *Journal of the History of Ideas* 28 (1967), 403–14.

——. "Medieval Empiricism: The Case of Grosseteste's Optics." *Speculum* 43 (1968), 306–21.

——. "Robert Grosseteste's Theory of the Rainbow. A Chapter in the History of Non-experimental Science." *Archives Internationales d'Histoire des Sciences* 77 (1966), 313–32.

Forest, Aimé. "Guillaume d'Auvergne, critique d'Aristote." In

Etudes médiévales offertes à Augustin Fliche, pp. 67-79. Vendôme, France, 1953.

Geyer, Bernhard, ed. *Friedrich Ueberwegs Grundriss der Geschichte der Philosophie. II:* Die patristische und scholastische Philosophie. 12th ed. Basel, 1951.

Gieben, Servus. "Bibliographia universa Roberti Grosseteste ab an. 1473 ad an. 1969." *Collectanea Franciscana* 39 (1969), 362-418.

Gilson, Etienne. *A History of Christian Philosophy in the Middle Ages.* New York, 1955.

―――. "Pourquoi saint Thomas a critiqué saint Augustin." *Archives d'Histoire Doctrinale et Littéraire du Moyen Age* 1 (1926-27), 5-127.

―――. "Réflexions sur la controverse S. Thomas–s. Augustin." In *Mélanges Mandonnet,* I, 371-83. Paris, 1930.

―――. "Les sources gréco-arabes de l'augustinisme avicennisant." *Archives d'Histoire Doctrinale et Littéraire du Moyen Age* 4 (1929), 5-149.

―――. "Sur quelques difficultés de l'illumination augustinienne." *Revue Néoscolastique de Philosophie* 36 (1934), 321-31.

Grabmann, Martin. *Der göttliche Grund menschlicher Wahrheitserkenntnis nach Augustinus and Thomas von Aquin.* Münster, 1924.

Hamelin, Alonzo M. *L'école franciscaine de ses débuts jusqu'à l'occamisme.* Louvain, 1961.

Heinzmann, Richard. "Wilhelm von Auvergne." In *Lexicon für Theologie und Kirche,* X, 1127-28. 2nd ed. Freiburg i. B., 1965.

Jansen, Bernhard. "Quomodo Divi Augustini theoria illuminationis saeculo decimo tertio concepta sit." *Gregorianum* 11 (1930), 146-58.

Jolivet, Jean. "Comparaison des théories du language chez Abélard et chez les Nominalistes du XIVe siècle." In *Peter Abelard,* pp. 163-78. Ed. E. M. Buytaert. Proceedings of the International Conference, Louvain, 10-12 May 1971. Louvain, 1974.

Jüssen, Gabriel. "Idee" (II, B, 3: Wilhelm von Auvergne). In *Historisches Wörterbuch der Philosophie,* IV, coll. 84-86. Eds. Joachim Ritter and Karlfried Gründer. Basel/Stuttgart, 1976.

―――. "Wilhelm von Auvergne und die Entwicklung der Philosophie im Übergang zur Hochscholastick." In *Thomas von Aquin im philosophischen Gespräch,* pp. 185-203. Ed. Wolfgang Kluxen. Freiburg/Munich, 1975.

Keicher, Otto. "Zur Lehre der ältesten Franziskanertheologen vom 'intellectus agens.' " In *Festgabe zum 70. Geburtstag Georg Freiherrn von Hertling,* pp. 173–82. Freiburg im Br., 1913.

Knowles, David. *The Evolution of Medieval Thought.* Baltimore, 1962.

Koyré, Alexandre. "The Origins of Modern Science: A New Interpretation." *Diogenes* 16 (1956), 1–22.

Kramp, Josef. "Des Wilhelm von Auvergne 'Magisterium divinale.' " *Gregorianum* 1 (1920), 538–84, and 2 (1921), 42–78, 174–87. (Latin version: 1 (1920), 585–616, and 2 (1921), 79–103, 187–95.)

Landry, Bernard. "L'originalité de Guillaume d'Auvergne." *Revue d'Histoire de la Philosophie* 3 (1929), 441–63.

Lang, Albert. *Die theologische Prinzipienlehre der mittelalterlichen Scholastick.* Freiburg im Br., 1964.

Leclercq, Jean. *Etudes sur le vocabulaire monastique au moyen âge.* Rome, 1961.

Leff, Gordon. *Medieval Thought. St. Augustine to Ockham.* Baltimore, 1958.

Longpré, Ephrem. "Guillaume d'Auvergne et Alexandre de Halès." *Archivum Franciscanum Historicum* 16 (1923), 249–50.

———. "Guillaume d'Auvergne et l'Ecole Franciscaine de Paris." *La France Franciscaine* 5 (1922), 426–29.

Lottin, Odon. *Psychologie et morale aux XIIe et XIIIe siècles.* I. Louvain, 1942.

Lynch, Lawrence E. "The Doctrine of Divine Ideas and Illumination in Robert Grosseteste, Bishop of Lincoln." *Mediaeval Studies* 3 (1941), 161–73.

McEvoy, James. "The Chronology of Robert Grosseteste's Writings on Nature and Natural Philosophy." *Speculum,* in press.

———. "La connaissance intellectuelle selon Robert Grosseteste." *Revue Philosophique de Louvain* 75 (1977), 5–48.

———. "The Metaphysics of Light in the Middle Ages." *Philosophical Studies* (Ireland) 26 (1979), 126–45.

Marrou, Henri-Irénée. " 'Doctrina' et 'disciplina' dans la langue des Pères de l'Eglise." *Bulletin du Cange* 10 (1934), 5–25.

Masnovo, Amato. *Da Guglielmo d'Auvergne a s. Tommaso d'Aquino.* 3 vols. 2nd ed. Milan, 1945–46.

———. "Guglielmo d'Auvergne." *Rivista di Filosofia Neo-Scolastica* 19 (1927), 132–45.

————. "Guglielmo d'Auvergne e l'Università di Parigi dal 1229 al 1231." In *Mélanges Mandonnet*, II, 191–232. Paris, 1930.

Mazzarella, Pasquale. *La dottrina dell'anima e della conoscenza in Matteo d'Acquasparta.* Padua, 1969.

Miano, V. "La teoria della conoscenza in Roberto Grossatesta." *Giornale di Metafisica* 9 (1954), 60–88.

Michaud-Quantin, Pierre. *Etudes sur le vocabulaire philosophique du moyen âge.* Rome, 1970.

Moody, Ernest A. "William of Auvergne and his Treatise *De anima.*" In *Studies in Medieval Philosophy, Science, and Logic*, pp. 1–109. Berkeley, Calif., 1975.

Muckle, J. T. "Isaac Israeli's Definition of Truth." *Archives d'Histoire Doctrinale et Littéraire du Moyen Age* 8 (1933), 5–8.

Palma, Robert J. "Grosseteste's Ordering of *Scientia.*" *The New Scholasticism* 50 (1976), 447–63.

————. "Robert Grosseteste's Understanding of Truth." *The Irish Theological Quarterly* 42 (1975), 300–06.

Pouillon, Henri. "Le premier Traité des Propriétés transcendantales. La 'Summa de bono' du Chancelier Phillippe." *Revue Néoscolastique de Philosophie* 42 (1939), 40–77.

Rohmer, Jean. "Sur la doctrine franciscaine des deux faces de l'âme." *Archives d'Histoire Doctrinale et Littéraire du Moyen Age* 2 (1927), 73–77.

————. "La théorie de l'abstraction dans l'école franciscaine de Alexandre de Halès à Jean Peckam." *Archives d'Histoire Doctrinale et Littéraire du Moyan Age* 3 (1928), 105–84.

Rossi, Pietro. "Un contributo alla storia della scienza nel Medioevo." *Rivista di Filosofia Neo-Scolastica* 67 (1975), 103–10.

————. "Per l'edizione del *Commentarius in Posteriorum Analyticorum Libros* di Roberto Grossatesta." *Rivista di Filosofia Neo-Scolastica* 67 (1975), 489–515.

Ruello, Francis. "La *divinorum nominum reseratio* selon Robert Grossetête et Albert le Grand." *Archives d'Histoire Doctrinale et Littéraire du Moyen Age* 34 (1959), 99–197.

Russell, Josiah C. "Phases of Grosseteste's Intellectual Life." *Harvard Theological Review* 43 (1950), 93–116.

————. "Richard of Bardney's Account of Robert Grosseteste's Early and Middle Life." *Medievalia et Humanistica* 2 (1944), 45–54.

————. "Some Notes Upon the Career of Robert Grosseteste." *Harvard Theological Review* 48 (1955), 197–211.

Schindele, Stephan. *Beiträge zur Metaphysik des Wilhelm von Auvergne*. Munich, 1900.

Serene, Eileen F. "Robert Grosseteste on Induction and Demonstrative Science." *Synthese* 40 (1979), 97–115.

Sharp, Dorothea. *Franciscan Philosophy at Oxford in the Thirteenth Century*. Oxford, 1930.

Stevenson, Francis S. *Robert Grosseteste, Bishop of Lincoln*. London, 1899.

Stock, Brian. "Experience, Praxis, Work, and Planning in Bernard of Clairvaux: Observations on the *Sermones in Cantica*." In *The Cultural Context of Medieval Learning*, pp. 219–62. Ed. John E. Murdoch and Edith D. Sylla. Dordrecht, Netherlands, 1975.

Thomson, Samuel H. *The Writings of Robert Grosseteste, Bishop of Lincoln, 1235-53*. Cambridge, 1940.

Valois, Noël. *Guillaume d'Auvergne, évêque de Paris (1228-1249), sa vie et ses ouvrages*. Paris, 1880.

Van Steenberghen, Fernand. *Aristotle in the West*. 2nd ed. Louvain, 1970.

———. *La philosophie au XIIIe siècle*. Louvain, 1966.

Veuthey, Léon. "Les divers courants de la philosophie augustino-franciscaine au moyen âge." In *Scholastica ratione historico-critica instauranda*, pp. 627–52. Acta Congressus Scholastici Internationalis, Rome, 1950. Rome, 1951.

Vignaux, Paul. *Philosophy in the Middle Ages*. Trans. E. C. Hall. Westport, Conn., 1959. (Trans. of *Philosophie au moyen âge*, 3rd ed., Paris, 1958.)

Vogt, Berard. "Der Ursprung und die Entwicklung der Franziskanerschule." *Franziskanische Studien* 9 (1922), 137–57. (Trans. in *Franciscan Studies* 3 [1925], 5–23.)

Wallace, William A. "Albertus Magnus on Suppositional Necessity in the Natural Sciences." In *Albertus Magnus and the Sciences*, pp. 103–28. Ed. James A. Weisheipl. Toronto, 1980.

———. "Aquinas on the Temporal Relation between Cause and Effect." *The Review of Metaphysics* 27 (1974), 569–84.

———. "Aristotle and Galileo: The Uses of Ὑπόθεσις (*Suppositio*) in Scientific Reasoning." In *Studies in Aristotle*. Ed. Dominic J. O'Meara. Washington, D.C., 1981.

———. *Causality and Scientific Explanation*. I: Medieval and Early Classical Science. Ann Arbor, 1972.

———. "The Scientific Methodology of St. Albert the Great." In

Albertus Magnus Doctor Universalis 1280/1980, pp. 385–407. Eds. Gerbert Meyer and Albert Zimmermann. Mainz, 1980.

Weinberg, Julius R. *Abstraction, Relation, and Induction.* Madison, Wis., 1965.

———. *A Short History of Medieval Philosophy.* Princeton, 1964.

Weisheipl, James A. "Classification of the Sciences in Medieval Thought." *Mediaeval Studies* 27 (1965), 54–90.

———. "The Nature, Scope and Classification of the Sciences." In *Science in the Middle Ages,* pp. 461–82. Ed. David C. Lindberg. Chicago, 1978.

Werner, Karl. *Die Psychologie des Wilhelm von Auvergne.* Vienna, 1873. (Reissued, along with other works of Werner, in a single volume: Amsterdam, 1966.)

———. *Wilhelms von Auvergne Verhältniss zu den Platonikern des XII. Jahrhunderts.* Vienna, 1873.

SECONDARY WORKS NOT CITED

Allard, Baudoin C. "Nouvelles additions et corrections au 'Répertoire' de Glorieux: à propos de Guillaume d'Auvergne." *Bulletin de Philosophie Médiévale* 10–11 (1968), 79–80.

Baeumker, Clemens. "Der Platonismus im Mittelalter." In *Studien und Characteristiken zur Geschichte der Philosophie insbesondere des Mittelalters,* pp. 139–79. Beiträge, XXV, 1–2. Münster, 1927.

———. "Zur Frage nach Abfassungszeit und Verfasser des irrtümlich Witelo zugeschriebenen Liber de intelligentiis." In *Miscellanea Francesco Ehrle,* I, 87–102. Rome, 1924.

Bataillon, L.-J. "Bulletin d'histoire des doctrines médiévales." *Revue des Sciences Philosophiques et Théologiques* 57 (1973), 157–62.

Belmond, S. "A l'Ecole de s. Augustin. Essai sur l'origine des idées d'après quelques-uns des maîtres de la scolastique du XIIIᵉ siècle." *Etudes Franciscaines* 33 (1921), 7–25 and 145–73.

Bertola, Ermengildo. "È esistito un avicennismo latino nel medioevo?" *Sophia* 35 (1967), 318–34, and 39 (1971), 278–320.

Bertsch, August. *Studien zur Summa philosophiae des Pseudo-Robert Grosseteste.* Braunschweig, 1969.

Bérubé, Camille. *La connaissance de l'individuel au moyen âge.* Montreal, 1964.

————. "La connaissance intellectuelle du singulier matériel au XIIIe siècle." *Franciscan Studies* 11 (1951), 157–201.

Boehner, Philotheus. *The History of the Franciscan School.* 2 vols. Typescript. St. Bonaventure, N.Y., 1943. (Mimeo. copy, Duns Scotus College, Detroit, 1947).

————. "A Milestone of Research in Scholasticism." *Franciscan Studies* 8 (1948), 295–300.

————. "The Spirit of Franciscan Philosophy." *Franscican Studies* 2 (1942), 217–37.

————. "The System of Metaphysics of Alexander of Hales." *Franciscan Studies* 5 (1945), 366–414.

Callus, Daniel A. "Philip the Chancellor and the *De anima* ascribed to Robert Grosseteste." *Mediaeval and Renaissance Studies* I (1941), 105–27.

————. "The 'Summa Duacensis' and the Pseudo-Grosseteste's 'De anima.'" *Recherches de Théologie Ancienne et Médiévale* 13 (1946), 225–29.

Chenu, Marie-Dominique. "Grammaire et théologie aux XIIe et XIIIe siècles." *Archives d'Histoire Doctrinale et Littéraire du Moyen Age* 10–11 (1935–36), 5–28.

Dales, Richard C. "The Influence of Grosseteste's *Hexaemeron* on the *Sentences* commentaries of Richard Fishacre, O.P. and Richard Rufus of Cornwall, O.F.M." *Viator* 2 (1971), 271–300.

Day, Sebastian J. *Intuitive Cognition: A Key to the Significance of the Later Scholastics.* St. Bonaventure, N.Y., 1947.

de Rijk, Lambertus Marie. "Die Bedeutungslehre der Logik im 13. Jahrhundert und ihr Gegenstück in der metaphysischen Spekulation." In *Methoden in Wissenschaft und Kunst des Mittelalters,* pp. 1–22. Ed. Albert Zimmerman. Miscellanea Mediaevalia, 7. Berlin, 1970.

de Vaux, Roland. "La première entrée d'Averroès chez les Latins." *Revue des Sciences Philosophiques et Théologiques* 22 (1933), 193–245.

De Wulf, Maurice. "Augustinisme et aristotélisme au XIIIe siècle." *Revue Néo-Scolastique* 8 (1901), 151–66.

————. *Histoire de la philosophie médiévale.* I and II. 6th ed. Louvain, 1934 and 1936.

————. *Philosophy and Civilization in the Middle Ages.* Princeton, 1922.

————. "Qu'est-ce que la philosophie scolastique?" *Revue Néo-Scolastique* 5 (1898), 141–53, 282–96.

Doucet, Victorin. *Commentaires sur les Sentences. Supplément au Répertoire de M. Frédéric Stegmüller.* Quaracchi, 1954.

————. "Maîtres franciscains de Paris. Supplément au 'Répertoire des maîtres en théologie de Paris au XIIIᵉ siècle' de M. le chan. P. Glorieux." *Archivum Franciscanum Historicum* 27 (1934), 531–64.

————. Prolegomena to Alexander of Hales. *Summa theologica* (Liber tertius). IV (prolegomena). Quaracchi, 1948. (Partial trans. in "The History of the Problem of the Authenticity of the Summa," *Franciscan Studies* 7 [1947], 26–41 and 294–312.)

————. "Quelques commentaires sur les 'Sentences' de Pierre Lombard." In *Miscellanea Lombardiana,* pp. 276–94. Novara, 1957.

Ehrle, Franz. "L'Agostinismo e l'Aristotelismo nella Scholastica del Secolo XIII." In *Xenia Thomistica,* III, 517–88. Rome, 1925.

————. "Der Augustinismus und der Aristotelismus in der Scholastik." *Archiv fur Litteratur- und Kirchengeschichte des Mittelalters* 5 (1889), 603–35.

————. "John Peckham über den Kampf des Augustinismus und Aristotelismus in der zweiten Hälfte des 13. Jahrhunderts." *Zeitschrift für katholische Theologie* 13 (1889), 172–93.

————. "Der Kampf um die Lehre des hl. Thomas von Aquin in den ersten funfzig Jahren nach seinem Tod." *Zeitschrift für katholische Theologie* 37 (1913), 266–318.

————. "S. Domenico, le origini del primo studio generale del suo ordine a Parigi e la Somma teologica del primo maestro, Rolando da Cremona." In *Miscellanea Dominicana,* pp. 85–134. Rome, 1923.

Emden, Alfred B. *A Biographical Register of the University of Cambridge to 1500.* Cambridge. 1963.

————. *A Biographical Register of the University of Oxford to A.D. 1500.* 3 vols. Oxford, 1957–59.

Endres, Joseph A. "Des Alexander von Hales Leben und psychologische Lehre." *Philosophisches Jahrbuch* 1 (1888), 24–55, 203–25, and 257–96.

Evans, Gillian R. *Old Arts and New Theology.* Oxford, 1980.

Gilson, Etienne. Introduction to "The Treatise *De anima* of Dominicus Gundissalinus." Ed. J. T. Muckle. *Mediaeval Studies* 2 (1940), 23–27.

――――. "La philosophie Franciscaine." In *Saint François d'Assise,* pp. 148–75. Paris, 1927.

Glorieux, Palémon. *Le Faculté des arts et ses maîtres au XIIIᵉ siècle.* Paris, 1971.

――――. *La littérature quodlibétique.* 2 vols. Le Saulchoir, 1925, and Paris, 1935.

――――. *Répertoire des maîtres en théologie de Paris au XIIIᵉ siècle.* 2 vols. Paris, 1933–34.

Grabmann, Martin. "Zur Erkenntnislehre der älteren Franziskanerschule." *Franziskanische Studien* 4 (1917), 105–26.

Herscher, Irenaeus. "A Bibliography of Alexander of Hales." *Franciscan Studies* 5 (1945), 435–54.

Hunt, Richard W. "Verses on the Life of Robert Grosseteste." *Medievalia et Humanistica* n.s. 1 (1970), 241–51.

Jolivet, Régis. "La doctrine augustinienne de l'illumination." In *Mélanges Augustiniennes,* pp. 52–172. Paris, 1931.

Jüssen, Gabriel. "Von Wilhelm von Auvergne zu Thomas von Aquin—und zurück." In *Thomas von Aquin im philosophischen Gespräch,* pp. 262–65. Ed. Wolfgang Kluxen. Freiburg/Munich, 1975.

Kaeppeli, Thomas. *Scriptores Ordinis Praedicatorum medii aevi.* I-II (A-I). Rome, 1970 and 1975.

Lértora Mendoza, Celina A. "Los comentarios de Santo Tomas y de Roberto Grosseteste a la 'Fisica' de Aristoteles." *Sapientia* 26 (1970), 179–208 and 257–88.

――――. "La 'Summa physicorum' y la filosofia natural de Grosseteste." *Sapientia* 26 (1971), 199–216.

Lindberg, David C. "The Transmission of Greek and Arabic Learning to the West." In *Science in the Middle Ages,* pp. 52–90. Ed. David C. Lindberg. Chicago, 1978.

Little, Andrew G. *The Grey Friars in Oxford.* Oxford, 1892.

Lohr, Charles H. "Medieval Latin Aristotle Commentaries." *Traditio* 23 (1967), 313–413; 24 (1968), 149–245; 26 (1970), 135–216; 27 (1971), 251–351; 28 (1972), 281–396; and 29 (1973), 93–127.

――――. "Medieval Latin Aristotle Commentaries. Addenda et corrigenda." *Bulletin de Philosophie Médiévale* 14 (1972), 116–26.

————. "Medieval Latin Aristotle Commentaries. Supplementary Authors." *Traditio* 30 (1974), 119–44.

Lottin, Odon. "Alexandre de Halès et la 'Summa de anima' de Jean de la Rochelle." *Recherches de Théologie Ancienne et Médiévale* 2 (1930), 396–409.

————. "L'influence littéraire du Chancelier Philippe sur les théologiens préthomistes." *Recherches de Théologie Ancienne et Médievale* 2 (1930), 311–26.

————. "Les traités sur l'âme et les vertus de Jean de la Rochelle." *Revue Néoscolastique de Philosophie* 32 (1930), 5–32.

McKeon, Charles K. *A Study of the Summa philosophiae of the Pseudo-Grosseteste.* New York, 1948.

Mandonnet, Pierre. *Siger de Brabant et l'averroïsme latin au XIIIe siècle.* 2 vols. 2nd ed. Les Philosophes Belges, 6–7. Louvain, 1911 and 1908.

Manser, G. "M. Johann von Rupella + 1245. Ein Beitrag zu seiner Charakteristik mit besonderer Berücksichtigung seiner Erkenntnislehre." *Jahrbuch für Philosophie und spekulative Theologie* 26 (1912), 290–324.

Mazzantini, Carlo. "Da Guglielmo d'Auvergne a s. Tommaso d'Aquino." *Giornale di Metafisica* 6 (1951), 408–21.

Minges, Parthenius. "De scriptis quibusdam Fr. Ioannis de Rupella." *Archivum Franciscanum Historicum* 6 (1913), 597–622.

————. "Die psychologische Summe des Johannes von Rupella und Alexander von Hales." *Franziskanische Studien* 3 (1916), 365–78.

————. "La teoria della conoscenza in Alessandro di Hales." *Rivista di Filosofia Neo-Scolastica* 7 (1915), 347–68.

————. "Zur Erkenntnislehre des Franziskaners Johannes von Rupella." *Philosophisches Jahrbuch der Görresgesellschaft* 27 (1914), 461–77.

Moody, Ernest A. "Empiricism and Metaphysics in Medieval Philosophy." *The Philosophical Review* 67 (1958), 145–63.

————. "Professor Pegis and Historical Philosophy." *Franciscan Studies* n.s. 5 (1945), 301–8.

Padellaro de Angelis, Rosa. *Il problema degli universali nel XIII e XIV secolo.* Rome, 1971.

Pegis, Anton. Introduction to *The Basic Writings of Saint Thomas Aquinas,* I, xxxv-liii. New York, 1945.

Pelster, Franz. Review of Lottin on John of la Rochelle. *Scholastik* 5 (1930), 456.

Pelzer, Auguste. *Répertoire d'incipit pour la littérature latine philosophique et théologique du moyen âge.* 2nd ed. Rome, 1931.

Pinborg, Jan. "Bezeichnung in der Logik des XIII. Jahrhunderts." In *Der Begriff der Repraesentatio im Mittelalter,* pp. 239–81. Ed. Albert Zimmerman. Miscellanea Mediaevalia, 8. Berlin, 1971.

————. *Die Entwicklung der Sprachtheorie im Mittelalter.* Beiträge, XLII, 2. Münster, 1966.

————. *Logik und Semantik im Mittelalter. Ein Überblick.* Stuttgart, 1972.

Quentin, Albrecht. *Naturkenntnisse und Naturanschauungen bei Wilhelm von Auvergne.* Hildesheim, 1976.

Salman, Dominique. "Jean de la Rochelle et les débuts de l'averroïsme latin." *Archives d'Histoire Doctrinale et Littéraire du Moyen Age* 16–17 (1947–48), 133–44.

————. "Note sur la première influence d'Averroès." *Revue Néoscolastique de Philosophie* 40 (1937), 203–12.

Stegmüller, Friedrich. *Repertorium commentariorum in Sententias Petri Lombardi.* 2 vols. Würzburg, 1947.

Teicher, Jacob. "Gundissalino e l'agostinismo avicennizzante." *Rivista di Filosofia Neo-Scolastica* 26 (1934), 252–58.

Thomson, Samuel H. "The *De Anima* of Robert Grosseteste." *The New Scholasticism* 7 (1933), 201–21.

Totok, Wilhelm. *Handbuch der Geschichte der Philosophie.* II: Mittelalter. Frankfurt a. M., 1973.

Van Steenberghen, Fernand. *Aristote en Occident.* Louvain, 1946.

————. "L'interprétation de la pensée médiévale au cours du siècle écoulé." In *Scholastica ratione historico-critica instauranda,* pp. 23–39. Acta Congressus Scholastici Internationalis, Rome, 1950. Rome, 1951.

————. *Siger de Brabant d'après ses oeuvres inédites.* II: Siger dans l'histoire de l'aristotelisme. Les Philosophes Belges, 13. Louvain, 1942.

————. "Travaux récents sur la pensée du XIIIe siècle." *Revue Néoscolastique de Philosophie* 42 (1939), 469–85.

Veuthy, Léon. "Augustinismus and Aristotelismus." *Wissenschaft und Weisheit* 4 (1937), 211–15.

Wallace, William A. "The Philosophical Setting of Medieval Science." In *Science in the Middle Ages,* pp. 91–119. Ed. David C. Lindberg. Chicago, 1978.

Index

Abelard, Peter, 91n, 97n
abstraction, 71–72, 113, 170,
206–8, 209, 267
accident, 40n, 41, 52, 53, 159,
182, 206; material, role in cognition, 56n, 70, 71n, 166n, 170,
173, 176. *See also* opinion
accommodation (*adaequatio*) as
truth, 81–85, 89, 92, 217–19.
See also conformity as truth; relation, as truth
action and passivity. *See* mind, active capacity of
Adelard of Bath, 65n
agent intellect, 58, 59, 64, 106
Albert the Great, 245n, 273n
Alexander of Hales, 19n
al-Ghazali, 34n, 273n
alternation, exclusive, 79
Anselm, 52, 155n; *Cur deus homo,*
236n; *De veritate,* 43n, 46n,
76n, 78n, 84n, 146, 147n,
149n, 219n; *Monologion,* 76n;
on truth, 42–43, 45, 146
ape, 66, 68, 294
a posteriori knowledge, 116
a priori knowledge, 116
Arabic philosophy, 10n, 14, 29,
34–35, 276, 284, 287. *See also*
al-Ghazali; Avicenna
archetypal world, 43–45, 47–49,
69, 168, 171. *See also* examplar,
divine; idea; intelligible, in
God
Aristotelianism, 8n

Aristotle: *Categoriae,* 118; *De
anima,* 20n, 189n; *De interpretatione,* 15; epistemology of,
19–21, 101, 116n, 120n,
198–99, 220n, 252–54, 267; on
habitus, 118; influence of,
15–17, 28–30; *Metaphysics,* 84n,
104n, 124, 209, 218n; *Nicomachean Ethics,* 131n; *Physics,* 65n,
102, 140, 245n; *Posterior Analytics,* throughout book; *Prior
Analytics,* 15; on science, 9, 99,
101–2, 166; on transparency of
glass, 279n; on truth, 39–40,
74–75
arithmetic, 255–56, 261, 262
art, 201, 205, 230n. *See also* skill
astronomy, 105, 175, 277. *See also*
eclipse of moon
Augustine: *De Genesi ad litteram,*
58; *De libero arbitrio,* 12–13; *De
magistro,* 198n; *De vera religione,* 149n; epistemology of,
7n, 11–13, 69, 150; influence
of, 10–13, 16–17, 30; noetics
of, 58–59, 60–61, 68; *Soliloquia,*
12, 153n, 155n; on truth,
12–13, 41n, 155n
Augustinianism, 5, 7n, 8n, 10,
29n
Aurillac, France, 27
authority, 3, 17, 27, 75, 108
Avicebron, 34n, 47; *Fons vitae,*
47n, 64, 184n
Avicenna, 29n, 34n, 59n, 64;

Library of Congress Cataloging in Publication Data
Marrone, Steven P., 1947–
  William of Auvergne and Robert Grosseteste.

  Bibliography: p.
  Includes index.
    1. William, of Auvergne, Bishop of Paris, d. 1249—
Knowledge, Theory of.   2. Grosseteste, Robert, 1175?–1253—Knowl-
edge, Theory of.   3. Knowledge, Theory of—History.   4. Truth—His-
tory.   I. Title.
B765.G824M37   1983   121′.09′022   82-61375
ISBN 0-691-05383-9